When All You Can Do Is Wait

*Triumphing Over Life's Trials
By Waiting on God*

Steve Roll

GRACE
Broken Arrow, OK

Unless otherwise noted, all Scripture references are taken from *New American Standard Bible*. Copyright © 1960, 1962, 1963, 1968, 1971, 1972, 1973, 1975, 1977, 1995 by The Lockman Foundation. All rights reserved. Used by Permission.

Scripture quotations marked HCSB are taken from *Holman Christian Standard Bible*. Copyright © 1999, 2000, 2002, 2003, 2009 by Holman Bible Publishers, Nashville Tennessee. All rights reserved. Used by permission.

Scripture quotations marked NKJV are taken from *New King James Version*. Copyright © 1982 by Thomas Nelson, Inc. All rights reserved. Used by permission.

Scripture quotations marked NIV are taken from *The Holy Bible, New International Version*. Copyright © 1973, 1978, 1984, International Bible Society. Used by permission of Zondervan.

Scripture quotations marked AMP are taken from the *Amplified® Bible*. Copyright © 1954, 1958, 1962, 1964, 1965, 1987 by The Lockman Foundation. Used by permission.

Scripture quotations marked KJV are taken from the *King James Version* of the Bible.

When All You Can Do Is Wait

Triumphing Over Life's Trials By Waiting on God

ISBN-13: 978-1-60495-005-2
ISBN-10: 1-60495-005-6

Copyright © 2014 by Steve Roll. Published in the USA by Grace Publishing. All rights reserved. No part of this book may be reproduced in any form or by any electronic or mechanical means, including information storage and retrieval systems, except as provided by USA Copyright law.

Contents

Introduction 5

Part 1: About Waiting

1. Hurry Up…and Wait! 11
2. W-a-i-t! A Good Four-letter Word 21
3. If You Want to Be Great, You're Going to Have to Wait! ... 41
4. If Waiting's Good, Why Is It So Hard? 55
5. What Can Happen if You Don't Wait 69
6. The Marines Aren't the Only Ones Looking 83
7. God's Waiting Rooms 97
8. God's Timing Is Everything 109

Part 2: Wait Training

9. Wait Training 101 129
10. Advanced Wait Training 155
11. How to Find Peace with God's Pace 185
12. Some Things Are Worth the Wait 205
13. Waiting for Your Dreams to Come True 231

Conclusion: It's Never Too Late to Learn How to Wait! 245

Endnotes: 251

Dedication

To my precious wife and life partner Jo Ann, whose patience with me speaks volumes about God's love and faithfulness. Her sincere, unwavering trust in God has stretched my faith and shown me the incomparable value of waiting on and trusting in the Lord.

Introduction

I don't know about you, but my favorite things don't include waiting. I'll confess right up front: I hate to wait!

With my high-energy, results-oriented, triple-type-A personality, I'm probably the last person on planet earth anyone would expect to write a book on the subject.

Patience is definitely not my forté. Just ask my wife, Jo Ann, who has jokingly (I think) threatened to plant Impatiens on my final resting place as a testimony to the world about my lifestyle. I guess we'll just have to wait to see how serious she is.

People like me tend to view waiting as the archenemy of our master plans to success. Our modus operandi: Do it now; get it done. Tomorrow is definitely too late for our "yesterday" deadlines. As far as we're concerned, waiting is worse than dying a slow, painful death. It's for lesser-motivated individuals who have nothing better to do than to sit around expecting their ship to come in.

Movers and shakers don't wait for ships. They build them. Then they send them out to sea, expecting them to return in record time fully laden with all kinds of goodies.

If you're like me, you have trouble sitting still. My grandmother used to say that I had the wiggles. Waiting has always tested every fiber of my being — an unnecessary nuisance to be avoided at all costs. It gets in the way of super enthusiastic people like me who are convinced that we're called to straighten out the world and save mankind… Now!

We live in an age that produces a lot of worry and weariness. Look around and you'll see multitudes of people stressing out, burning out and falling out because they've lost sight of God's formula for rest and renewal.

The Bible tells us *those who wait upon the Lord will renew their strength…* (Isaiah 40:31), yet many people are going bust because they seldom wait for anything because they've come to expect instant gratification. They expect even God to jump at the snap of their fingers and fix all of the problems their impatience has created.

Waiting may not be fashionable. It certainly isn't popular or politically correct. But waiting is fruitful and profitable. The majority of us in this culture need to spend less time with advisors, therapists, and so-called experts, and more time with God!

Waiting before the Lord to receive the things we need produces a peace that passes understanding and a confidence that can conquer any challenge!

It is the greatest investment we can make in life. It's all about faith. It means we must trust in God's wisdom and timing to deliver what He has promised to His believing children. To those who understand that *He works on behalf of those who wait for Him* (Isaiah 64:4), Wall Street will never yield a return like the Almighty can.

A single mom raising two pre-school children came to my office for counseling. She had gone through a divorce that left her financially destitute. In addition to having to adjust to life after divorce, within the span of a week prior to our appointment she'd received an eviction notice from her landlord; her car had expired on the expressway; she was laid off from her part-time waitressing job; there were no groceries in the house; and the mother she loved deeply and looked to for support and encouragement died of a heart attack.

Overwhelmed by her circumstances, this young woman was emotionally depleted. Tears streamed down her face as she said, "Pastor Steve, I'm all alone and I have nothing left but Jesus."

My heart was broken by her heavy burden. "I know your situation looks bleak. But you're right. You still have Jesus, and He'll help you through this difficult time. Let's look to God together and wait on Him for comfort, healing, strength and the solutions to the problems you're facing," I told her.

In miraculous ways over the next few weeks God affirmed His love for this single mom and her children. Waiting produced relief and renewed faith that the Lord was bigger than her troubles.

When life crashes in, and all we can do is wait, waiting on God is critical to overcoming what overwhelms us.

God comforts our hearts and heals our hurts through the process He designed. While we wait, we discover His good, acceptable, and perfect plan for our lives. Time spent waiting produces the revelation and wisdom necessary to solve our problems. As we wait on the Lord, He provides the vision and provision we need to succeed.

Waiting on God builds faith. It renews us for the next phase of the battle. If we're willing, the time we spend waiting can teach us how to walk in the wisdom and anointing necessary to succeed in God's will for us.

Considering the priceless, timeless treasures that we must possess if we're to achieve success, none of us who name the name of Christ can afford not to wait upon the Lord!

The waiting process that produces patient and persevering character is no longer my personal foe. It has become a faithful and trustworthy friend. I have learned that to be like Christ, I must wait on the Lord. The Bible and life's school of hard knocks have taught me that the very best things in life come to those who wait.

I've learned some important things about waiting on God, and I want to share them with you. Some will tickle your funny bone; some will seriously challenge your concepts about waiting.

Hopefully, my journey through waiting will motivate you to make some attitude adjustments and take some positive steps that will result in reaping the benefits and blessings of waiting upon the Lord.

One final thing before we begin: I need to add a disclaimer. I'm far from perfect in this patience business. Trust me. The Lord and I are still working on this waiting thing. I'm the proverbial work in progress. It will take my lifetime to nail it down!

And you know what? I wouldn't have it any other way! I'm thankful to God every day that He's so patient with me. I stand amazed at His willingness to continue to work on this piece of imperfect, but improving clay.

The time you invest in reading this book will be worth the results. So why wait any longer? Let's get going and discover how to *be still and know* that He is God (Psalm 46:10) when those times come in life when all we can do is wait!

About Waiting

Chapter 1
Hurry Up…and Wait!

In the wee hours of the morning our plane touched down on the tarmac at Lindberg Field in San Diego. Outside, the harbor and downtown skyline were shrouded in a dense fog.

With a handful of new acquaintances from Washington State, I hustled across the tarmac to a waiting bus. The doors slammed behind the last passenger, and we headed into the unknown.

After weaving his way through pre-dawn traffic, our driver turned into the entry of a gated compound guarded by armed military personnel. Permission granted, the bus rolled into the complex and stopped at the edge of a paved area that seemed to stretch for miles.

Sitting in total silence, we were wondering what we had gotten ourselves into when, from seemingly nowhere, a broad shouldered guy boarded the bus. Voice booming, he delivered a speech I will never forget!

"Attention! Welcome to the United States Naval Training Center. You now belong to Uncle Sam. This base will be your new home for the next six weeks. My job is to turn you sissies into sailors. You are not on vacation. This is boot camp. I am your drill instructor and I will be in your face twenty-four hours a day. By the time I finish with you, you mamma's boys will know what it means to be a man. Grab your gear, get your lazy tails out of this vehicle, and fall in formation on the parade field on the double."

Intimidated to the max, fearing this man maybe even more than we did the devil or God, we rookie recruits scrambled off the bus while our government-appointed father figure screamed in our ears: "Move it! Move it! Move it!"

None of us knew what a formation was. But we were scared enough (some would call it motivated) that we formed a reasonable facsimile of a straight line. We stood stiffly in the early morning darkness, not daring even to bat an eyelash.

Pacing like a panther on the prowl, our instructor looked us over, sizing up his ragtag company of ex-civilians. Then, he left without another word.

Sufficiently paralyzed by fear, we stayed riveted at attention as minutes that seemed like eternity ticked by. Wiggling and twitching was out of the question; our drill instructor must be lurking somewhere in the shadows.

Part 1: About Waiting

We stood, and we stood, and we stood some more! My feet and legs burned with pain. As I did my best to hold out and not fall out, I remembered a conversation with my stepfather, who had served in the Korean War. He'd advised me that if I enlisted, I would become intimately acquainted with the standard operating procedure of the armed forces — hurry up and wait. "It's simple," he said. "You wait. Then move to another place. And wait. Waiting's the name of the game in the military. No matter how much you may dislike it, you hurry so you can wait."

When our first predawn formation was finally dismissed, we were further introduced to, and indoctrinated in, the waiting process. First, we waited in line to have our paperwork checked. Next we waited in line to exchange our civilian clothes for our government-issue shirts, dungarees, socks, and combat boots. Then, the shot line. Imagine waiting in line to have both arms and one hip popped with an air-powered immunization gun while watching those ahead of you — men much more macho than you — faint dead away!

Next it was time for a trip to the barbershop. When shoulder length hair, extended sideburns, goatees, beards, mustaches, and any and every combination thereof the norm, we newbies looked like hippies waiting to sit in the chair. And after a few surgically precise strokes of the clippers transformed unique individuals into hairless cone heads, it was pretty unsettling to look around and not recognize anyone, including yourself!

After four years with the Navy, I can say without reservation that I came to thoroughly understand what "hurry up and wait" means. I did my share of it — in chow lines, phone lines, shower lines, mail call lines, commissary lines, paycheck lines, equipment lines, sick call lines, and plain old line lines. If there was a line, I hurried to stand and wait in it!

I learned a lot about waiting from Uncle Sam. I learned that I didn't like it, and that it wasn't much fun.

Hurry up and wait isn't the exclusive domain of the military. It's fact of life.

Have you ever gone to a popular amusement park? Anticipation running high, you arrive at the park early. Thousands of wide-eyed children and their parents crowd together behind a restraining rope waiting for the park to open.

When the park opens people surge in en mass, fanning out in all directions. Some people literally run to the attractions, hoping to be first in line. But their hurrying is for naught; they dutifully take their place waiting in the infamous lines of the most popular rides.

As you wait, you inch along through mazes created by daisy-chained ropes. Eventually you come upon a brightly colored sign informing you "From this point, the wait is one hour." Only 60 minutes before you can enjoy your three-minute ride!

Isn't it amazing how we're willing to hustle around an amusement park to wait in obscenely long lines for a short ride that sends chills down our spines and forces screams from the depth of our being? Then, when the ride ends, we stagger out announcing to those waiting their turn in line, "What an awesome ride!" and telling our companions, "Let's do it again!"

In Ecclesiastes 3:1-11, God's Word through Solomon tells us God has set *an appointed time for everything* (v 1) and God *has made everything appropriate in its time* (v. 11). We read about *a time to give birth, and a time to die, a time to plant, and a time to uproot what is planted, a time to kill, and a time to heal, a time to mourn, and a time to dance.*

Time involves waiting. Because God has *set eternity in our hearts* (v.11), it is vitally important that we get a grip on waiting.

Let's repeat: Waiting is the rule, not the exception in life.

Children wait until they are big enough to ride bicycles. Teenagers wait to be old enough to drive cars. Young people wait for their first dates. Students wait for high school diplomas and college degrees.

We wait for Mr. or Ms. Right to come along so we can get married. We wait as we prepare for our career; we wait to get into our career; we wait for our career to prosper and succeed. We wait for that perfect job, the big promotion, the fat pay raise. We wait to have children, then we wait to send those children out of the nest. We wait to take out a mortgage, and we wait for what seems like a millennium to pay the mortgage off. We wait for grandchildren. We wait to retire. We wait to die. And Christians wait for the second coming and glorious appearing of our Lord and Savior Jesus Christ!

Like it or not, waiting plays a major role in our lives. We can't escape it.

Because God perfectly times every season of life, waiting for His time is the wisest thing we can do. But we Americans want what we want the way we want it, when we want it. And, we want it now!

We try hard to speed everything up, don't we? Have you ever caught yourself standing in front of your microwave exhorting it to hurry? Or urged your computer to download a little quicker? I plead guilty, and you probably should too. But God isn't into hurry. According to Galatians 5:22-23, our Creator and Redeemer is into things like holiness and holy living that produces *love, joy, peace, patience, kindness, goodness, faithfulness, gentleness, and self-control, the fruit of the Spirit.*

Most of us know we need to learn patience, but many of us are trying to find a place where we can take a crash course. Rubber-meets-the-road living doesn't work that way. Waiting that produces patience, which is the mark of mature character, is not instant gratification.

If we're honest, most of us would admit we'd rather do just about anything else. In fact, if the truth were known, some of us would rather do wrong than wait.

Time and time again in the course of counseling I hear stories from brokenhearted people who chose to make poor decisions rather than wait a little longer for God's wisdom and direction. Consequences follow choices.

> *Do not be deceived, God is not mocked: for whatever a man sows, that he will also reap. For the one who sows to his own flesh shall from the flesh reap corruption, but the one who sows to the Spirit shall from the Spirit reap eternal life. And let us not lose heart in doing good, for in due time, we shall reap if we do not grow weary.*
>
> Galatians 6:7-9

To act impulsively according to the desires of our flesh and to choose not to wait before the Lord for His plan can only bring disappointment and disaster. We can fight the process and be frustrated, or we can flow with it and be fruitful.

Just as it takes time for physical fruit to grow, spiritual fruit takes time to produce. And the process requires patience.

Biblical salvation is about personal wholeness, wellness and healthy relationships with God and people. Waiting is an essential ingredient in the wholeness process. Waiting on the Lord is a prerequisite for receiving the benefits and blessings our Heavenly Father has built into His universe for those who trust in Him.

The abundant and eternal life Jesus came to give (John 10:10) belongs to those who aren't in a hurry to acquire some shallow religious experience. They come to those who are willing to wait on the Lord, receive Him by responding to His invitation to believe in Him and to enter into a personal relationship with the Son of the Living God. (John 1:12)

Christians must be careful and watchful about the forces that press in on us from all sides to condition and conform us to this hurried and harried age in which we live. Rather than give into subtle pressures to sidestep the waiting process, we need to step up our resistance and rise to a higher level of endurance when we are tempted to cave in to the easy, but costly, path of impatience.

My patience level and ability to endure certainly get put to the test regularly. Can you identify with some of life's little scenarios that really put the heat on us?

- waiting to see the doctor when we have poison oak!
- being late for an appointment, the expressway speed limit is 65, and the fast lane is limping along at 50!
- being in a hurry to mail a package at the Post Office during the Christmas rush when the line is out the door and all but one of the service windows say "This window closed."
- flying standby and getting stuck behind a non-English speaking tour group at the airline ticket counter.
- finding yourself and your six items behind a mother with two unruly preschoolers and an overloaded grocery cart…and the express lane is closed.
- standing at the counter while your carry-out pizza is in sight and getting cold, but inattentive, inexperienced employees can't seem to get their act together.
- going to the Department of Motor Vehicles to renew your license.

I'm sure you have the picture by now and can probably add some of your own. Life really does push and pull on us. Patience, acquired through waiting, will help us prevail over the push/pull pressures of modern life.

Each of us experiences times in life when things happen that we can't control. Things happen that we don't understand, that don't seem to make sense. These events and experiences stretch our waiting abilities to the limit.

I grew up in a family of six boys raised by a single mom. Talk about hurry up and wait! We had to take our turns to wait for the bathtub, the Sunday roast beef

Part 1: About Waiting

platter to round our corner of the table, new school clothes, a bicycle, and so on. We waited. But we had a lot of fun along the way. Being part of a large family instilled in me a strong desire to have my own family someday.

Jo Ann and I had been married five years when we felt it was time to become a family. While I was attending seminary in Kentucky, she announced to me, using a pair of baby booties as a visual aid, that we could look forward to the arrival of a little Roll. Six weeks into the pregnancy, she miscarried. It was a frightening and devastating experience for a young couple who so desired to be parents. We had waited five years, had prayed a lot about becoming a mom and dad and felt peace that it was time for the Lord to bless us with a child.

Yet we lost the baby.

Miscarriage is a personal loss that must be grieved. Psalm 107:20 tells us *God sent His Word and healed them and delivered them from all their destructions.* As He always is, the Lord was merciful and gracious toward us. He comforted and strengthened us as we worked through the healing process. The Holy Spirit came alongside a heartbroken couple, soothed our spirits, and strengthened us emotionally as we looked to the Word for healing and recovery.

After a season of sorrow, and sensing that we had recovered sufficiently from our loss, we were convinced more than ever that we wanted a child. We decided to try again. Jo Ann conceived. First trimester miscarriages are fairly common in first-time pregnancies. Having one behind us, we looked forward with renewed anticipation to a precious gift from God. Eight weeks later, miscarriage revisited the Rolls.

We were crushed. We had waited for years. During that time we had happily watched our friends have healthy babies. We had been careful to seek counsel and to wait on the Lord for His direction. We had even experienced and overcome one miscarriage. We'd believed it was still His will for us to have children. We'd conceived a second time. Then life crashed in. It didn't feel like we would ever have a baby.

Wait! hit us head on. We had many questions with few answers in sight. Two miscarriages forced us to wait on God, whether we felt like it or not.

Immediately following my graduation, Jo Ann flew home to be with her folks. I remained behind to pack up our belongings and transport them to our home church in San Diego where we were going to take a ministry position.

Preparing to move proved to be an extremely painful experience for me. We had turned one of the bedrooms into a cheerfully decorated nursery. Looking at and touching soft baby blankets, cuddly stuffed animals and a child's first toys drove the knife of disappointment deep into my grieving heart. I hurt beyond description for Jo Ann, myself, and our loss.

I couldn't remain in the room. Unable to handle the waves of grief any longer, I cried out, asking the Lord why we couldn't have a baby. Seminary friends were having babies. Others in our morally warped society were aborting and abusing children. I tried to convince God we should be parents. We loved children. We were solid, committed Christians, headed for full-time service as pastors. God could count on us to take seriously our responsibility to raise our children according to biblical principles.

"Surely, Lord you know that we would make excellent parents," I reasoned. "We've waited so long and have gone through so much. Why, Father, are we unable to become a family?"

After praying and pouring out my personal pain, a soothing quietness overshadowed my anguished spirit. I sensed from the Holy Spirit that God was very near and wanted to speak to me. As I knelt in my usual place of prayer and tried to focus on the Lord, I heard that still small voice whisper in my spirit, "Steve, if you never have children, will you still serve Me?"

Taking a shuddering breath, I mustered the grace and courage necessary to respond, "Lord, you know me. I love you with all my heart. Yes, I will serve you all the days of my life even if we aren't blessed with a little one. But You do know that I would like to be a daddy."

A deeply comforting, spiritual peace settled over me as I left the desire to be a daddy in God's hands. Releasing my disappointment opened up in me an even stronger desire to be a father. The Lord used that season of grief to deepen my trust in His perfect will for Jo Ann and me. We entered a season of waiting.

Our Heavenly Father cares very much about our heart's desires. Psalm 37:4 tells us: *Delight yourself in the Lord, and He will give you the desires of your heart.* God's process for fulfilling our heart's desires is for us to delight or take pleasure in Him first. Then, He promises to fulfill our God-given desires.

Sometimes we must wait so that God will know that our delight is in Him. In His wisdom, He will bring us to a place where we will be tested to determine if He is indeed first in our lives.

In Genesis 22 we read that Abraham was tested when asked to sacrifice his only son, Isaac, on Mt. Moriah. Abraham passed the test. He walked through a long and rewarding life with his son because he had been willing to let him go. Through the testing process, not only was Abraham's faith proven, God showed him again that waiting on the Lord is the pathway to His richest blessings! God kept His covenant promise to Abraham.

Miscarriage and disappointment forced us to wait. But *everything is appropriate in its time.* "Its time" is God's time. We waited nine years before our son was born. Three years later a daughter joined our family.

Our two red-haired, blue-eyed blessings are miracles. From the ash heap of miscarriage, God raised up two incredibly amazing children for us. Jo Ann and I are indeed blessed. We praise the Lord every day for granting us the desire of our hearts.

If you want a good, godly desire to be fulfilled, delight in the Lord first. Life under God's control and within His timing is abundant and fulfilling.

Not only do we wait, God waits on high in heaven to bless us. Isaiah 30:18 reveals something very precious about the heart of God for His children:

> *The Lord longs to be gracious to you; and therefore, He waits on high to have compassion on you. For the Lord is a God of justice; How blessed are those who long for Him.*

Every time I read this verse, my spirit jumps with joy! The Lord longs to be gracious toward us. *Us* means you and me. When we're experiencing one of those waits, it's wonderfully comforting and reassuring to know that God desires, even longs, to extend grace to us. Who doesn't need grace in a time of testing and waiting?

Our Creator not only desires to be gracious to us, He also waits on high, in the heavenly places, to have compassion on us. Did you catch that? God waits.

The Almighty actually waits for opportunities to pour His compassion into our hearts! Is that good news or what? The Lord is a God of justice who knows how unfair and unjust some situations in life can be. He helps make them tolerable and conquerable through the great love that He gives us through the sacrifice of His Son, Jesus Christ. Paul reminded us in Romans 8:37-39 that nothing in life, and that certainly includes waiting experiences, can separate us from His love:

In all these things we overwhelmingly conquer through Him who loved us. For I am convinced that neither death, nor life, nor angels, nor principalities, nor things present, nor things to come, nor powers, nor height, nor depth, nor any other created thing, will be able to separate us from the love of God, which is in Christ Jesus our Lord.

All of us encounter seasons of the soul on our journey through life, seasons of loss and grief, setback, tragedy, unexpected reversals, transitions and change, adjustments, negative and positive passages and more. Sometimes the only, and the best thing we can do is wait when they test and try the mettle of our spirits. A do-it-now, get-it-now, fix-it-now mentality won't work when life crashes in and all we can do is wait.

Having noted that our Heavenly Father longs to be gracious and waits to be compassionate, let's look at what we must do if we want to be blessed. To paraphrase David: How blessed (happy, oh, how happy) are those who long for (strongly desire and are willing to wait) for Him.

If God longs for us and waits for us, how much more do we need to long for Him and wait on Him?

It has taken me considerable time and effort to come to the conclusion that waiting is good. But if God waits, and if He counsels and invites us to wait, then waiting must be good. "Hurry up and wait" doesn't have to be a negative experience. It can be one of the most positive, productive and personally profitable experiences we can have if we will look to the Lord and wait on Him for His solution to our problems.

It's time we look at those situations in a different light…the light of God's Word. Scripture reveals that waiting can definitely be God's will and His way for blessing those who want to walk through life victoriously!

If we look to the Lord when all we can do is wait, life's test and trials can turn into good things.

Chapter 2
W-A-I-T! A Good Four-Letter Word

"No waiting at register six," a feminine voice announces.

"No waiting" barely escapes her lips, before a stampede of shoppers rush to get there first.

I admit, I've been one of those people determined to beat the others. You probably have too at least once.

When exhausted shoppers are stacked in line ahead of me, their carts overflowing with who knows what, and that little pulsating light clicks on requesting some member of management to come to my checkout lane, I think John 13:27: *Whatever you have to do, do quickly!* (Author's paraphrase)

In America, the land of the free, the home of the brave, and the society of the selfishly impatient, waiting cuts against the grain of our satisfy-and-gratify-me-now natures. Our philosophy to look out for number one precludes us from entertaining the thought that someone else might like — or even need — to be first once in a while.

Imagine a line opening and shoppers turning to each other and saying, "Please, go ahead. I'd love for you to go first. It would make my day."

We erroneously conclude that waiting isn't good. God forbid that we approach this waiting business in a positive way. So the probability of our high-tech culture turning into an other-centered, service-oriented society in our lifetime is probably slim to none!

Our averseness to waiting originates from at least four sources: **Self-Centeredness, Cultural Conditioning, Negative Experiences** and **Spiritual Warfare.**

Self-Centeredness

The self-centered, self-absorbed, sinful nature we inherited doesn't like to wait (Romans 5:12-21). Rebellion, disobedience and self-will were at the root of Adam and Eve's sin (Genesis 3). At the core of their disastrous decision we see an impatient, selfish spirit that chose to disregard God's Word and take for themselves what He had forbidden.

Think about this for a moment. Our first parents resided in the Garden of Eden, a paradise on earth. God's very best would always be theirs if they would simply put their faith in Him and obey His Word. God said what He meant, and meant what He said (Genesis 2:15-17). Yet Adam and Eve chose to act on their selfish, carnal impulses (Genesis 3:6) and they lost everything (Genesis 3:24). They should have trusted God, but they didn't believe He had a better plan for their lives than they did.

The selfish nature of Adam and Eve lives in each of us. The only way we can overcome that old, sinful nature is to put on the sinless nature of Christ (Ephesians 4:20-24). The Apostle Paul, the Bible's proclaimer and guardian of grace, shows us what Jesus did to deliver us from the sinful and deadly nature of Adam.

> *If by the transgression of the one [Adam], death reigned through the one, much more those who received the abundance of grace and the gift of righteousness will reign in life through the One, Jesus Christ. So then as through one transgression there resulted condemnation to all men, even so through one act of righteousness there resulted justification of life to all men. For as through one man's disobedience [Adam] the many were made sinners, even so through the obedience of the One [Jesus] the many will be made righteous.*
>
> Romans 5:17-19

Do you see the good news in these three verses? Self, and self-absorption, can be dethroned. Jesus Christ provided a new way for sinners to live. We don't have to remain in a state of condemnation because of our self-centered nature inherited from Adam. We can choose to believe in Jesus, the second Adam, and identify with His sinless, selfless nature. According to 2 Corinthians 5:14-21, our old life passes away. As new creations in Christ, all things are made new.

It's the great exchange — Jesus Christ's nature for Adam's nature. When we receive Jesus into our hearts by faith and walk in obedience to His commandments, He abides in us. Because of His holy presence in our hearts, we have the potential, the power, and the promise to become the people that we need to be — trusting, patient, willing to wait for the Father's will. Instead of banishment, the inheritance of those who put off Adam and put on Christ is blessing.

The daily presence of Jesus Christ in our hearts helps us wait on the Lord and, through the Holy Spirit, receive the good things He intends for us.

Cultural Conditioning

American society suffers from a "wait loss" that is turning us into a nation of emotionally unhealthy people.

From earliest childhood, significant people and events in our lives communicate to us that waiting is not a good thing.

- What do we teach children who stubbornly insist on having what they want Now! and get it because the adults in their lives want to avoid confrontation?

- What happens to our children when they observe the way we handle traffic? You know the drill: Traffic flows unbearably slowly. Lights in your direction seem permanently stuck on red. Distracted drivers are yacking on cell phones, texting, gawking out windows, "rubber-necking" and paying very little attention to their driving in general.

    Mom or Dad the driver gets frustrated and upset, and say what a bummer it is to have to wait for traffic to move. They honk the horn at a driver who delays a second or two before starting through a green light, or who ever-so-slowly eases onto the roadway without signaling. They make rude comments when someone in front of them drives too slowly.

Impressionable eyes and ears are on full alert. What messages do we send children who are watching us like hawks?

I'm ashamed to admit it, but my offspring vocalize and echo some of my past driving comments. My orations on the evils of having to wait in traffic have registered well and are repeated verbatim. My impatient behavior behind the wheel has sent a message to the next generation of Roll family drivers that waiting in traffic is something just short of sinful. Waiting in line behind an endless column of cars, or waiting for a light to change couldn't possibly have any positive benefit in life!

When we display our displeasure at having to wait, whether in line for a hot dog at the ballpark, in the waiting area of the pediatrician's office, because our phone call is put on hold for several minutes, or for whatever reason, we're sending powerful messages that influence our children and become deeply imprinted in their conscious and subconscious memories.

The attitudes of parents, relatives, peers, the media, and society in general shape the attitudes of our children. Regardless of what we may tell them they should do, our children do what we do. Our actions really do speak louder than our words.

- When was the last time you watched a television commercial that extolled the virtues of waiting?

- How many infomercials exhort us to take our time about making a decision: Go ahead, sit back, relax before grab your credit card and call the number on the screen whenever you're ready.

- Television shows set people up to believe we don't have to wait for anything. Love, romance, power, influence, material things, even major life problems are worked out during the twenty to forty minutes of fanciful story line sandwiched between commercials! It's a travesty to think that in the short span of a feature movie presentation tragedies can be healed and everyone lives happily ever after.

- Minute Rice; best-selling books like *The One-Minute Manager*; microwaveable meals; no down payment, no payments, and no interest for six months credit plans; instant pudding; quick lubes; drive-through dry cleaners; eye glasses in about an hour; same-day loan approval; and speedy checkout lanes all impress a negative worldview of waiting in our minds.

- Why wait on the old-fashioned, tried and tested way of losing weight sensibly and safely through healthy eating habits and regular exercise? If you want to lose 30 pounds in 30 days, simply melt those unwanted pounds away by swallowing a few pills and spending $30.

- Don't want to take the time to talk to someone? Text!

Our culture definitely conditions us to view waiting as a liability rather than an asset. One of the reasons we have so many anxious, hurting, depressed, unstable and unfulfilled citizens in America is because we have been duped by the devil and have bought into the lie that waiting can't possibly contribute anything positive to our lives. Anything that looks like it might make us wait must be avoided at all costs!

Negative Experiences

Past negative experiences often impact our attitudes in situations that require patience.

Every person can vividly recall times when waiting ended in grief. Maybe it was a night spent in a hospital emergency room. Or waiting for a much-needed job. Maybe it was waiting for that special day when you would be married, but your fiancé changed their mind, leaving you alone.

Perhaps you've waited for a healing that didn't happen, money that didn't materialize, a relationship that didn't blossom…hopes and dreams that didn't come to fruition!

Sometimes, past experiences have been so disappointing that we work hard to suppress the memories of those events.

Often, when we don't want to deal with something, we ignore it, telling ourselves it will disappear in time. But the mind doesn't work that way. Repression isn't freedom. It's bondage. Negative experiences enslave us when we deny the pain they cause.

If we aren't careful, life can cause us to turn a cold shoulder to this waiting business. The only thing that will set us on the road to healing and freedom is to acknowledge those negative experiences, release them, and replace them with positive ones.

Spiritual Warfare

In the average American's vocabulary, wait is akin to a not-so-nice four-letter word. It's probably near the bottom of, or not even on, most people's priority lists.

When was the last time you intentionally included some waiting time in your schedule?

As Christians, we have a real spiritual enemy who doesn't want us to wait…especially on God. We will discuss this dimension of spiritual warfare in greater detail in chapter four. For now, just remember that John 10:10 tells us the enemy of our souls is a *thief [that] comes only to steal and kill and destroy.*

Using his own arsenal of spiritual weaponry, Satan and his demons will do everything they can to steal our time with God and discourage us in our walk with the Lord. His mission is to kill our faith and destroy our relationship with our Lord Jesus Christ.

Part of gaining victory over our negative perception about waiting is to remember that the devil is ultimately behind everything that would steer us away from waiting for the Lord. As Christians, we must believe and know that the devil has been defeated.

The Son of God appeared for this purpose, to destroy the works of the devil.

1 John 3:8

Greater is He [Jesus Christ] who is in you, than he [the devil] who is in the world.

1 John 4:4.

Whatever is born of God overcomes the world; and this is the victory that has overcome the world — our faith.

1 John 5:4

Thanks be to God, who always leads us in triumph in Christ, and manifests through us the sweet aroma of the knowledge of Him in every place.

2 Corinthians 2:14

While multitudes of voices scream at us that waiting is bad, another voice softly vies for our attention. It's the comforting, compassionate voice of the Holy Spirit who seeks to reveal to us that while society says waiting is bad, Scripture declares that waiting is good!

When it comes to waiting, we're confronted with a choice. We either believe the world's negative assessment, or we lay hold of God's positive revelation.

To wait for means "to look for with a view to a favorable reception." Waiting, in the biblical sense, has to do with an expectation, a hope that believes it will be received by God and be blessed by Him.

The book of Lamentations is an Old Testament record of Jeremiah's grief and sorrow over the condition of the Jewish people. The five chapters of Lamentations are songs of mourning. They vividly express the anguish of the children of God at the utter ruin of Jerusalem and its holy Temple, and the displaced population under the Babylonians who conquered and carried them away into captivity in 586 B.C.

"My groans are many and my heart is faint," Jeremiah wrote (1:22). Temporarily losing hope for better days, Jeremiah struggled before God — weeping and troubled in spirit, feeling walled in and chained, filled with bitterness, having forgotten happiness…hopeless (2:11; 3:7; 3:15, 17-18).

At the depth of his despair, God's Word helped Jeremiah remember some things about the God who never fails His children.

> *Remember my affliction and my wandering, the wormwood and the bitterness. Surely my soul remembers, and is bowed down within me. This I recall to my mind, therefore, I have hope. The LORD's lovingkindnesses indeed never cease, for His compassions never fail. They are new every morning; Great is Your faithfulness. "The LORD is my portion," says my soul, "Therefore, I have hope in Him." The LORD is good to those who wait for Him, to the person who seeks Him. It is good that he waits silently for the salvation of the LORD.*
>
> Lamentations 3:19-26

With the dawning of each new day, the Lord's lovingkindness and faithfulness met Jeremiah's needs. In the middle of a crushing captivity, the weeping prophet was reminded of God's compassion. As he remembered the foundation of his hope, Jeremiah was reminded he was to seek after the Lord. To wait for Him.

Why was Jeremiah reminded to seek the Lord? Because the Lord is good to those who wait for Him, to the person who seeks Him. Note how *good* and *wait* are linked together in Lamentations. Again in verse 26: It is good (not bad!) that we wait silently for God's salvation.

We'll discuss how to wait on God successfully in later chapters. For now, realize that *wait* and *good* go together. Kind of like vanilla ice cream and chocolate syrup!

Good things come through waiting.

God is a good God (Psalm 86:5). He plans good things for people who seek Him and are willing to wait for His solutions to life's problems (Jeremiah 29:11-13).

The pages of the Bible are filled with good things from the hand of a good God. Salvation is good. Healing is good. Peace is good. Restoration is good. Prosperity is good. Promotion is good. Wisdom is good. Guidance is good. Deliverance is good. Protection is good. Correction is good. Renewal is good. Waiting is good. And of course, heaven is good. God wants to give His children a host of other good things (Psalm 34:10, Romans 8:32).

Receiving the good things God wants to give us often require us to wait. It's part of the process for receiving our inheritance in Christ. (Romans 8:14-17)

If you're facing a situation right now that has you at the "end of your rope," grab on to the hope offered here. Your help, healing and happiness are found in the Lord. Wait on Him…humbly, expectantly, confidently and patiently.

In Psalm 145:15 David wrote: *The eyes of all look to You, and You give them their food in due time.* David, testifying from personal experience, teaches us that when we look to God He will provide whatever we need at the right time.

Waiting Requires Focus

Many people feel helpless and hopeless because they focus on their surroundings instead of their Savior. Circumstances, not Christ, direct their choices and actions. Desperate, hoping against hope, they wait in vain for the world to come through for them. Unfortunately, the world system is a hopeless system. The way of the world is devoid of moral principle and is powerless to do for us what we can't do for ourselves.

Only Almighty God can deliver what we need. Hebrews 12:2-3 not only encourages us, it also tells us where to look for our needs to be met.

> *Fixing our eyes on Jesus, the author and perfecter of faith, who for the joy set before Him, endured the cross, despising the shame, and has sat down at the right hand of the throne of God. For consider Him who has endured such hostility by sinners against Himself, so that you may not grow weary and lose heart.*

No matter how severe our situation, we don't have to lose heart. Jesus Christ is our hope.

God rebuilt and restored Judah (Jeremiah 30:17; 31:1-17). The people's days of mourning turned into dancing. Their despair turned into delight because they waited for the Lord and His salvation.

According to Acts 10:34, God is no respecter of persons. What He did for Judah, He will do for us. To receive from God, we must do what Jeremiah and Judah did. Wait for the Lord!

Wait is a wonderful word for those who want to line their lives up with the Word of God.

> *As for me, I am like a green olive tree in the house of God; I trust in the lovingkindness of God forever and ever. I will give You thanks forever, because You have done it, and I will wait on Your name, for it is good, in the presence of Your godly ones.*
>
> Psalm 52:8-9

In God's kingdom, waiting is a good thing. Instead of believing the world, like the Psalmsist we can choose to focus our faith on what God says about waiting. We can decide that *wait* is a good four-letter word.

Waiting Renews and Re-Energizes Us

The single most important decision we will ever make is to surrender our lives to Jesus Christ as our personal Savior and Lord!

At the onset of my Christian life, a brother in Christ taught me that maturity in Christ would come over time. My faith would grow step by step. I would be strengthened and grow in God's grace as I waited on the Lord.

Waiting doesn't come naturally to most of us. It certainly wasn't a part of my nature. It was something I would have to learn if I were to become Christlike.

God knew I would have to go through His school of waiting. So He began teaching me how to wait on Him the day after I was converted to Christ. The Holy Spirit, who lived in me, assumed the role of my resident teacher. The Spirit of God began showing me how to walk with my Maker and enjoy fellowship with Him.

I suppose every Christian has a favorite verse or passage in the Bible that means something special to them. Early in my Christian life, the Lord gave me my life's passage and verse all in the same package. Isaiah 40:25-31 contains the spiritual truth and treasure that I draw upon on a daily basis:

> *"To whom then will you liken Me, that I would be his equal?" says the Holy One. Lift up your eyes on high and see who has created these stars, The One who leads forth their host by number, He calls them*

*all by name; because of the greatness of His might and the strength of His power, not one of them is missing. Why do you say, O Jacob, and assert, O Israel, "My way is hidden from the L*ORD*, and the justice due me escapes the notice of my God"? Do you not know? Have you not heard? The Everlasting God, the L*ORD*, the Creator of the ends of the earth does not become weary or tired. His understanding is inscrutable. He gives strength to the weary, and to him who lacks might He increases power. Though youths grow weary and tired, and vigorous young men stumble badly, yet those who wait for the L*ORD *will gain new strength; they will mount up with wings like eagles, they will run and not get tired, they will walk and not become weary.*

The prophet Isaiah was writing to a people experiencing extremely hard times. The nation had drifted far from the Lord. Difficult days were their lot in life. They complained that God wasn't just. Life wasn't fair. In their arrogance, they accused Him of hiding from them. Forgetting them.

Having already lost sight of their faith and now fast losing heart, God's weary children were spiritually and emotionally tempted to seek self-centered, self-serving solutions to their problems. His chosen people considered looking to the powerful, pagan nation of Assyria to care for them. National disaster loomed on the horizon. If they weren't careful, if they rejected God's invitation to wait on the Lord, they would reap remorse and reside in a land of regret.

Mercifully, God raised Isaiah to vehemently protest their lapse into disobedience and their imminent spiritual downfall.

Life is not fair, and it never will be. It can wear us down and wear us out. At times we wonder if there is, or ever will be, justice on this earth. Circumstances out of our own control deceive us into questioning whether God knows our name or where we live anymore! Our frustration can lead us to doubt our faith.

During moments of spiritual weariness, Satan comes as a wolf in sheep's clothing, tempting us to look to some other source (such as a powerful Assyria) for the renewal and resources we need.

Both Isaiah and Jeremiah agree that the Lord is the One to satisfy our needs.

I satisfy the weary ones, and refresh everyone who languishes.

Jeremiah 31:25

The Psalmsist wrote in Psalm 130:5-6: *I wait for the Lord, my soul does wait, and in His Word do I hope. My soul waits for the Lord, more than the watchmen for the morning; indeed, more than the watchmen for the morning.*

More than anything, David desired to wait and watch for the Lord and a word from Him.

God's people found themselves in trouble because they were unwilling to wait on the Lord to renew their strength.

The passage from Isaiah shows us four things that are good for us: **Perspective, Providence That Is Personal, Power, and Exchanging Weakness for Strength**. All are connected to waiting on the Lord.

Perspective

Proper perspective is critical to successful living. Our perspective is determined by where we choose to look.

Many people have no clue as to what the big picture of life is all about. The average person's world is pathetically small, bordered by I, me, mine, and myself. Caught up in an obsessive preoccupation with themselves and their concerns, self-absorbed people focus on what they can see around them. Their shortsighted focus is creature and creation oriented. Sight, not faith, guides their lives.

Looking inward is the way of the world. Introspection, self-study, inner analysis, and self-improvement are the politically and intellectually correct things to do. But while there is a place for healthy self-examination, looking within often causes anxiety and frustration. Focusing exclusively on ourselves can lead to discouragement and even despair when we realize that we don't measure up to our expectations.

We must look to God if we're to see things as God sees them. Our self examination should always be done using prayer as our guide and the Bible as our standard for determining how we measure up to God's expectations for our lives.

God's spiritual spokesman exhorts us, *"Lift up your eyes on high."* Look up. Shift your focus. Get your eyes, and thoughts, off yourself. Look through spiritual eyes and see the Creator who stands above and behind His creation. Focus on the One who made everything and put the universe in motion.

Unfortunately, many people created after the image of God are looking in and down. As a result, our society has become highly impersonal. In fact, we don't even look around much anymore. Observe people in public. You won't find very many people walking with their heads up. Most people won't lift their gaze to look at you when you pass by, either. They stare at the ground in front of them.

Try this exercise. Turn your gaze toward your feet. Look toward the ground. Come on, you can do it. No one will see you! Look down.

What did you see? You saw yourself, didn't you? Nothing but you. Your body, your clothes, your shoes. You, you, you. That's the result of the downward look. The downward look causes people to be consumed with themselves. God is nowhere to be found when we look in and down.

Now, turn your gaze toward heaven. That's right, look up. Lift your gaze to a higher place. What do you see? You don't see yourself, do you? That's good, because most of our problems originate from ourselves.

I once heard a preacher say if he I could kick squarely in the seat of the pants the person who caused him the most trouble, he wouldn't be able to sit down for a week! There's a lot of truth for all of us in that statement.

While looking up you don't see yourself. You see a much bigger world, and that is very good! In fact, the higher we look, the better it gets!

According to Isaiah 40:25-31, God invites us to look up and see Him. Why? He is the solution to our problems. The Creator knows how to care for His creation. He is the only One qualified to deliver us from our dilemmas.

David wrote in Psalm 123:2:

> *Behold, as the eyes of the servants look to the hand of their master, as the eyes of a maid to the hand of her mistress, so our eyes look to the Lord our God, until He is gracious to us.*

The emphasis here is on the eyes of the servants and maids looking to their masters. Servants depend on their masters to meet their needs. In like manner, God's servants are to look to Him. He will be gracious to those who do.

Over the past three decades, I have had the privilege of providing pastoral counsel for many people who have been wounded by life. Most come to my office looking down and in. They focus on their feelings and their troubles. I seek God's wisdom to motivate them to redirect their spiritual eyes. Hurting people can begin to triumph over their troubles when they look up, to Jesus Christ. Our Creator, Redeemer and Healer can bind up our wounds and heal our hurting hearts (Psalm 30:2; Jeremiah 30:17; Psalm 147:3).

God can help us like nobody else can, because there is nobody like Him!

Modern missionary statesman J. Sidlow Baxter said there is no substitute for Jesus because there is no equivalent.

Isaiah declared there is none to compare with the Holy One. Jeremiah also had something to say about the Everlasting God, the Creator of the ends of the earth.

> *Are there any among the idols of the nations who give rain? Or can the heavens grant showers? Is it not You, Oh LORD, our God? Therefore, we hope in [wait for] You, for You are the one who has done all these things.*
>
> Jeremiah 14:22

There's nobody like God. Period. Never has been, never will be. That's why we are to lift up our eyes on high and look to Him. We enlarge our perspective on life by looking to the Maker, Giver and Sustainer of life. The upward look trumps the downward and inward look every time!

Providence That Is Personal

I may be a bit old-fashioned, but I still believe in the personal touch.

Though I can survive without these things, I do enjoy being noticed by others, hearing my name, and occasionally having people ask how I'm doing, what I'm doing, and where I'm going. I'm not some nameless, faceless entity simply identified by a nine-digit Social Security number. Psalm 139 makes it clear that I'm a uniquely special person, wonderfully and fearfully made by a personal God.

The world system tries to convince us otherwise. We're told the name of the game is to be the same as everyone else.

Conscious and unconscious efforts to squeeze everyone into the same mold are producing nothing but a bunch of confused and identity-less citizens. If you think about it long enough (30 seconds should be adequate) who wants to be like everybody else anyway? I don't. You don't either. If there were no differences between us, life would be boring with a capital B!

God has a better idea. Abundant, satisfying life flows from being the unique, one-of-a-kind, wonderfully special person He created you to be.

God is a god of the personal touch. That's good news for you and me, who live in an intensely impersonal culture where taking a number is more important than being called by name. In the passage we read from Isaiah 40 note what verse 26 says about God. The Lord Himself created the stars. Billions upon trillions of them. Numberless. Not only did He create them, He leads them, He calls all them by name, and not one of them is missing!

If by the greatness of His might and the strength of His power God literally hangs each one of the twinkling stars in this endless universe, assigns each one of them a name, and knows where each one of them is so that not a single, fiery ball of gaseous matter is missing from roll call, what does that mean for us?

It means that if He cares that much about stars, He cares much more for you, a person made after His own image (Genesis 1:26-28). He sent His only Son to die so you could be saved for time and eternity! (John 3:16)

It should be absolutely mindboggling to think we are that important to God! We are the real stars of the universe. Because we are, we need to lift our eyes up on high to the star maker, our Lord and Savior Jesus Christ.

Nothing escapes God's notice concerning His children. He watches over us. He wants us to know we are never forgotten (Isaiah 44:21) and never forsaken (Hebrews 13:5). Just as He skillfully and personally leads the stars in the skies, He purposefully and graciously directs the paths of His faithful children living on planet Earth.

To remind myself of this, I've made it a habit to regularly step outside at night to gaze upon the heavens. When I lift my face up to stare at the stars, perspective and purpose come into focus. I lift my hands, as well as my eyes, to my Creator and praise Him for His personal care for me. I enjoy my sky-watching moments most when I feel stressed, when life's pressures press in on me. When I'm tempted to look down at myself, or look around to my situation, I know it's time to look up!

If you want to experience a refreshing spiritual lift, get out of your house and look up into the night sky. Lifting your eyes on high to see God is the first step to waiting on the Lord.

There really is a personal God who loves us very much. Life turns around when we turn our eyes to the Lord.

As Robert Schuller once said, we can turn our scars into stars.

Power

The pastor at the other end of the phone connection needed to talk. Next Sunday he would be resigning his position, he told me. He didn't really want to. But shortly after he'd arrived at his church two years earlier, the devil went to work on discrediting the pastor's ministry and dividing the congregation. The damage the enemy inflicted led to a church split. "Steve, I've been fighting this thing for over two years. I'm bone-weary. I checked into a hotel for a couple of days to rest and regroup. Sitting poolside, I wondered if anyone as tired as me had sat in the chair I was occupying. I feel that I can't go on," he confided. "I guess I'm out of gas."

Out of gas. Ever been there? Maybe your spiritual gas tank is hovering just above empty right now. Maybe you feel like your life is running on fumes. We've all been there at one time or another.

God spoke to Israel through Isaiah because Israel was out of gas. The Lord's handpicked people lacked the spiritual power needed to find refreshment and move forward. They were worn out and wondering what to do.

Isaiah 40:28 tells us the Lord asked them questions designed to jog their spiritual memories: *Do you not know? Have you not heard?* Of course they knew, and had heard many times. But they had forgotten. They needed a spiritual nudge. God reminded them *the Everlasting God, the* Lord, *the Creator of the ends of the earth does not become weary or tired.*

In other words, God said, "Listen up, Israel. It is obvious you're tired and worn out. But I'm not. I never get tired. It's not possible for Me to ever become weary. Tiredness is not one of the Trinity's attributes. I never have to sleep. I'm always wide-awake, rested, on the alert, and ready to refresh you when you're weary."

Weary friend, God never runs out of gas! He doesn't for one simple reason: He's God!

I'm sometimes reminded of a series of television commercials Reekbok once ran featuring famous young athletes. The scenarios varied, but each ad concluded with a similar scene. As cameras zoomed in on the athlete's Reebok-clad feet, he or she declared, "This is my planet."

Young people loved it. Why? Because youth thinks it's invincible. Adolescents and young adults are convinced — by their peers and a horde of happy hormones —life is theirs for the taking; youth can do anything: Tackle every trial. Conquer any challenge. Move every mountain.

Their prowess fools them into believing that they're all-powerful. — Bring it on life. You can't wear me out or wear me down. I'm young and I never run out of gas.

Though young people want to believe they're in control and have never-ending personal vigor, they're mistaken. Their misguided notion of endless human power and inexhaustible strength simply isn't true.

Psalm 24:1 declares *the earth is the Lord's, and its fullness....* Our planet is God's, not ours. He made it. Everything in, on and above the earth, including us, belongs to Him. God owns everything, runs everything and sustains everything by His power.

Thinking we own the earth and are all-powerful can cause us to forget who is in charge and where we need to go to be recharged when our "batteries" are running low. Our sole source of unlimited, inexhaustible strength is God. David knew this, and directed our spiritual attention to the One who is our help.

> *I will lift up my eyes to the mountains; from where shall my help come? My help comes from the Lord, Who made heaven and earth. He will not allow your foot to slip; He who keeps you will not slumber. Behold, He who keeps Israel will neither slumber or sleep.*
>
> Psalm 121:1-4

God's Word tells us God shows up and meets our needs when we're tired and need help. The Lord knows something about young people. In Isaiah 40:30, the prophet plainly stated that even youths grow weary and tired. Then, the writer added that even vigorous young men stumble badly. What a message for our youth-crazed culture! Not only do even the most buff, conditioned athletes tire and stumble in life — they stumble badly.

Stumbling is descriptive of the age we live in, isn't it? People are tripping up and falling down everywhere you look. Our culture is wearing everybody out. Even mega-vitamin packs, caffeine, instant energy drinks, steroids, and pep pills can't stem the tide of stumbling that surrounds us. News headlines and magazine covers offer shocking stories about people who stumble and tumble because life is too much.

We don't have to stumble. Not only is God strong, never sleepy, and full of power (*power belongs unto God* Psalm 62:11), *He gives strength to the weary, and to him who lacks might He increases power* (Isaiah 40:29).

What a welcome promise for weary warriors! God doesn't keep His strength and power to Himself. He gives it to those of us who are weary, exhausted, ready to throw in the towel. It isn't God's will for us to wear out and stumble. When we admit our need and look to Him, He steps in to empower us to go on.

Human prowess and charismatic personality are not enough to get through life successfully. We need Almighty God's power, and we need it daily. Each day of our earthly existence, we need to rely on our Redeemer!

Look to the Lord as your remedy. God will not allow your foot to slip!

Exchanging Weakness for Strength

God's plan for us includes exchanging our weakness for His strength, our powerlessness for His power. Paul elaborates on this in 2 Corinthians 12:9-10:

> *He has said to me, "My grace is sufficient for you, for power is perfected in weakness." Most gladly, therefore, I will rather boast about my weaknesses, that the power of Christ may dwell in me. Therefore I am well content with weaknesses, with insults, with distresses, with persecutions, with difficulties, for Christ's sake: for when I am weak, then I am strong.*

Weakness is part of life. It isn't a sin. Being weak just means we're human and we need God's strength. Within our weakness is the potential for us to be strong. Paul wrote that when he was weak, he was strong. How? Christ's power worked in Paul.

Because everything in the passage from Isaiah (40:28) is true (we get tired and stumble but God never does), verse 31 tells us what we need to do to be renewed:

> *Those who wait for the Lord will gain new strength; they will mount up with wings like eagles, they will run and not get tired; they will walk and not become weary.*

We surrender our weakness and lack of power when we wait on the Lord, because waiting on the Lord means we are relying on Him instead of ourselves.

We demonstrate our reliance upon God by going to Him when we are weary and stumbling through life.

God's highest purpose for His children is not for them to rush through life tired, stumbling, fumbling, fainting, or falling out somewhere along the way. Not at all!

His children are to mount up with wings as eagles. To rise above their problems, and soar effortlessly and efficiently — spiritual eagles on the wings of the Holy Spirit!

We are to run and not get tired. That means we can run our race without running out of steam.

And, God's children will walk and not become weary. When we walk step by step in faith, we are refreshed and renewed by the Lord.

Scripture tells us renewal comes to those who wait on God, because He gives them new strength. That means, we can enjoy our journey with Him though life empowered by God!

The specific meaning of the word translated as *wait* in Isaiah 40:31 is to twist or to stretch in order to become strong.

Life can definitely stretch us every day with its unpredictable twists and turns. God's purpose in the twisting and stretching process is to turn us toward Him.

I certainly understand being stretched to become strong through twists and turns. Years ago, acute reactive depression landed me in a hospital for a month. A personal crisis left me troubled in spirit and haunted by suicidal thoughts.

I wasn't prepared to walk through the valley of depression. Struggling to survive the onslaught of despair, I found it nearly impossible to raise myself up from under the dark shadows of its cloud. My faith was tested to the limits of my endurance, exhausting not only my spiritual resources, but also my emotional and physical resources.

When I entered the hospital for treatment I was completely spent. Life had taken a turn I didn't welcome or understand. In the middle of my pain and confusion, the Lord reached out to me with His merciful and compassionate hand. He overruled, and turned this life-threatening ordeal around for my good, showing me in the midst of everything how great His love is for me.

My only way out was to wait on the Lord. Though weaker than I had ever been in my life, I believed that God's strength would overcome my weakness. I looked to God and trusted Him that in weakness I would become strong in Christ.

Psalm 59:9 says it well: *Because of his strength I will watch* [wait] *for You, for God is my stronghold.*

God didn't fail me in my hour of desperation. On the contrary, He did for me what I couldn't do for myself. As I waited for Him, He waited on me. The Lord healed my heart and restored me to physical, emotional and spiritual health.

Those who wait for the Lord do indeed gain new strength. Renewal does come when we wait. It may not always make sense, but when all we can do is wait, it's God's path to His best work in our lives.

Take the word of someone who has plummeted to the depths and come back stronger than ever: Waiting is good when we wait on God.

The secret to receiving good things from God is to wait.

"I will restore you to health and heal your wounds," declares the Lord.
Jeremiah 30:17

Chapter 3
If You Want to Be Great, You're Going to Have to Wait!

While I was in seminary I attended a motivational seminar. The keynote speaker was a Christian businessman with a national reputation for inspiring people to believe in themselves and fulfill their dreams. His topic: How to Be Great God's Way.

His message was perfect for me! I believe God has called every Christian to greatness. I desired more than anything to be successful; I would soon become involved in full-time ministry; I wanted to succeed God's way.

I could hardly wait to learn from this herald of God.

Immediately after being introduced, the speaker bounded to the podium, leaned over it, and said, "If you want to be an overnight success, it will take about ten years!"

The crowd broke out with a roar of approval followed by an enthusiastic round of applause. It set the tone for the rest of the evening. What a night! We listened, laughed, cried, and cheered.

I took notes and soaked up every bit of wisdom I could.

If I learned anything from that successful leader, it was this: There's no such thing as overnight success. Success takes time.

You might be thinking, "Wait a minute! What about those overnight successes that shot to the top like a meteor streaking across the starlit sky?"

We do live in an age of splash, flash, and dash. Everybody wants to make it big…Now! Fifteen minutes of fame will do. Anything, just so people will know who you are. How people strive to do something great; become rich and famous; write a best-selling book; star in a box office smash; hit the World Series winning home run; win a lottery! Have you ever heard the expression "a person who makes a big splash may be a person who has fallen overboard"?

The world applauds mere mortals and equates their moments of earthly celebrity with greatness and success, but ultimately life in the fast lane of worldly success can be shallow and unsatisfying!

Success is a journey, not a destination — especially in the Kingdom of

God. Biblical success and biblical prosperity come to those who wait. The Lord approves of godly men and women whose hearts are set on being fruitful for time and eternity. Greatness and success, God's way, involves a purifying process. Over time waiting produces the type of faith and character that He can trust with His true riches.

Most people will tell you heaven is their ultimate destination. But have you ever noticed how few of us seem to enjoy the journey that takes us there? We can miss much in our hurry to get somewhere. Neglecting to soak up the special moments in life that God graciously grants us on the path to paradise will steal our joy and peace. We should be willing to slow down and wait a little while along the way.

WAITING BUILDS GREAT CHARACTER

Consider this.
- Golda Meir came out of retirement at 71 to become Israel's Prime Minister.
- Colonel Harlan Sanders of Kentucky Fried Chicken fame was 66 and bankrupt when he began to promote his style of cooking and create an empire!
- Grandma Moses began painting in her mid-70s after giving up embroidery because of arthritis.
- Nelson Mandela was almost 76 when he was elected president of South Africa after spending 27 years in prison.
- Ray Kroc, who built the McDonald's Corporation from a handful of hamburger stands into the world's largest fast food chain, didn't sell his first burger until age 52. Before that he was a paper cup salesman, pianist, DJ, and traveling milkshake machine salesman (for 17 years).

Overnight? Hardly! As Ray Kroc said, "I was an overnight success all right, but 30 years is a long, long night."

Successful people who are honest and humble will tell you that it was a long, arduous climb to the top, with many periods of waiting and preparation.

Abraham Lincoln was great because he knew how to wait.

Born in 1809, and receiving less than one year of formal schooling in his childhood, Abraham Lincoln endured and overcame formidable obstacles on his journey to the Oval Office.

Event	Age	Year
Mother died	9	1818
Lost his job	22	1831
Defeated in run for Illinois General Assembly	23	1832
Failed as business owner, went bankrupt	24	1833
Elected to Illinois State Assembly	25	1834
Sweetheart died	26	1835
Suffered a nervous breakdown	27	1836
Defeated for Speaker of Illinois House of Representatives	29	1838
Proposal to Mary Owens declined	31	1841
Defeated for Congress	33	1843
Elected to U.S. House of Representatives	36	1846
Defeated for Re-election to Congress	39	1848
Sought the job of land officer in his home state – rejected	40	1849
Son, Edward, died	41	1850
Defeated for U.S. Senate	46	1855
Defeated for Vice President	47	1856
Lost Republican Senate nomination to another candidate	50	1859
Elected President of the United States	51	1860
Attack on Ft. Sumter began Civil War	52	1861
Son, William, died	53	1862
Re-elected President	54	1864

Defeats, failures, setbacks, misses, misfortune. Call them what you will. Lincoln waited a long time, making lots of little splashes (and stepping in some puddles too!) before the glory of his presidential greatness! He dreamed, worked, and waited all the way to the White House. Abraham Lincoln was a great man, not because he had lived in a log cabin, but because he got out of it! He was not idle. He worked hard to pursue his dream. His hard work took time. President Lincoln's experienced many waiting periods on his incredible journey from a log cabin in Kentucky to the White House in Washington D.C.

Those times of waiting made the man who made history during the most turbulent, troubling and ultimately triumphant period in our nation's history. Where would our country be today if Lincoln had decided not to persevere and wait to be great?

If Lincoln had chosen to give up and quit somewhere along the way, we would not be blessed with the Gettysburg address, the Emancipation Proclamation, or the healing and reuniting of a nation that had been torn apart by the hellish pain of Civil War.

The Bible records stories of people who were great at waiting.

- At a time when there had never been rainfall, righteous Noah worked on the Ark for 120 years, waiting for the flood God said would come to cover the earth (Genesis 6-9).
- Abraham and Sarah waited 25 years before they held the son of promise, Isaac, in their arms (Genesis 12-21).
- Joseph waited 13 years before his dream came to fruition as prime minister of Egypt. As a result, Joseph saved his family, the covenant God made with his forefathers, and the world (Genesis 37-50).
- Moses spent 40 years on the back side of a barren desert before God sent him to declare to evil Pharaoh, *"Let my people go!"* (Exodus 3-15).
- The Hebrew nation waited thousands of years for their Messiah.
- When *the fullness of time had come*, Jesus came (Galatians 4:4).
- Simeon, the righteous servant of the Lord, and Anna the prophetess, waited in the temple in Jerusalem for decades for the day when they beheld with their own eyes the Son of God (Luke 2:21-38).
- Saul the Pharisee, now Paul the tireless proclaimer of salvation *by grace through faith* (Ephesians 2:8-9), spent three years waiting on God in the wilderness. He unlearned religion, receiving instruction and insight into the Good News that transformed him into the great Apostle of grace (Galatians 1:17-18).

- A physically ill woman who had exhausted all of her resources had waited 12 years for medicine to heal her, until one afternoon, boldly exercising her faith, she touched the hem of Jesus' coat and was instantly made whole (Mark 5:25-34).

Throughout the Word of God, fulfillment of prophecy, healings, signs and wonders, miracles, salvation, and blessings of every kind came to those who waited.

In Psalm 149:4, David, who was also great because he had learned how to wait, penned these precious words: *The Lord takes pleasure in His people; He will beautify the afflicted ones with salvation.* What a tremendous thought! God takes pleasure in (is delighted and gets excited) us! If we will wrap this truth around our hearts, it will turn our day around.

It's a scriptural fact that God delights in us and desires to make us great if only we will learn to wait on Him. In fact, He has called His people to greatness. If you need to be convinced, study what Jesus said in Matthew 20:20-28. In verses 25-28, the Lord made it crystal clear about how to be great in the Kingdom of God.

> *Jesus called them to Himself and said, "You know that the rulers of the Gentiles lord it over them, and their great men exercise authority over them. It is not so among you, but whoever wishes to become great among you shall be your servant, and whoever wishes to be first among you shall be your slave; just as the Son of Man did not come to be served, but to serve, and to give His life a ransom for many."*

The context (what comes before and after) and setting of this teaching is very important. The mother of James and John had approached Jesus, asking for preferential treatment for her sons in the coming Kingdom (vv. 20-21). She went so far as to request that Jesus command that they be His right and left hand men. Jesus straightened her out by telling her that she didn't really understand what she was asking for (vv. 22-23). Service and self-sacrifice were at hand. Not superiority and showmanship. James and John would share in Christ's cup of suffering. But the decision as to who would sit where in heaven was not His to make. Those heavenly appointments belonged to the Father.

When the other ten disciples became indignant when they heard what was going on (v. 24), the stage was set for Jesus to set the record straight about how greatness is achieved in God's Kingdom. He called the disciples to Himself.

Any time Jesus called the twelve in close and tight, He had something important to impart to them. Teaching by contrast, He reminded them how the world operates. Greatness in this world system is gained when men assume positions of power over others. *"The rulers of the Gentiles lord it over them, and their great men exercise authority over them,"* He said. Out in the world, Jesus said the great person is the one who controls and commands others. The world measures greatness by how many people serve you. Living in a Jewish culture under the rule of the Romans, the disciples understood what Jesus was saying.

Lesson half-finished, the Lord proceeded to deliver the meat of the message Mrs. Zebedee, her two sons, and the ten jealous disciples needed: The world functions in you-serve-me fashion, but My followers should not. In God's Kingdom greatness is defined differently. To be great, you must serve everybody else. To be first, you must wait on others, a willing slave to their needs, not your own.

According to Jesus, service is the badge of greatness in the Kingdom of God. True greatness is not about commanding others to do things for you; true greatness is about doing things for others.

In his New Testament commentary on the book of Matthew, William Barclay made insightful comments concerning greatness God's way.

> The world may assess a man's greatness by the number of people whom he controls and who are at his beck and call; or by his intellectual standing and his academic eminence; or by the number of committees of which he is a member; or by the size of his bank balance and the material possessions which he has amassed; but in the assessment of Jesus Christ, these things are irrelevant. His assessment is quite simply…how many people has he helped?[1]

In Christ's Kingdom, we are instructed to not follow the examples of the world. The believer's example is Jesus, not some corporate president or wealthy celebrity. Greatness is not found in position or power, but in personal character.

Christ-like character that serves and gives is what God considers great. Jesus came to give His life through service and sacrifice; therefore, we give our lives in service to Him and others (v. 28).

Serving, giving, and being like Jesus demands that we wait on the Lord.

WAITING MEANS PARTNERING WITH GOD

As we have seen, God takes pleasure in His people. He has also entered into a partnership with those who love Him. Isaiah 64:4b states: *Who* [referring to Almighty God] *acts in behalf of the one who waits for Him.* Do you see the divine/human partnership? God works (acts) when we wait. Success in God's Kingdom is dependent upon a His part/our part system. God does His thing (works on our behalf) when we do our thing (wait for Him).

The great missionary statesman William Carey clearly understood this partnership principle. He said, "Expect great things from God; attempt great things for God." God works and does great things when we wait expectantly on Him.

Now, let's look at an important concept. Scriptural waiting is not passive; it's proactive. It doesn't involve hanging out on the couch eating potato chips expecting God to break through and meet our needs while we do nothing. Waiting on God requires us to work while we wait. Thomas Edison once said, "Everything comes to him who hustles while he waits!" That's the attitude of winners.

Many people never see God work because they don't work while they wait. They don't do their part. If you use a concordance and a good word study, and trace the word *wait* through Scripture you'll find that it means several things: "to look for; to stay in a place of expectation of; to await an event; to stand by expectantly; eager expectation and longing for something from God; to attend as a servant; to be active in looking for a favorable reception or response from the Lord." *Wait* is an active word, demanding activity on our part. Waiting is all about initiating — taking action that demonstrates to God that I trust in Him and depend on Him to meet my need.

The principle is this: I wait and work and God works.

Christians can get off track and fall into two ditches when it comes to this waiting business. The first: God does everything and I do nothing. The second: I do everything so God doesn't have to do anything.

The God-does-everything crowd sits around staring into spiritual space, waiting for the Big Guy in the Sky to bless them while they lift no finger to assist in the process. This bunch of misguided believers needs to seriously consider this: Most of the time the best helping hand you will ever find is at the end of your own arm. Or as a popular leadership saying goes: Don't wait for something to turn up, get a spade and dig for it!

The passive waiting process relieves its adherents from any personal responsibility. No playing a part in God's miraculous intervention in our lives! A supernatural/natural partnership is unnecessary because God is going to take care of everything without needing my involvement.

It sounds great, but this view is a few slots left of biblical center.

On the opposite end, the I-do-everything group is a few slots right of biblical center. They overemphasize the natural at the expense of the supernatural: I must do it. I do, do, do — so God won't have to!

Many people who live by this credo populate our churches. They are the works/righteousness crowd. They reason they can work their way to God's favor, blessings, and heaven. Man takes center stage in this unscriptural scheme of things, while God waits in the wings to have the opportunity to someday help His children.

Keeping biblically centered and balanced will ensure a proper understanding of the supernatural/natural partnership God has set up.

Take these people, for example.

Abraham's part was to believe God. God's part was to fulfill the covenant. (Romans 4)

Noah's part was to build the Ark. God's part was to send the flood, judge mankind, and start all over again with righteous Noah's family. (Genesis 6-9)

Moses' part was to hold the rod over the Red Sea and believe for a miracle. God's part was to make a way of safe escape through the imposing seawall for Israel, and a watery grave for Pharaoh and his pursuing army. (Exodus 13-15)

David's part was to speak faith, load his slingshot with rocks, and launch. God's part was to fell the giant Goliath. (1 Samuel 17)

The poor widow's part was to bring all the empty vessels she could round up to Elijah. God's part was to fill them with oil. (2 Kings 4)

Elijah's part was to confront the prophets of Baal, build an altar, soak it with water, and pray. God's part was to send fire from heaven. (1 Kings 18)

Daniel's part was to stand firm in his faith and not fear a den of hungry lions. God's part was to make the wild beasts harmless and show a heathen king who is really in charge. (Daniel 6)

The servant's part was to fill the water pots for the wedding. God's part was to turn the water into fine wine. (John 2)

The little lad's part was to surrender his fish and flatbread lunch to Jesus. God's part was to multiply it and miraculously feed nearly 20 thousand hungry people. (Mark 6)

Blind Bartimaeus' part was to call out to Jesus for mercy. God's part was to restore his sight. (John 9)

Mary and Martha's part was to be comforted and trust Jesus. God's part was to raise Lazarus from the dead! (John 11)

Jesus' part was to submit to the Father's will in the Garden of Gethsemane. God's part was to strengthen and empower His only begotten Son to forgive sinners, die on the Cross, and be raised in glory and power on the third day (Matthew 26-28).

Note: When we forgive others (our part)…then God forgives us (His part). (Mark 11:25-26)

Our part in these last days of the last days is to keep the faith while looking for the second coming of Jesus. God's part is to send Jesus back at the proper time (Acts 1:9-11)!

Do you get the picture? God's work gets done His way when there's balance between His part/our part, the supernatural/natural…the waiting and working principles we have explored. Stated simply: We work while we wait and God works because we wait.

Wait and work, work and wait. That's the way to being great in God's Kingdom! If you want to be great…Wait!

Daniel 11:32 tells us *the people who know their God will display strength and take action.* The King James Version reads *"the people that do know their God shall be strong and do exploits."* No matter how the translation renders this verse, I get excited about the take action, shall be strong, and do exploits stuff! *To do exploits* means "to accomplish heroic deeds and acts." Wow! Biblically, that means being heroes and heroines for God! Sounds like greatness to me.

The clear key to being strong and taking heroic action is knowing God. Many people desire to do great things for God, but they don't know Him. Many want experiences without experiencing *Him*. But Scripture says the doing is in the knowing. And knowing is in the waiting.

We get to know God when we wait on Him. We can't do great things for God when we don't know Him. We can't know Him unless we spend time with Him. And we can't spend time with Him unless we do our part (action) and wait on Him.

When I met Jeff he was 17 and in the hospital suffering from cystic fibrosis. Jeff struggled for almost every breath. For a 17-year-old, his body was underdeveloped and underweight. It was very difficult for him to undertake any strenuous activity. Most of the time he was confined to a bed or wheelchair.

A nurse who attended my church had called me to the hospital. She had been assigned to care for Jeff, and in the process, had become quite attached to the very likable young man.

Jeff had taken a huge turn for the worse. His doctors were concerned that they might lose him. His lungs were filling with fluid. His heart was beginning to fail under the stress on his system created by his chronic condition.

When I entered his room, I sensed I had come into the presence of someone very special. As I became acquainted with Jeff, feeling became certainty.

Jeff asked me to pray for his healing — a complete recovery. He said he believed in Jesus as his personal Savior. His family didn't attend church or care for the things of God. But this guy loved the Lord! A warm, bright glow lit up Jeff's eyes when he mentioned the name of Jesus. He told me that he wanted to be well so he could witness more boldly to his unsaved family and friends. He desired to minister to other cystic fibrosis victims. Jeff wanted to get out of that bed and do something great for God!

His desire to serve and do something great for God stirred my heart. I thought of so many healthy, able-bodied, talented believers I knew who could and should, but wouldn't do anything for the Kingdom.

What was the difference between Jeff's attitude and that of others I know? It was heart. Jeff, with all his limitations and handicaps, had the heart of Jesus. He told me that while in bed or wheeling around in his chair, he spent most of his time praying, reading the Bible, and sharing his faith with patients and hospital staff.

He was waiting on the Lord in that hospital room. By waiting, Jeff was getting to know God. Knowing God produced His heart in Jeff.

I left that day warmed deep in my spirit by a young man who, despite his serious situation, had everything going for him because he knew how to wait on the Lord, and God was working on His behalf.

Jeff got better and went home, witnessing up a storm to his family and friends! What a winner…a real winner!

Psalm 31:23-24 reminds me of, and is my prayer for, Jeff: *The LORD preserves the faithful.…Be of good courage, and He shall strengthen your heart, all you who hope in the LORD. (NKJV)*

When it comes to waiting, we have to be careful about what we're waiting for. Don't confuse the spectacular with the supernatural. Our entertainment-driven society thrives on sensationalism and showmanship. Unfortunately, many people are looking for something similar from God. What they really need is to show up themselves and flow in the power of the Holy Spirit.

Jerry Savelle once shared a very relevant message on this subject. He was covering Job 22:21-30 and was talking about knowing God. To paraphrase, he said, "Being intimately acquainted with Him is what the Christian life is all about. Waiting on God is how we become intimate with the Lord. We need to pursue the Provider…not the provision. Seek His face, not His hand! Seek the Healer, not the healing." Wise words for those who want to be great for God!

GOD'S SON, THE GREATEST

God so loved the world, that He gave His only begotten Son, that whoever believes in Him shall not perish, but have eternal life.
John 3:16

This chapter is about being great, and the fact that greatness comes to those who wait.

Muhammad Ali, former American professional boxer and one of the most recognized sports figures of the past 100 years, is considered by many to be among the greatest heavyweights in the sport's history. He certainly boasted he was The Greatest. Many agreed, including *Sports Illustrated*, which named him Sportsman of the Century.

But with all due respect and admiration for him and his many admirable accomplishments, in God's book The Greatest is Jesus Christ. He is the real heavyweight champion of the world. Christ fought valiantly and victoriously, soundly defeating Satan, sin, death and the grave! His death and resurrection was the knockout punch for all time!

Jesus was (and is) great because He waited on the Father. He sets the pace for those who want to be great! Think about some of the moments that we call great in Jesus' life and see how He waited on God.

- The Lord waited 30 years before beginning His public ministry.
- He waited for John the Baptist to recognize Him as the Lamb of God, baptize Him in the Jordan River, and to hear the Father's voice of approval from heaven. (Matthew 3)
- He waited 40 days in the wilderness, being tested by Satan, using the Word to resist temptation, and received strength from ministering angels. This desert time of waiting on God helped prepare Him for His ministry and journey to the Cross. (Matthew 4)
- He waited on the Father all night in prayer before He chose the twelve disciples. (Luke 6)
- He regularly left the disciples behind and went up into the mountains to pray and wait on God for spiritual refreshment and to receive power to perform miracles.
- He waited to raise Lazarus from the dead so God would be glorified, Mary and Martha would be comforted, the witnesses would be amazed and some would be saved. (John 11)
- Jesus waited in the Garden of Gethsemane to surrender His will to the Father's will before He went to Golgotha. (Matthew 26)
- He waited before the Father as He hung on the Cross, forgiving His accusers before breathing His last earthly breath. (Luke 23)
- He waited in the grave and descended into the hell for three days before He was gloriously resurrected from the dead by the power of the Holy Spirit! (1 Peter 3:18-22, Matthew 28)

- After His post-resurrection appearances and ministry to the twelve, He waited to ascend to heaven. (Acts 1:9-11)
- He waited to send the Promise of the Father (the Holy Spirit) upon His followers who were gathered together in the Upper Room at Pentecost. (Acts 1-2)
- He waits now, at the right hand of His Father, praying for us and listening for the word to return for His holy bride, the church!

The Lord Christ is our example of greatness and waiting. If we desire to be like Christ, we have to wait to be great.

Successful waiting is a process. First Peter 2:4-5 tells us that believers are *living stones...being built up as a spiritual house for a holy priesthood, to offer spiritual sacrifices acceptable to God through Jesus Christ.*

If you've never experienced the processes involved in building a house, let me share some important truths wrapped up in those two verses.

After 17 years of marriage, my wife and I had the opportunity to own our first home. When we decided to build, the Lord led us to a Christian homebuilder, under whose skillful guidance that home became a reality.

At first, progress was fast. The lot was cleared and graded. Footers were poured. Plumbing was put in place. Foundation poured. While the foundation was being smoothed out, lumber for framing arrived on site. After the concrete had cured, framers began their job. They measured, sawed, hammered and raised the skeleton of the superstructure. The house was taking form.

The roof came next. To lay the asphalt tiles the roof rats, as they called themselves, scaled steep peaks under an unbelievably hot summer sun.

Roof on, visible progress slowed to a virtual crawl for a results-oriented guy like me. It seemed as if little or no progress was being made. Activity was ongoing, but installation of electrical wiring and switchboxes, although necessary, is not very exciting to watch. The heating and cooling ducts, stairwells, kitchen cabinets, and fireplaces went in at a slow snail's pace.

When the drywallers showed up, the pace picked up. The house started taking a shape I could recognize.

Our future home began looking more and more like the architect's drawings. But what a mess! Building debris and construction junk littered the entire lot.

From my point of view, about two weeks before the scheduled closing date, the construction process ground to a screeching halt. Nothing seemed to be happening. I started to panic.

My veteran homebuilder assured me that everything would pull together in the next 14 days. I just needed to trust his word and experience.

He was right. The finish carpenters, wood stainers, painters, fixture people, carpet layers, window cleaners, and landscapers all swarmed the house at once. What a three-ring circus! Workers in and out, up and down, all around our home putting on the finishing touches. Closing day, the landscapers laid out an entire sod lawn. The yard went from Oklahoma red-dirt to green Bermuda grass in a couple of hours.

When we took possession of our home, seeing everything shining in its proper place took our breath away. All of the hassles and waiting were worth it.

In a similar, and much more important way, Christians are building a spiritual house upon the foundation of Jesus Christ. God wants each of our spiritual houses to be great houses... places of praise and adoration for our wonderful Savior! But a lot of clearing out, laying the foundation, curing, framing, roofing, shaping, and detail work must take place in order to finally achieve our Architect's vision. Sometimes the going's slow, sometimes not. But it takes time, and can be a messy process. If we're going to be great spiritually, we have to wait on the process of perfection that makes us like Jesus. As Daniel Webster once said, "A solemn regard to spiritual and eternal things is an indispensable element to all true greatness."

Chapter 4
If Waiting's Good, Why Is It So Hard?

The devil does everything he can to distract us from waiting on the Lord.

To this point we have studied how, from God's perspective, waiting is a good thing. God's richest benefits and blessings belong to those who wait.

But if waiting is so good, why is it so hard? Good and great things are never easy. They demand our best effort.

The fact that we're waiting to be blessed by God doesn't go unnoticed, either. Those of us who wait are well aware that we have an enemy who wages war on us. This formidable foe has no desire to see us receive God's gifts; just the opposite. He spares no energy or effort in mounting an all out assault against anyone who chooses to wait on the Lord.

Who is this adversary who attacks those who wait on God? Scripture identifies the devil as our adversary. The word *adversary* means "opposer or enemy, one that contends with, one who resists." Satan is a spiritual opponent who resists our efforts to live for God. The Bible describes our archenemy this way:

> *Be of sober spirit, be on the alert. Your adversary, the devil, prowls around like a roaring lion, seeking someone to devour. But resist him, firm in your faith, knowing that the same experiences of suffering are being accomplished by your brethren who are in the world. And after you have suffered for a little while, the God of all grace, who called you to His eternal glory in Christ, will Himself perfect, confirm, strengthen and establish you.*
> 1 Peter 5:8-10

If you're under attack, you're not alone. Christians everywhere are experiencing the same kind of difficulties you are.

Peter knew that. Through his own failure, he learned some valuable lessons about waiting on the Lord. He exhorted believers in Christ to be on the alert. He told us we need to be of sober spirit, at our post, awake and spiritually sharp on the lookout, because an enemy is prowling around searching for someone he can destroy. Note that word, *someone*.

Don't be among the spiritually misinformed people who live in a state of perpetual panic. Don't think the devil devours (tears and consumes) any poor old soul who happens to wander in his vicinity.

The truth is: The devil can only devour those who are devourable. What does that mean? It means we don't have to become his food. Let's remember we're his adversaries!

Peter encouraged believers to *resist* the devil. Peter also told his brothers and sisters in Christ not to worry. So don't run and hide. Resist with all your might. Courageously and boldly oppose the evil one. Fight back by standing firm in your faith. Refuse to surrender an inch of ground. Know what Scripture tells us so you can give the devil a good lick or two in the name of Jesus Christ!

Peter was a man of realistic faith. He knew Christians would suffer in this world. Suffering comes with the territory when serving the Lord. But seasons of suffering are temporary. Tough, trying times don't last forever.

The Psalmist's attitude toward his adversaries is refreshing and inspiring.

> *You are my King, O God; command victories for Jacob. Through You we will push back our adversaries; through Your name we will trample down those who rise up against us. For I will not trust in my bow, nor will my sword save me. But You have saved us from our adversaries, and You have put to shame those who hate us. In God we have boasted all day long, and we will give thanks to Your name forever.*
>
> Psalm 44:4-8

The good news is that in the midst of the battle, while the smoke is rolling and the dust is flying, by His grace God Himself will perfect, confirm, strengthen, and establish you! Why? Because He didn't call you and save you so that you should suffer and be devoured by the devil! Tough times never last…but tough people in Christ do!

Our Father in heaven redeemed us by the power of His love. Through the death and resurrection of His Son, God calls us to eternal glory. Christian living is a life of victory and overcoming in Christ. Our triumph comes through our personal faith in Jesus Christ. The beloved apostle John describes our victory over the world in which we live this way: *Whatever is born of God overcomes the world; and this is the victory that has overcome the world — our faith!* (1 John 5:4)

Yes, our adversary, the devil, is real. He isn't a mythological creature. Nor some fanciful, fairy tale character dreamed up to make stories more dramatic. He is alive and well on this earth, an entirely evil spiritual being set on destroying the human race.

In 2 Corinthians 2:11 Paul tells us we should not allow Satan to take advantage of us because *we are not ignorant of his schemes.* This means as Christians we shouldn't be in the dark when we deal with the prince of darkness. We shouldn't be ignorant concerning his tactics and strategies. By reading and studying Scripture we will know who the devil is and how he operates. And when we understand who the devil is and what he does, we can counteract his strategies in a spiritually intelligent and victorious manner.

We will know who he is because of his many names in Scripture. He is called accuser (Revelation 12:10), adversary (1 Peter 5:8), angel of the bottomless pit (Revelation 9:11 KJV), Belial (2 Corinthians 6:15), Beelzebub (Matthew 12:24), god of this world (2 Corinthians 4:4), murderer (John 8:44), the prince of the devils (Matthew 12:24 KJV), prince of the power of the air (Ephesians. 2:2), prince of this world (John 14:30 NIV), serpent (Genesis 3:4), tempter (Matthew 4:3), and the evil one (Matthew 13:19 KJV).

We live in an age of so many distractions, few people are focused on what matters in life. Satan knows this. And because distraction makes people vulnerable, he pulls no punches in using it against our faith.

To successfully resist the devil, we must first realize that he is out to distract us. In Ephesians 6:10-13, the Apostle Paul reminds us of the spiritual struggle we're engaged in.

> *Be strong in the Lord, and in the strength of His might. Put on the full armor of God, so that you may be able to stand firm against the schemes of the devil. For our struggle is not against flesh and blood, but against rulers, against the powers, against the world forces of this darkness, against the spiritual; forces of wickedness in the heavenly places. Therefore, take up the full armor of God, so that you will be able to resist in the evil day, and having done everything, to stand firm.*

The clear emphasis here is on resisting the enemy (the spiritual forces of wickedness in heavenly places) and on standing firm (repeated three times!) against the schemes of the devil.

The prince of this world is a cunning strategist who plots intentional evil against God's people. He works overtime devising ways to disrupt and sidetrack Christians while they're waiting on God. Our real enemy is never human flesh. (Although at times we think some people we know are the devil.) People are not our primary problem. Satan, the malevolent serpent, and his hellish hordes are.

Samuel Chadwick, a seasoned saint who had tremendous insight into war that is being waged in the spiritual realm noted, "Satan dreads nothing but prayer. His one concern is to keep the saints from praying. He fears nothing from prayerless studies, prayerless work, prayerless religion. He laughs at our toil, he mocks our wisdom, but he trembles when we pray."

The evil one will tolerate all types of ineffective religious activity. But prayer taps the power that topples his kingdom. (See Mark 9:14-29.) Knowing this, Satan attacks all who would wait on God in prayer.

Have you wondered why it is such a struggle to pray sometimes? Why on some occasions, is the spiritual opposition so thick that you could "cut it with a knife"? When Satan spots a saint about to pray, he aims his *flaming arrows* (Ephesians 6:16) of distraction.

How many times have we put off our prayer time because the phone rings, the children invade our space, a business associate has to see us, we remember something we just have to do immediately…and on, and on, and on?

Satan will send distraction after distraction designed to keep us from God because he wants us to live stressed and anxious each day instead of walking daily in quiet faith and confidence in the Lord.

Paul's response to the devil's distraction was to tell Christians to be strong in the Lord and the strength of His might (Ephesians 6:10). Paul commanded Christians to put on and take up the whole armor of God (described in Ephesians 6:14-20) then, having done everything God instructs his spiritual soldiers to do, to stand firm (vv. 11-13).

Make no mistake about it, the devil will never cease to wage war against us. The spiritual strength and overcoming power we need to stand firm and not budge when under attack comes from waiting on the Lord in prayer.

An enemy is defeated in battle when the opposite side has a superior force and reliable intelligence regarding his battle plans. As born-again believers, Christians are the superior force in Christ. Jesus Christ, the captain of our salvation and our spiritual commander-in-chief, and His heavenly host is all the army we need! (See 2 Kings 6:8-23.)

Peter and John overcame Satan through faith in Christ. No wonder Peter exclaimed, *"To Him be dominion forever and ever! Amen!"* (1 Peter 5:11)

We possess accurate, real-time spiritual intelligence. The Word tells us how Satan conducts himself. When we know how he will attack, we can counter him and conquer him in the name of Jesus. The battle is the Lord's (2 Chronicles 20:15) and *victory belongs to the Lord* (Proverbs 21:31).

Solomon wrote in Proverbs 8:34-35: *Blessed is the man who listens to me, watching daily at my gates, waiting at my doorposts. For he who finds me finds life and obtains favor from the Lord.*

The blessed man is the one who daily watches and waits at God's gate. He listens for the voice of the Lord. Hearing God's voice, he finds life. Not only does he find life when he finds God, he also obtains the Lord's favor or advantage.

We should expect assaults from the devil when we're drawing close to the Savior. When we watch and wait for the Lord, the enemy of our soul strikes. He doesn't want us to be blessed or walk in God's favor and power.

Our flesh resists watching and waiting, so one of our adversary's surest strategies is to assault our flesh. Matthew 26:36-46 shows us a prime example:

> *Jesus came with them to a place called Gethsemane, and said to His disciples, "Sit here while I go over there and pray." And He took with Him Peter and the two sons of Zebedee, and began to be grieved and distressed. Then He said to them, "My soul is deeply grieved, to the point of death; remain here and keep watch with Me." And He went a little beyond them, and fell on His face and prayed, saying, "My Father, if it is possible, let this cup pass from Me; yet not as I will, but as You will." And He came to the disciples and found them sleeping, and said to Peter, "So, you men could not keep watch with Me for one hour? Keep watching and praying that you may not enter into*

> *temptation; the spirit is willing, but the flesh is weak." He went away again a second time and prayed, saying, "My Father, if this cannot pass away unless I drink it, Your will be done." Again He came and found them sleeping, for their eyes were heavy. And He left them again, and went away and prayed a third time, saying the same thing once more. Then He came to the disciples and said to them, "Are you still sleeping and resting? Behold, the hour is at hand and the Son of Man is being betrayed into the hands of sinners. Get up, let us be going; behold, the one who betrays Me is at hand!"*

Jesus was heading steadily toward His date with destiny on the Cross. The disciples had accompanied Him to the Garden of Gethsemane. Deeply distressed about bearing the burden of mankind's sin, Jesus invited Peter, James and John, His closets followers and friends, to go deeper into the garden to wait and pray with Him. *"My soul is deeply grieved to the point of death; remain here and keep watch with me,"* He told His inner circle (v. 38).

Can you imagine what the Lord was feeling? I can't comprehend the immense pressure He was under, taking on our sins and knowing He was about to be betrayed. Scripture tells us that His sweat was blood.

He who knew no sin was to become sin for us. In His hour of deepest anguish, Jesus requested that His disciples stick close and watch (wait) with Him. The Lord struggled through His human side, surrendered His fleshly desires, and submitted to do the Father's will.

What did the disciples do while Jesus waited on the Father for the grace and strength He needed to become the sacrifice for the sins of the entire world? They napped! His most trusted, loyal supporters dozed off at their posts.

Three times Jesus came and found them asleep. In verse 45, you can almost feel the personal sorrow behind Jesus' question, "Are you still sleeping and resting?"

Was this the way they waited, watched, and prayed? What were they thinking? The appointed hour had arrived. Jesus would soon be betrayed and delivered into the hands of His enemies. The peaceful garden scene in Gethsemane would shortly give way to a tortuous path to crucifixion on Golgotha.

Jesus was prepared for what was coming. The disciples weren't.

Verse 43 tells us Jesus had found the three sleeping because *their eyes were heavy*. Heavy eyes. That's a flesh thing. For Christ's followers, the physical outweighed the spiritual.

The disciples could have kept watch. And they should have. Jesus would soon lay down His life for them. Surely, they could have toughed it out, kept their eyes open and watched with Him for one measly hour! While Jesus sweat blood battling for the souls of mankind, His closest followers checked out! How could that have possibly happened? What could account for the disciples' lack of devotion and self-discipline?

The disciples were physically tired. Worn out. Satan used their weariness as a weapon to distract them. If they were asleep, they couldn't support the Son of God while He made the decision to die so men could live. The disciple's flesh knocked them out of the spiritual fight surrounding them.

In verse 56 we read of disastrous consequences of their lack of devotion:, *All the disciples left Him and fled*. When push came to shove, Christ's physically and spiritually sleeping followers abandoned Him when he was hauled off to Pilate.

From our vantage point today, it's easy to point accusing fingers at the disciples for failing Jesus. But we should be slow to criticize or condemn them. We're no different from those first century followers of the Son of God. Our eyes get heavy too. Our flesh gets in the way of our spiritual life. We're tempted to fall asleep at our spiritual posts just like they did. Most likely we would have been assaulted in the same manner, and responded in the same way.

As His disciples, we need to heed the words of Jesus: *"Keep watching and praying, that you may not enter into temptation; the spirit is willing, but the flesh is weak"* (v. 41).

The words translated *watching* and *praying* are a continuous present tense. That means unceasingly, all the time, without interruption. Watching and praying continuously is an important part of waiting on God. Why should we watch and pray continuously? So we can resist temptation. Our spirit is willing to do the right thing. But our flesh is weak and more than willing to do the wrong thing.

A willing spirit coupled with weak flesh sets up a titanic tug of war within our will. (In Romans 7:14-25 and Galatians 5:16-25 Paul identifies the battle between the flesh and spirit.)

In warfare, military commanders never attack their enemy at his strong point. They strike the enemy at his most vulnerable spot. Satan knows how weak human flesh is. Encased in a pleasure-seeking physical body, our natural senses crave to be gratified and satisfied. Fleshly appetites and desires are averse to waiting. Human flesh cries out, "Satisfy me and gratify me now!"

Satan knows he can't defeat believers in Christ by hitting us head on spiritually. So, his favorite tactic is to attack flesh. The devil deploys his demonic forces to outflank and overrun us by overwhelming our flesh with temptation.

Believing in Christ sets people free to know the truth.

Scripture tells us Satan is a liar, a thief, a murderer, and destroyer. These descriptions give us all the intelligence information we need to defeat the devil. Let's look more closely.

SATAN AS A LIAR

John 8 tells us the Lord Jesus got into a spiritual battle with the Jews over the issue of truth. Jesus told them truth sets people free, and He was the truth.

The unbelieving Jews struggled with accepting Jesus as their Messiah. They tried to justify their unbelief by hiding behind their heritage, claiming that it was enough to have Abraham as their spiritual father. Jesus responded by telling them that if they were of Abraham, they should do the deeds of Abraham (v. 39). Without mincing words, He told them who their father really was.

> *"You are of your father the devil; and you want to do the desires of your father. He was a murderer from the beginning, and does not stand in truth, because there is no truth in him. Whenever he speaks a lie, he speaks from his own nature; for he is a liar, and the father of lies."*
>
> John 8:44

The Son of God delivered a scorching spiritual rebuke when He told the doubting Jews their father was the devil.

Under conviction and unwilling to confess their failure to acknowledge what is true, the children of the father of lies were offended. They picked up stones intending to throw them at Jesus (v. 59), but He slipped away.

The devil is a deceiver, a liar. It's his nature. He never deals in truth. Whenever he speaks, whatever he speaks, it's a lie.

Christians are children of the truth who walk in truth (3 John 3-4), and because the devil can't overcome truth, he does his best to undermine truth with lies.

In the Garden of Eden a lying serpent deceived Adam and Eve. The devil's "did God say?" cast doubt in Eve's mind. Building on her doubt, the devil suggested that Adam and Eve wouldn't die if they ate the fruit God had forbidden (Genesis 2:4-5). He notched up the lie by telling Eve that God knew that if they ate the fruit, their eyes would be opened and they would become like Him. Those words were a cleverly calculated lie designed to derail Adam and Eve's faith in God. Paradise was lost because Adam and Eve believed that lie.

What does Satan being a liar have to do with us watching and waiting today? Everything. Believers know the truth that God blesses those who wait. The devil also knows this. So Satan shows up to deceive us into doubting the value and necessity of waiting on the Lord. He doesn't approach us as some gruesome, grotesque, or scary thing. The angel of the abyss, the god of this world, *disguises himself as an angel of light* (2 Corinthians 11:14). And so the lie begins.

Satan lies to every generation. Sly and subtle, ever so cleverly, he whispers into our spiritual ears, "You're intelligent and perceptive. You know how to make decisions on your own. You're just too busy today; there's no time to get alone with God. You really don't need to wait on Him. Do you know anybody else praying and reading their Bibles all the time? You don't have to be super-spiritual. What will people think if you turn into a Jesus freak?

"Go ahead. Trust your instincts. Take care of yourself. Have it your way. Do what feels good and looks good. God's busy; He has more important things to attend to than your prayers and requests for help. Waiting's a waste of time. Take action. Do something. Don't miss the opportunity before you. He who hesitates loses."

Satan has similar scripts custom designed for each of his targets.

Have you ever heard this saying: "Beware of half-truths; you just might get hold of the wrong half"? Maybe you are very busy. Being busy is all the more reason to take time to wait on the Lord. Maybe you are mature in the things of God. Because you're seasoned spiritually you should know that you must wait on Him if you are to remain wise.

Your Father in Heaven waits for you to come and sit at His feet. You, His child, are the most important priority in all the created universe!

Don't let the devil bring truth decay into your spiritual life. Lies always look good and appeal to our fleshly nature. Refuse to be fooled and taken in by the father of lies. Fight with truth! You can silence Satan's lying tongue by speaking the truth in Christ.

SATAN AS A THIEF

The Bible also depicts the devil as a thief. John 10:10 clearly tells us: *The thief comes only to steal and kill and destroy.*

Thief, robber, burglar, shoplifter, pickpocket. One who steals what isn't his. That describes Satan. He does everything he can to rip-off the righteous.

In contrast, Jesus describes Himself as the Good Shepherd, *"I came that they might have life and might have it abundantly. I am the good shepherd; the good shepherd lays down His life for the sheep"* (vv. 10-11).

Jesus, the Good Shepherd, gives to His sheep and provides them with abundant life. Satan steals from them and seeks their destruction.

Just what does Satan steal?

He steals solitude. He works hard to keep us so busy we don't slip away to be alone and quiet before the Savior.

He steals our time. There just aren't enough hours in the day, especially to wait on God, right? Wrong. The enemy of our souls will steal minutes and hours from us in order to keep us from spending precious moments before the Lord. The tyranny of the urgent is one of the devil's favorite fiery darts. Some things can and should be rescheduled or postponed while we attend to the really important things. When we make waiting on the Lord a priority, we discover there is time, plenty of time in fact.

He steals our discipline. He appeals to the lazy side of our flesh. If he can keep us unfocused, disorganized, unprepared, and self-indulgent, he can make us ineffective Christians. He deceives us into indulging ourselves in selfish pleasure rather than spending quality time with the Lord. He wears us down by keeping us agitated over worldly pursuits. Unfocused, worried, drained, we become unable to concentrate on God, His Word and the work of His Kingdom.

The prince of this world attempts to steal our faith, hope, dreams, joy, strength, peace, patience, endurance, relationships, assets, and our resources.

How can we avoid it? We must stay alert; be on guard; keep watch. In other words, be on the lookout for the slick-handed trickery of the thief from the bottomless pit. And we do this by reading and knowing God's Word, spending time in prayer, and building a personal relationship with Christ.

The day is coming when truth will trump his lies for good. Satan will find himself chained in the depths of spiritual darkness, paying eternally for his thievery against humanity!

SATAN AS A MURDERER AND DESTROYER

Murder is the most heinous crime against humanity.

Who is the face and force behind murder? Satan. In John 8:44 Jesus said that the devil was *a murderer from the beginning.* John 10:10 also calls him a thief and destroyer.

Throughout history, the devil has been bent on killing off the human race. As a deceiving liar, thief and murderer, he destroys lives.

He not only murders physically, he does all in his power to murder people spiritually. His mission is to curse and destroy everything and everyone God has created and blessed. In fact, he's determined to destroy everything decent, holy, and right. How?

He disrupts relationships between God and men. He stalks those of us who would wait on the Lord, seeking any opportunity to snatch us away spiritually, if not physically. His strategy? Murder our visions, dreams, hopes and plans for the future.

Proverbs 29:18 tells us *where there is no vision, the people are unrestrained (perish KJV); but happy is he who keeps the law.*

Sadly, many people today are living without vision, dreams, or plans for God. Satan knows people with vision prosper. So, on any given day, in spiritual dark alleys the devil and his demon gang jump the unsuspecting, beating belief out of their souls in an attempt to murder their spiritual hunger for the things of the Lord. Afterward, those people might be alive physically, but they are spiritually dead, living a nightmare instead of God's dream for their lives. They become insensitive and uninterested in God's plan for their present and future.

But good news! Dreams are born in the prayer closet. Plans become clear and steps crystallize when we wait before the Lord.

In 1 John 4:4, the Bible tells us this: *You are from God little children, and have overcome them; because greater is He who is in you than he who is in the world.*

Even though Satan, the murderer, slips into the sheepfold to take the lives of the sheep, The Good Shepherd gives His life so that the sheep can live life abundantly.

It may be hard to wait sometimes, but waiting on the Lord brings victory! Satan is no match for those who are the temple of the Living God!

WAITING ON GOD WORKS

When life looks hopeless and we feel helpless, how can we stand against the destroyer? The truth is, we don't have to! Someone else stood up for us. In 1 John 3:8 we find these incredibly inspiring words:

> *The one who practices sin is of the devil; for the devil has sinned from the beginning. The Son of God appeared for this purpose, to destroy the works of the devil.*

This verse declares that the destroyer has been destroyed! Christ's primary purpose in coming to earth was to destroy the devil and deliver us from sin, death and the grave. Satan was stripped of his power when Jesus rose from the dead in resurrection glory!

It's easier to defeat the devil when you know you have the victory in Christ. Standing firm in faith in the victory Jesus has secured for us is our key to overcoming the evil one. We stand by waiting on the Lord.

Those who wait walk in triumph. What better way to conclude this chapter than to look at one of Christ's triumphs over Satan. It occurred early in His earthly ministry and is recorded in Matthew 4:1-11.

Following His water baptism by John the Baptist *Jesus was led up by the Spirit into the wilderness to be tempted by the devil* (Matthew 4:1). After fasting 40 days and nights, Jesus was hungry. The devil sought to take advantage of Christ's physical distress. In verses 3-19 we see that Satan tempted Jesus three times to take some shortcuts on the way to becoming Savior of the world.

The devil appealed to the flesh: "Command these stones to become bread." He appealed to pride: "Throw yourself down…the angels will watch over you." And he appealed to the lust of the eyes: "If you will fall down and worship me, I will give you all the kingdoms of the world." The three-pronged temptation was Satan's strategy to sidetrack Jesus from waiting on the Father for these legitimate needs to be met.

What did Jesus do? He resisted and rejected the devil by meeting him head on with the Word of God. Three times tempted; three times replying, "It is written…." God's Word backed the wicked one down each time. Matthew 4:11 tells us after the third time Jesus commanded Satan to be gone *the devil left Him; and behold, angels came and began to minister to Him.*

Satan ran. Angels came and ministered to the Lord's needs.

Jesus won in the wilderness because He waited with the Word of God. His watchword and His victory was, "It is written"!

Without doubt it's hard to wait. The devil does everything he can to make it difficult.

During seasons of difficulty my resolve to wait on the Lord is severely tested. It seems as if everything depends on waiting on God, and everything is pulling against me. Have you ever been there?

Once, waiting on the Lord for His guidance was the only way out of my dilemma. I had exhausted every avenue of things I knew to do. This trial demanded nothing less than an answer from God — a clear path from Him through the spiritual/emotional wilderness I was experiencing. I needed to see some roads signs pointing my way out.

The pressure was intense. Satan tried to seduce me into despair by suggesting that I had tried everything I knew to do without success. I could almost feel him breathing down my neck, harassing and intimidating me, "Where's your God now?"

Fed up, I determined to take a deep spiritual breath and rise up equipped with the whole armor of God. I pushed through the pressure to not wait on the Lord. Ultimately, I received the answers and direction I needed. I walked out of the wilderness, defeating the devil, because I waited on the Lord.

Jesus waited and won. Because He lives in us through the Holy Spirit, we can wait and win too! In all honesty, it may be hard to hang in there sometimes, but God's blessings are worth the wait. And believe it or not, the more we wait on God, the easier waiting becomes!

CHAPTER 5
WHAT CAN HAPPEN IF YOU DON'T WAIT

In 1967, New Orleans was granted a National Football League franchise, to be named the Saints. The French Quarter partied long and loud when the news broke that the Crescent City would field an expansion team.

Expansion teams aren't expected to make it to the Super Bowl in their first year. Few expect franchise teams to win many games, either. It takes time to develop a winning club.

Their inaugural season the New Orleans Saints started and ended on a record setting pace. Their season began with a 94-yard opening kickoff return for a touchdown. And even though their 3–11 season finish put them in last place, those three wins matched the most for an expansion team.

Yet the rookie team from Louisiana soon became the laughing stock of the league. They went 20 seasons in a row — and 10 head coaches, some of whom were dismissed mid-season — before their first-ever winning season. They didn't score their first playoff win until 2000.

By 1980, fans were up to their eyeballs with embarrassment and humiliation. After the team lost the first 14 games, fans showed up with brown paper bags over their heads. Adding insult to injury, the "bagheads" had scribbled *Ain'ts* across the forehead of their masks. The name stuck. The team became know as The New Orleans Ain'ts.

The Saints lost more games than they won during 40 seasons in the National Football League. Their losing ways finally came to an end when, in February 2010, playing in their 43rd season, they won the Super Bowl.

What has that got to do with me, you're thinking.

The Apostle Paul opened his letter to the Philippians by addressing them as *all the saints in Christ Jesus who are in Philippi* (Philippians 1:1). According to *Strong's Exhaustive Concordance*, the word translated as *saint* is used more than 100 times in Scripture. It simply means "holy ones."

In fact, in God's eyes, saints are much more than a small, select group of pious people who have been recognized for some superior spiritual performance. As far as God is concerned, everyone who names the name of Christ is a saint; every person who has a personal relationship with the Lord Jesus Christ is a holy one. And His holy people are set apart for a sacred purpose.

Unfortunately, instead of saints, there are a lot of ain'ts running around — people who choose not to wait on God, erringly thinking they can use their time more wisely doing their own thing; they can make it through life successfully on their own because waiting on the Lord is a waste of time.

The truth is, people going it alone blunder a lot. We stumble and fumble through life when we refuse to let God be our coach. We simply can't win without Him! We need the Lord if our lives are to amount to anything worthwhile. Jesus said it simply and well: *"Without Me, you can do nothing"* (John 15:5 NKJ).

The only way to turn losses into wins is to team up with the Holy One who shows His holy ones how to play to win. God's holy ones, those who know Christ and are known by Him (2 Timothy 2:19), are the people with the greatest potential for being blessed and being a blessing.

Champions aren't made overnight. Neither are God's saints. Winning requires waiting.

God's champions who accomplish great things are produced through the process of patiently waiting on the Lord. God's winners learn to wait on Him and walk through life with Him.

People who are unwilling to wait make big mistakes. In Numbers 21:4 we read revealing words regarding the patience of Israel.

> *They set out from Mount Hor by the way of the Red Sea, to go around the land of Edom; and the people became impatient because of the journey.*

That last phrase bears repeating. *The people became impatient because the journey.* On the pathway to glorious freedom where the bountiful blessings of the Promised Land awaited, God's chosen people became impatient with the process! The trip was taking too long. They got tired of waiting! Oh, they wanted to *be* there; they just didn't want to have to *get* there!

Patience and self-control were not among Israel's noblest virtues on their God-ordained journey. Their impatience bred discontent. The people spoke against God and Moses saying, *"Why have you brought us up out of Egypt to die in the wilderness? For there is no food and water and we loathe this miserable food"* (Numbers 21:5).

What Can Happen if You Don't Wait

God hadn't delivered the Hebrews from slavery in Egypt for them to die in the desert. His perfect will was for them to prosper, not perish. But the children of God lost their perspective. Instead of seeking the Lord and submitting to His will along the way, they spoke against Him, venting their displeasure with His plan. The result? God's judgment fell. In verses 6-9 we read that fiery serpents and death plagued the Hebrews because they became impatient with the journey.

Impatience occurs when our spirit is out of control. God's people didn't discipline themselves. Undisciplined, they became enslaved to impatience. Fleshly desires went uncontrolled and unchecked. Impatience led to indulgence and indulgence reaped the indignation of God. Instead of being blessed, these people found themselves cursed.

Like impulsive Israel, we can become impatient with our journeys. Unwillingness to wait will bring all types of troubles into our lives, too. Solomon warned in Proverbs 25:28: *Like a city that is broken into and without walls is a man who has no control over his spirit.*

A city without walls around it was unprotected and vulnerable to invasion from hostile forces. Many people's lives today are like cities without walls. Impatient people who don't control their fleshly impulses find themselves defenseless when Satan attacks. If we look to ourselves to manage our lives without waiting on God for protection and deliverance, our legacy will be broken lives that are falling apart and headed for destruction

America has become a culture of shortcuts with a No Waiting approach to life and success.

Microwave cooking. *SparkNotes.* No bake cookies. Acrylic nails and quick drying nail polish. Mail order diplomas, degrees, and licenses. Instant messaging. Text messaging. Social media. High speed Internet. Drive in and drive through restaurants and banks. Shortened sermons and streamlined religious services. All bear testimony to our aversion to waiting.

Americans may be the slickest shortcutters in modern history; but we are also short-circuiting for the sake of pursuing the seductive prize called success! Record numbers of people can't function unless they're using prescription antidepressants. Violent crime and sexually transmitted diseases run rampant. The divorce rate is at all time highs, in part because too many people know little about commitment to anything requiring loyalty, faithfulness, and stick-with-it-ness. Even the use of heartburn medication has skyrocketed.

Shortcuts don't cut it! Painting mascara and glossy lipstick on a preteen girl and dressing her up in the latest styles doesn't make her a woman. Short-term courtships raise the stakes against couples enjoying long-term marital happiness. Cramming things in drawers and under furniture doesn't make a clean and tidy home.

Get the picture?

There are no shortcuts to success. To be successful we must live correctly. We can't force, manipulate, or rush important issues. To be successful as God intended, we have to learn to wait. Patience is a vital part of the process.

DECISIONS DETERMINE DESTINY

Numbers 13-14 record a pivotal point in the spiritual journey of God's chosen people. Israel, led by the Lord, arrived at Kadesh Barnea, the entry gate to Canaan. Having sent spies to check out the land, Israel was poised to enter in and possess the land flowing with milk and honey that God had promised them.

What happened at Kadesh Barnea was a watershed event for Israel. The task before them wasn't difficult: Charge ahead and conquer Canaan. No big deal. Their success was already guaranteed. Almighty God had prepared the way. All they had to do was to continue to wait for His commands and obey them. But the Hebrews made two epic mistakes that determined their destiny for generations to come.

First, they held back when they should have gone forward. They received two vastly different reports from the twelve spies they had out sent to scout the land. The majority report, given by ten of the scouts, was negative and demoralizing (13:25-33). Those ten men couldn't see past the giants and fortified cities they'd observed. Their report terrified the people and paralyzed their faith.

The minority report, submitted by Joshua and Caleb, was positive and motivating (13:30, 14:6-9). They had observed the same giants and high-walled cities as the other spies, but these two men never lost sight of their awesome God. They passionately exhorted the people, *"We should by all means go up and take possession of it, for we shall surely overcome it!"* (13:30).

Caleb and Joshua declared: Canaan is ours. Giants and all! These obstacles are meant to be overcome! God's already gone ahead of us and removed the giants' protection from them. They're our prey! We're not grasshoppers. We're God's army! We shouldn't fear any man. We fear and serve the Living God! The land lays before us for our taking. So don't be afraid. Don't rebel against the Lord. Let's go forward by faith and claim what's ours! (Author paraphrase)

After the two men's impassioned speech the people rose up in unison and charged into Canaan, right?

Wrong! Intimidated Israel decided to stay put. God's chosen people wept, grumbled and rebelled (14:1, 9). They went so far as to suggest God didn't know what He was doing.

While the Hebrews considered stoning Moses, Aaron, Joshua and Caleb and returning to Egypt, the Lord paid a visit. He wasn't in a particularly good mood, either!

Then the glory of the LORD appeared.
Numbers 14:10

Showing up in all of His grandeur and glory, God told Moses, "I'm not putting up with this rebellious people anymore. They've seen all the mighty miracles I've done on their behalf and they still spurn Me. I've had it! I'm going strike them down with dreadful diseases, then disown them. I'm going to start from scratch again. You, Moses, and your family will become a great nation." (Numbers 14:11-12 Author paraphrase).

Moses knew the seriousness of God's displeasure and interceded on behalf of the people (Numbers 14:13-19). Amazingly, the Lord relented and pardoned Israel. But there were consequences for their unbelief and rebellion. The pardon carried a high price tag: The ten scouts who had given negative reports dropped dead. For the next 40 years — one year for each day the scouts had been in the land — the Hebrews would wander in the desert, until the last of the grumblers who were now over the age of 20 died (Numbers 14:21-37). Worse yet, the children would suffer for 40 years because of their parents' unfaithfulness (Numbers 14:34).

Can you imagine what it must have been like for an innocent generation to watch their parents and grandparents die in the desert? One by one. Family by family. Two generations, gone.

Israel paid a phenomenal price. Why? They weren't willing to wait on God and follow His lead into the Promised Land!

God is serious not only about waiting on Him, but also trusting in Him and moving forward when He says to.

In Numbers 14:39-45 we have an account of plain old spiritual stupidity. Israel refused to budge when they should have moved forward in faith. Then they moved forward when they should have waited. God's stubborn people, already under divine penalty, now decided they wanted to go up and possess the land. Moses confronted them and told them their efforts wouldn't succeed because they had turned from following God and He was no longer with them.

They went anyway. They were beaten back and disgraced by people they were supposed to have conquered.

Israel should have submitted to God's correction and judgment, paid their dues, and moved on after the 40-year wandering period was over. But no. They convinced themselves that if God said the land was theirs, it was theirs, no matter when they decided to go. Why wait 40 years? So they took matters into their own hands. Go now. Show God we can do it. We're strong enough!

They forgot that their strength was in the Lord! What was the result of their insolence and rebellion? Defeat, destruction, and death. All because they refused God's timing.

There is no anointing, power, covering, protection or blessing without God!

Imagine what they thought a year after their disastrous decision. Do you think they experienced more than a few regrets while searching for food and water in the heat of the unrelenting desert sun?

Like Israel, Christians who try spiritual shortcuts to avoid having to wait on God wind up wandering in the wilderness instead of feasting on the fruit of the Promised Land.

In fact, many people today reside in the desert of regrets. Frequently, people who come to me for counseling often lament, "If only I hadn't decided to do that," or "If only I'd made a better choice," or "If only I'd looked to the Lord for His direction and guidance," or "If only I'd waited a little longer."

Regret casts a dark shadow that blocks the sunshine of God's blessings from reaching His people.

When my son was a teenager, we talked one day about who real heroes are.

Like most young people, he was into hero worship. I took him to Hebrews 11 and we studied the people in the Bible's Hall of Fame of Faith. It led him to ask some questions about men and women in the Bible who messed up and failed.

We dug into the Word to discover people who fell short of God's best for their lives. We discussed their disappointing lives and the disastrous consequences they experienced that disqualified them from being outstanding moral and spiritual role models. Afterwards, my son observed, "Dad, it looks like God has a Hall of Shame in the Bible as well as a Hall of Fame!"

He was right! Consequences follow choices. Decisions determine destiny. We reap what we sow. (See Galatians 6:7.) We can gain wisdom by learning from those who have preceded us.

Let's take a look at the flaws of a few biblical characters who acted more like ain'ts than saints. Some of them repented of their sins, re-adjusted their attitudes, learned from their mistakes and made better decisions. We can learn important truths and principles from their experiences.

As we begin, we must remember that we're not much different than these people. All of us experience times in our lives when we act more like ain'ts than saints! The good news is, Christianity is all about new beginnings! Grace always abounds where sin once abounded (Romans 6:1-6). Ain'tness doesn't have to be terminal!

Abraham

Spiritual father of the faith. Covenant receiver and keeper. A main character in God's Hall of Fame of Faith. Certainly, Abraham made a less-than-stellar decision at least once.

God promised Abraham and Sarah a son (Genesis 15:1-4). Ten years later they remained childless. For whatever reason, they grew weary of waiting and took matters into their own hands. Sarah gave her personal maid, Hagar, to Abraham. The result was a son named Ismael (Genesis 16).

When Abraham and Sarah's personal desires and impatience caused them to step outside of God's perfect plan, they paid a tremendous price. Ismael and his descendants became a perpetual thorn in the side to Israel and the world.

Israel

God's people left Egypt. They camped at the foot of God's holy hill, Mt.

Sinai, while Moses went up on the cloud-covered summit to meet with God. But Moses took longer than expected to return. Exodus 32:1 begins: *Now when the people saw that Moses was delayed to come down from the mountain....*

And there begins the rest of the story. Instead of accepting this divine delay gracefully, while Moses prayed and waited on God, the people made a golden calf and began worshipping it (vv. 1-8).

After the Lord directed Moses to go down to the people, Moses found them out of control, indulging in their sins. Their unwillingness to wait brought the wrath of God down on them.

In my ministry I meet a lot of people who get impatient when God's work in their lives seems to get held up by divine delays. What do they do? They give up on God. They run out and worship some idol. They toss out their convictions and commit sin. Then, when calamity comes, they're surprised.

Moses

Moses had been assigned a thankless task. Imagine leading a few million grumbling people across the desert to Canaan! No one in ministry leadership will ever have to put up with as much as Moses did (even though at times we might think we do).

Moses made a major mistake that cost him personally. In a moment of frustration driven by impatience, Moses struck a rock twice. He wasn't supposed to strike the rock at all. God had directed him to speak to it (Numbers 20:8-13). But instead of what God said to do, Moses did it his own way. The price? Moses was allowed to see Canaan, but his feet never touched the soil of the Promised Land (Deuteronomy 34:1-6).

The great deliverer of Israel missed his moment in Canaan's glory because of a frustrated outburst of impatience.

Achan

When Israel crossed the Jordan River and miraculously conquered the Canaanite city of Jericho (Joshua 6), God instructed His people not to touch the anything in the city. Those spoils belonged to God and were to be deposited into His treasury (6:18-19). The people were warned that if anyone took anything for personal use it would bring a curse upon all of Israel.

Even so, Achan stole some of the forbidden treasure and hid it in his tent.

When the Hebrews marched up to the next city to do battle, they were soundly defeated (Joshua 7:1-5).

Through the discernment of the Spirit Joshua learned of Achan's treachery (Joshua 7:16-23). God's punishment: Along with the hidden loot, Achan, his entire family, animals and possessions were taken to the Valley of Achor where they were stoned to death, burned with fire, and buried under a huge pile of stones!

Achan's sin? Greed and impatience. He wasn't willing to wait on the Lord to provide for his needs. By taking the forbidden spoil (Joshua 6:11), Achan reaped his death, the death of his wife and children, the deaths of Israelite soldiers and the defeat of God's people who were never supposed to lose a battle!

JACOB

Jacob was a bona fide ain't for part of his life. This ain't became a saint after a personal encounter with God Himself (Genesis 32: 24-32). Prior to that turning point in his life, Jacob was a conniving deceiver.

Genesis 27 records how Jacob deceived his father, Isaac, and stole his brother, Esau's, blessing and inheritance. Jacob would have been bountifully blessed if he had left the blessing business to God. But he didn't. Instead of being patient and waiting for God to move, Jacob acted out of jealousy and greed. Sowing seeds of deception, he reaped Isaac's grief, Esau's wrath, and God's displeasure. Jacob spent 20 years in emotional pain and misery, all because he refused to wait for God's choice of blessings.

When will we learn that we really can wait on God to provide us all we need and more? (Philippians 4:19, Ephesians 3:20-21, 2 Corinthians 9:8)

SAUL

King Saul was a roller-coaster-type man of God — up and down and all around in his faith walk.

First Samuel 13 tells us after waiting for Samuel for seven days, Saul entered the Temple to offer the burnt offerings and sacrifice (v. 9). But this responsibility belonged to the prophet Samuel, not Saul. As king, Saul knew better than to usurp the prophet's role. Yet, unwilling to wait for Samuel's arrival, Saul did something he was not ordained to do.

When Samuel confronted Saul, Saul tried to justify his improper behavior. Neither the prophet nor God accepted Saul's excuses for his misconduct. For his impatience he lost his kingship. (See vv. 13-14.)

JONAH

Jonah wound up in the belly of a big fish because he disobeyed God (the book of Jonah). God told Jonah to go to Nineveh because He was going to save the wicked city. But Jonah, passing his personal judgment on the evil Ninevites, felt they were unworthy of salvation. He boarded a ship heading in a direction opposite from God's assignment. The Lord pursued him, disciplined and re-dispatched him. Jonah finally obeyed God. According to God's plan, the city did experience revival.

Jonah went through a lot of unnecessary hardships (a violent storm at sea, being tossed overboard by his fellow travelers, spending three days in a fish's stomach, and reaping the displeasure of God) all because instead of waiting on God and obeying His will, he chose to judge God's will and do his own thing.

It took the belly of a smelly fish to straighten Jonah out!

ANANIAS AND SAPPHIRA

Acts 5:1-10 records a dramatic incident in the Bible. Ananias and Sapphira lied to the Holy Spirit over the amount of money they'd received from a piece of property they'd sold. Peter, directed by the Spirit, confronted them individually. For trying to deceive God and the church, both dropped dead in the presence of Peter and the disciples.

Monetary greed and personal gain was behind their lying scheme. They could have reported the right price, turned it all in and trusted God to use their gift and return manifold blessings to them. Instead, they acted without God and literally died over a few dollars!

PETER

Peter committed numerous blunders on his way to spiritual maturity. One incident stands out as a perfect demonstration of the result of his impatience. In John 18 we read that Judas betrayed Jesus. When the Jews and Roman soldiers arrived to arrest Peter's Lord, impetuous Peter drew his sword and lopped off the ear of Malchus, the high priest's slave.

Peter's sword should have remained in its sheath. Jesus had forewarned him about what was coming. Remember, Peter fell asleep during the prayer time in Gethsemane. Because he dozed off instead of prayerfully waiting on God with the Lord, Peter was not spiritually ready when the Roman soldiers arrived. His impetuousness caused another human being injury.

Do you see yourself in any of these examples? Not waiting can definitely lead to some disturbing and embarrassing consequences. I got a glimpse or two of myself in some of these episodes, and I ain't particularly happy with what I saw!

Satan wants none of this sainthood stuff for us. That's what Job's trial was about. This man, *blameless, upright, fearing God, and turning away from evil* (Job 1:1), had his faith stretched to the max. Job waited through extremely miserable conditions to see the goodness of God. The *patience of Job* (James 5:11 KJV) is best expressed in his personal declaration of unwavering faith in His Maker. At the height (or depth) of his testing, Job confidently said, *"Though He slay me, I will hope* [trust in, wait for] *in Him"* (Job 13:15). In Job 14:14, Job continued, *"If a man dies, will he live again? All the days of my struggle I will wait until my change comes."*

Job knew from first-hand experience the value of waiting. His patience was severely tested in the crucible of real-life tragedy: loss of wealth, death of loved ones, personal illness, mockery by friends, and his wife encouraging him to curse God and die. These would have tempted anyone to give up on God. But Job waited on the Lord. He knew who His Creator really was, and he reaped a double reward as a result. (Job 42:1-17)

Job determined to endure whatever misfortunes came to him without losing his faith in God. I believe *the Lord blessed the latter days of Job more than his beginnings* (v. 12) because his faith was unwavering. Job chose to be patient in the perfecting process.

Job's faith is relevant to our faith today. No matter what comes our way, we need to trust in the Lord and wait on Him. The psalmist rehearses Israel's rebelliousness and the Lord's deliverances in the 106th Psalm. Verses 13-33 make for some pretty powerful reading. Our focus in this chapter is on what can happen when we don't wait on God. Verses 13-15 provide some eye-opening insight into why the Lord chastened Israel.

> *They quickly forgot His works, they did not wait for His counsel; but craved intensely in the wilderness, and tempted God in the desert. So He gave them their request, but sent a wasting disease among them.*

One reason we need to wait regularly on the Lord and seek His counsel is because we tend to forget His works. Quickly. We need to wait at His feet often so we can remember all the great things He has done for us in the past. What He did then, He will do now.

We must seek His counsel to be successful and avoid negative consequences.

For example, a middle-aged couple came to me for pre-marital counseling. They believed they were in love and were perfect for each other. After exchanging pleasantries, I inquired about their personal backgrounds. She had been married and divorced twice, he once. They had known each other 14 days! They had met answering a personal ad in the local newspaper. The man had received Christ as his personal Savior only four days earlier. They wanted to "get the counseling done" in a month and be married within six weeks.

What a recipe for disaster! All the ingredients for another failed marriage were readily apparent…except to them. I wouldn't consider uniting this couple in holy matrimony. Too many things were wrong for their romantic fantasy to be right. They needed to take a long wait on the Lord and seek His counsel.

Our culture is overly populated with emotional rebounders. Rebounding is great in a basketball game. Crashing the boards to grab the ball and get another shot at the basket is exciting and potentially productive. But rebounding from one hurtful relationship to another isn't smart.

It's wise counsel for people to take at least two to three years after a divorce to get their lives together and healed from their loss before even considering looking for another life's partner. And then they better be sure it is God's will!

Jumping into — and out — of marriages without checking in with the Lord is crazy. No wonder we have so much heartache in America.

We find His will by waiting on Him and searching His Word.

I met Doris and her daughters over 35 years ago. Doris, a member of a church I also attended, was an exceptionally kind and gracious lady. Her two daughters were with her every Sunday and Wednesday. Doris served the Lord faithfully and joyfully. She sang in the adult choir, taught children's Sunday school and always showed up to help with special church projects.

Doris' husband never darkened the door of God's house. When Doris hosted a church event in her home, her husband was always conspicuously absent. Behind her gracious smiles, Doris seemed to have a cloud of unhappiness hanging over her. I had a feeling that something wasn't right.

As I became better acquainted with her two daughters, I learned why Doris was so dejected. She had a horrible marriage. Her husband was rude and downright crude around her. They fought constantly, never agreeing on anything that mattered. She cooked his meals but they seldom shared the same table. They had slept in separate bedrooms for years. Friction, tension and conflict bordering on spousal abuse marked their marriage.

Doris was a Christian before she married. Her husband was a non-believer who had no desire to serve the Lord. Doris, knowing full well that she was marrying a man out of God's will (See 2 Corinthians 6:14-18.), married him anyway, hoping he would get saved somewhere along the line and become the godly man she had dreamed of for a husband. Her dream became a nightmare. His heart only hardened with time.

Doris has hoped against hope for decades, praying and doing everything she knows how to do to honor her commitment and to keep her family together. She continues to pay a terrible price — a miserable, emotionally abusive marriage —because she didn't wait on the Lord before she tied the knot with an unbelieving mate. She pays every day for a decision she made that she did not receive from the Lord.

We've all done dumb things that reaped negative consequences. I've injured a muscle playing racquetball and not waited long enough for it to heal properly. I've painted something and not waited for the coat of paint to dry thoroughly before applying a second coat.

Neither racquetball injuries nor poor paint jobs are earthshaking. They certainly don't impact eternity. The consequences that come from not waiting on God can be very costly, however.

- We can miss God's will completely.
- We can mess up God's timing.

- We don't fulfill God's dream for our lives.
- We frustrate the people around us.
- Our children won't learn how to wait if we don't
- People may not come to know Christ.
- We'll be on our own, without His help.
- We'll miss out on God's richest blessings.

Pretty serious stuff, isn't it? I can't speak for you, but I know I don't want to miss anything the Lord has for me!

Second Kings 6:33 includes a statement by a man who was frustrated with certain events that had taken place in his life. He said despairingly, *"Why should I wait for the Lord any longer?"*

Why? Good things happen to those who wait. And bad things happen to those who don't. It's as simple as that.

Why be an ain't when you can be a saint? Wait on God. Become the winner only He can make you.

Chapter 6
The Marines Aren't the Only Ones Looking

When James A. Garfield was president of Hiram College, a man brought his son as a candidate for entrance as a student. He wanted a shorter course of study than normal for him. "The boy can never take it all in," said the father. "He wants to get through quicker. Can you arrange it for him?" Mr. Garfield, a minister-educator, replied, "Oh yes. He can take a short course. It all depends on what you want to make of him. When God wants to make an oak He takes 100 years, but he takes only two months to make a squash!"

Mighty oaks stand tall, unbending, persevering through the rough storms of life. The best we can say about squash is that they get baked and eaten. Few towering oaks dot the landscape of humanity these days. Human squash abound.

Becoming an oak or squash depends on whether we sign up for the short course or long course in character formation.

It's painfully obvious that we're facing a character crisis in America today. Celebrity and talent is esteemed more highly than character and integrity. The world is full of characters who lack character.

Character is about good reputation, moral excellence, personal integrity and godly behavior. Our character is defined by the sum total of the attributes and features of our lives that distinguish us as individuals. Character is a matter of the heart and spirit. Who we are on the inside is what really matters. As Ralph Waldo Emerson said, "What lies behind us and what lies before us are tiny matters compared to what lies within us."

Have you ever heard the old saying "ability may get you to the top, but it takes character to keep you there"? A lot of able and capable people manage to make it to the top rung of the ladder. But many of them are also the same people whose sad stories of falling from fame and glory are splashed across the covers of supermarket tabloids. Character is required to keep people in high positions of authority, influence and power; godly character is absolutely essential if we are going to go anywhere in life that counts.

Booker T. Washington, a distinguished gentleman of noble and inspiring character, once declared, "Character is power." The world system in which we must operate lusts after power. Power means control. The world's heroes are those who rise to positions of power and influence in their particular field of endeavor. Politics, athletics, business, education, the military, the entertainment industry, and even many churches base their selection of who makes their Who's Who lists on how much power they possess. Society is enamored with the intellectually elite, the athletically gifted, the talented, the entertaining, and the politically correct. But many people in positions of power don't possess the power of good character. A lot of characters lacking character are running around running our country.

Something is amiss when:

- pop stars who boldly flaunt their disdain for decency and morality are the most recognized and idolized men and women in the world.
- the NFL, AFL, NBA and ABA are riddled with scandal, drug use, and felony convictions, yet players are admired and awarded multi-million dollar contracts.
- our political system is administered at all levels of government by self-serving, self-righteous public officials who openly ridicule and reject righteous principles and replace them with borderline — even blatant — illegal and immoral legislative procedures.
- high-profile pastors and televangelists fall from grace because of personal moral failure and unethical ministry practices

Something is wrong, terribly wrong with this great nation that once prided itself on virtue, values, and right living.

The Bible's book of practical wisdom, Proverbs, opens with these words:

> *The Proverbs of Solomon, the son of David, king of Israel: To know wisdom and instruction, to discern the sayings of understanding, to receive instruction in wise behavior, righteousness, justice, and equity, to give prudence to the naive, to the youth knowledge and*

discretion, a wise man will hear and increase in learning, and a man of understanding will acquire wise counsel.

Proverbs 1:1-5

Solomon, inspired by the Holy Spirit, wrote words of wisdom that would help his naive young son discern truth and receive instruction in *wise behavior, righteousness, justice and equity*. Today, more than ever, our young people need instruction in godly wisdom and knowledge.

The devil, the devouring deceiver, is leading our youth astray, destroying them and their future because of *a lack of knowledge* (Hosea 4:6). The prophet Hosea, who was brokenhearted over Israel's unfaithfulness to the Lord, wrote these final words: *Whoever is wise, let him understand these things; Whoever is discerning, let him know them. For the ways of the Lord are right, and the righteous will walk in them. But transgressors will stumble in them* (14:9). A very timely word for such a time as this!

The central theme of Proverbs is wisdom. Solomon traces the source of wisdom, how to acquire wisdom, and most importantly, how to walk in wisdom.

Wisdom flows from God's character, and it's exhibited by character that is like His. The characters God uses in the work of His Kingdom are those who walk in His wisdom.

Wise behavior, righteousness, justice, and equity are at the core of godly character.

Our live-and-let-live society sorely lacks these virtues our Maker has given His stamp of holy approval. Godless character is the rule rather than the exception. Unwise behavior, unrighteousness, injustice, and inequity abound in America. Good, wise men and women, who can be trusted and looked up to, are few and far between. The result, millions of our citizens are frustrated, confused, despairing, and cynical, because the constantly changing times we live in call for godly character.

For decades the United States Marine Corps used the phrase "looking for a few good men" as its recruiting slogan. For longer than the Marine Corp has existed, God has been looking for a few good men and women, quality people to fight the good fight of faith and carry on the cause of Christ.

Scripture tells us the eyes of the Lord roam the earth searching for hearts that are devoted to Him. God promises to *strongly support those whose heart is completely His* (2 Chronicles 16:9). The Creator is looking for more than a few good men and women of character.

Character makes a person. Abraham Lincoln knew this. He remarked, "Character is like a tree and reputation is like its shadow; the shadow is what we think of it, the tree is the real thing." Many of the "characters" influencing our society propose agendas and programs that look good on the surface (shadows). But after the rhetoric ceases, the hype settles down, and we search the records, their actual conduct (the trees) reveals the real persons they are.

Financier J.P. Morgan was once asked about the best collateral a customer could give him. He replied, "Character!"

Meditate for a few moments on the following quotes concerning character.

- Character is not made in a crisis…it is only exhibited.
- Your spare time is the acid test of your character.
- Character is what you are when nobody is looking.
- Character is the sum total of what a man is after he has won all, and it is the sole thing after he has lost it all!
- If you want to get a true estimate of a man, observe what he does when he has nothing to do.
- No amount of riches can atone for poverty of character.
- A true test of a man's character is not what he does in the light, but what he does in the dark.
- People determine your character by what you stand for, fall for, and lie for.
- Live your life in such a way so that when people tell lies about you, no one will believe them.

One of my favorite quotes about character comes from the preacher-orator Phillips Brooks who preached in Boston over 100 years ago. He said, "Character may be manifested in the great moments, but it is made in the small ones." People who make the most of the smaller, everyday moments and seasons of life score moral successes and ethical victories.

We can't ascend the summits of success unless we successfully develop character in the more mundane moments of life. It really is the little things that make the big things.

The unwise squander the little moments in life. They don't use them as building blocks of godly behavior and holy conduct that ensure a successful, satisfied life. So, the lives they build crumble and crash down around them when the storms batter them. Proverbs 28:18 declares: *He who walks blamelessly will be delivered, but he who is crooked will fall all at once.*

God blesses blameless behavior and curses crooked conduct. Deliverance comes to those who walk right, while disaster comes to those who walk wrong.

The theme of this book is how waiting on God produces Christ-like character that triumphs over life's trials. You've read this far because you desire to be one of those Christ-like persons who triumphs over the trials of life. You've decided you don't want to be part of that company of characters who dominate our culture. You want to have character, not be one! So let's get to work.

BUILDING CHARACTER GOD'S WAY

CHARACTER FLAWS

Every one of us has character flaws. It's part and parcel of our inherited sin natures, personality types, backgrounds and individual experiences. Character flaws are similar to a blind spot in your car —you just can't see what's there. You need some help from a passenger or passerby to make sure it's clear before you venture into harm's way!

More than once my navigator wife has helped me avoid bashing into another automobile because she could see in the blind spot when I couldn't. God has also used her a time or two to assist me in overcoming some of my character flaws that I've been blind to.

Whether we like to admit it or not, each of us knows deep down in our hearts where our character battles are.

The Lord Jesus Christ can change, mold, modify, purify and tweak our character when we wait on Him. But because waiting on the Lord isn't the socially or politically correct thing to do today, many people find themselves stuck, spinning their spiritual wheels in character ruts, acting out the same foolish, immature behaviors day after day. Someone with some smarts said you're young only once, but you can stay immature indefinitely.

The Apostle Paul was a man of immense spiritual influence and power in the early church. He lived in such a manner that he could write with humble confidence: *The things you have learned and received and heard and seen in me, practice these things, and the God of peace shall be with you* (Philippians 4:9). His Christian conduct was so exemplary that he could also write: *Brethren, join in following my example and observe those who walk according to the pattern you have in us* (Philippians 3:17). In 1 Corinthians 11:1 he wrote: *Be imitators of me, just as I also am of Christ.* Paul wasn't being arrogant or self-righteous. Only a man of proven character such as Paul could invite others to walk as he walked and get away with it.

In Romans 5:1-5, Paul used the term "proven character" and laid out the process for developing the godly graces that help us overcome in life:

> *Therefore, having been justified by faith, we have peace with God through our Lord Jesus Christ, through whom also we have obtained our introduction by faith into this grace in which we stand; and we exult in hope of the glory of God! And not only this, but we also exult in our tribulations, knowing that tribulation brings about perseverance; and perseverance, proven character; and proven character, hope; and hope does not disappoint, because the love of God has been poured out within our hearts, through the Holy Spirit who was given to us.*

No wonder Paul was the "John Wayne" of the New Testament church, chasing and beating up the devil while cutting holy trails for his children in Christ to follow. He charged out into the unbelieving world, spiritual guns ablazing, courageous and confident because he was *justified by faith* (v. 1). Being justified (regarded and treat as righteous) brought *peace with God* (v. 1).

When we are right with God and are at peace with Him — all made possible through Jesus Christ — we can walk victoriously through life.

Proven Character

Paul went on to write that because of faith we have been introduced to a wonderful place of grace where we stand. As believers in Christ *we exult (rejoice, shout about) in hope of the glory of God* (v. 2). Because of grace, and by faith, we have come to know Him, have peace with Him, and find our hope in Him. Great news for all who desire to get right with God and live right for God!

If Romans 5:1-2 were the heads side of a coin, in most people's eyes verses 3-5 would be the tails side of that coin. But these verses are actually two heads of the same coin — a double-headed coin. This coin is all about rejoicing in the character and nature of Christ at work in our lives. Note the Apostle of grace says not only do we rejoice in our hope in Christ, but we also rejoice in our tribulation and trials too!

Rejoice in tribulation? Come on. The two can't possibly be named in the same sentence, can they?

Yes they can. Born-again believers rejoice in trials because they know something the unbelieving world doesn't. A spiritual process of perfection results in proven character. Different Bible translations bring this concept alive with clear, rich meaning.[2]

- *endurance, approval* (Alford)
- *endurance, strength of character* (Twentieth Century New Testament)
- ripeness of character (Weymouth)
- tested character (Williams)
- proof that we have stood the test (New English Bible)
- *We can rejoice, too, when we run into problems and trials for we know that they are good for us. Trials help us to learn to be patient. And patience develops strength of character in us and helps us trust God more each time we use it until finally our hope and faith are strong and steady.* (The Living Bible)
- *endurance (fortitude) develops maturity of character...that is, approved faith and tried integrity. And character (of this sort) produces (the habit of) joyful and confident hope of eternal salvation. Such hope never disappoints or deludes or shames us, for God's love has been poured out in our hearts through the Holy Spirit Who has been given to us.* (AMP)

Proven character is a wonderful and powerfully positive goal to strive for. According to the Bible, character formation is a process that progresses step by step. Tribulation produces perseverance. Then perseverance produces proven character. Proven character produces hope…the kind that doesn't disappoint. God's love is in the whole process. Our Heavenly Father pours His love in our hearts by the Holy Spirit who was given to us and abides in us (v. 5).

The phrase *proven character* is the focal point of this process of grace in our spiritual lives. The root meaning behind this phrase is experience, the process of proving, probation, approvedness, a spiritual state that has shown itself proven under trial. The original language conveys the idea of metal that has passed through the furnace and had all the impurities purged out of it. The fire causes the metal to become the real thing, pure, no junk, 100% metal.

Most people would say that proven character is desirable. But few are willing to pay its price. We would just as soon skip the tribulation, perseverance, endurance stuff and jump right over to the being like Mr. Jesus side. But maturity God's way doesn't work like that.

Hardship shapes character. Pressure produces patience. Our characters (metal) need the fire to become pure and of real substance. Paul says proven character (character that has been demonstrated or verified without a doubt — character which is like Christ) is produced as we pass through life's trials and are battle tested. Perseverance reproduces the Lord's character in us to such an extent that our faith becomes strong, our hope becomes solid and we don't end up disappointed.

If there is nothing for us to endure, we can't learn endurance. How can we hang in there, persevere and prove our character unless something pulls on our personality and tests our mettle (strength of character)? Proven character is the result of a process. People who are lacking in proven character sidestep the process. Instead of waiting on God, they wriggle out of tough times. No wonder their character comes up short under fire.

James, the brother of Jesus, also had something significant to say about this character producing process:

> *Consider it all joy, my brethren, when you encounter various trials, knowing that the testing of your faith produces endurance. And let endurance have its perfect result, that you may be perfect and complete, lacking in nothing.*

The Marines Aren't the Only Ones Looking

James 1:2-4

In many respects this passage parallels Romans 5:1-5. Note count it all joy (v. 2) when you encounter various trials (v. 2). Paul said to rejoice in tribulation. James said to count trials as joy; then James used the word *knowing* just as his fellow apostle did. Knowing what? That the testing of your faith — Paul highlighted faith two times in the Romans narrative — produces endurance.

We're told again that we know (an experiential knowing) there is a positive process of perfection that requires the fire of trials and the tests of endurance. God's goal for us is whole, complete, perfect character, lacking in nothing.

Character is cultivated, not created. Proven character is complete character — character that isn't missing or falling short in any spiritual qualities that mark mature believers.

The Bible reveals the character qualities that are Christlike. Paul's pastoral counsel to young minister Timothy regarding the qualifications for spiritual leadership in the church (1 Timothy 3:1-13) is woven together by the common thread of character. Overseers and deacons must possess godly character. The fruit of the Spirit listed in Galatians 5:22-23 — love, joy peace, patience, kindness, goodness, faithfulness, gentleness, and self-control — are character virtues.

Peter also had something to say about the character qualities God is seeking.

> *For this very reason also, applying all diligence, in your faith supply moral excellence, and in your moral excellence, knowledge, and in your knowledge, self-control, and in your self-control, perseverance, and in your perseverance, godliness, and in your godliness, brotherly kindness, and in your brotherly kindness, love. For if these qualities are yours and are increasing, they render you neither useless nor unfruitful in the true knowledge of our Lord Jesus Christ. For he who lacks these qualities, is blind or shortsighted, having forgotten his purification from his former sins. Therefore, brethren, be all the more diligent to make certain about His calling and choosing you; for as long as you practice these things, you will never stumble.*
>
> 2 Peter 1:5-10

Peter had learned some life lessons from his early days serving Christ. He had stumbled numerous times. Having matured spiritually and emotionally,

Peter strongly exhorted believers to be diligent to develop these godly character qualities because they will ensure usefulness and fruitfulness in the service of the Lord.

Character, as laid out by Peter in this challenging and inspiring passage, is God's guarantee for counting for the Kingdom. Life is the proving ground for the development of these godly character qualities. The passion of our hearts should be to live and labor in such a way that we will be found faithful, useful to the Master and bearing much fruit for the glory of Lord that will endure throughout time and eternity.

That's the way it was for Jesus and the early church. That's the way it is for us if we desire to be the real thing…like Him!

CHARACTER AND PATIENCE

A sign in a country store in Texas read: "Be patient. None of us am perfect." How true! None of us is perfect. But we are in a perfecting process. Christians are called to pursue spiritual maturity and Christlike character every day.

The spiritual lessons we learn from the lives of people in the Bible who have gone before us assist and encourage us to press on in pursuit of Christlike character. The writer of Hebrews reveals in 11:39-40 that the great men and women of God, who gained His approval through their faith are waiting and depending on us to successfully run our race so they can be made complete.

> *All these, having gained approval through their faith, did not receive what was promised, because God had provided something better for us, so that apart from us they would not be made perfect [complete].*

These verses tell us all the saints of God are connected in pursing Christlike character. The faith race of the Hall of Famers, and our faith races matter. We really do need each other to be complete! And we have to be patient in the character-forming process.

In Genesis 13, we find a powerful story about Abram and Lot, an uncle and nephew, who lived on the opposite poles of character. An appropriate way to wrap up this chapter on character is to take a close look at the lives of these two biblical characters. One was a man of character (the proven type) and the other was just a character (unproven in godliness).

God called Abram to leave his country and family and travel to the land the Lord would show him (Genesis 12). God promised to make Abram a great nation that would be blessed and be a blessing to all the families of the earth. At age 75, Abram went forth and followed the Lord's leading. Lot went with him.

Because Abram left not knowing exactly where he was going, the Lord appeared to him again, on his journey, assuring him that his descendants would inherit the land God was giving him. Abram stopped, built an altar, and worshiped the Lord. He journeyed on to the east, survived a famine in Egypt, and then left Egypt. Lot was still with him. (Genesis 12)

During this time of traveling by faith and obedience, God blessed Abram according to His promise. Abram became a very wealthy man, rich in livestock, silver and gold. It became his habit wherever the Lord led him, to erect an altar and worship the Lord.

A serious situation arose on the journey to the land God had promised Abram. Strife broke out between the herdsmen of Abram and Lot. The relatives' herds had multiplied to the point that they could no longer graze together because they needed so much room. Frustrated and grieved by the situation, uncle Abram approached nephew Lot with a gracious proposition.

In an attempt to keep peace with Lot *(for we are brothers – v 8)* Abram suggested they separate. He offered Lot first choice of where to settle: *"Is not the whole land before you? Please separate from me; if to the left, then I will go to the right; if to the right, then I will go to the left." (v. 9)*

Now we'll see an example of how choices reveal character, and consequences follow choices.

Abram had offered Lot an opportunity, a potentially prosperous prospect. In verses 10-13, Scripture tells us Lot *lifted up his eyes and saw the valley of the Jordan, that it was well-watered everywhere.* Enticed by the prospect, *Lot chose for himself* all the good land and *moved his tents as far as Sodom.*

The phrase "Lot chose for himself" reveals much about Lot. Given the opportunity to choose, he certainly didn't think of the faithful, elderly uncle who was responsible for caring for him and making him rich in the first place. No, Lot lusted after the pleasant valley he saw with his natural eyes, and, carnally motivated, he grabbed it for himself. He settled his family in Sodom and lived among the sinners (Genesis 14:12).

He didn't choose wisely. His association with the Sodomites brought him nothing but trouble. Verse 13 tells us *the men of Sodom were wicked exceedingly and sinners against the Lord*. Abram had to rescue Lot and his family from a confederation of kings that captured and conquered Sodom and Gomorrah.

Lot became a character without character. His association with the wicked men of Sodom showed he didn't possess proven character. The city was so evil God told Abram he was going to wipe it from the face of the earth.

In Genesis 18, we read of Abram's intercessory effort to convince God to spare the city where his nephew lived. Chapter 19 chronicles Lot's ungodly and utterly shameful conduct.

When two angels from the Lord visited the doomed city, the homosexual Sodomites wanted to have sexual relations with them. Lot harbored God's messengers in his house, trying to protect them.

Under pressure to release the angels, Lot offered the men his daughters — his own, innocent flesh and blood — in trade for the angels. Go ahead fellow citizens of Sodom. Do anything you want to them. Just don't touch my houseguests! Lot was shamefully sick in his soul.

The angels told Lot they had come to destroy Sodom. They exhorted him to warn his family of the wrath to come, and to flee. It's hard to understand, but Lot waivered when God told him to leave if he wanted to live. The Word says *he hesitated* (Genesis 19:6). That hesitation revealed Lot's true character.

Because of God's compassion toward Lot and his family in response to Abram's prayer on their behalf, His angelic rescuers hustled Lot and his family out of the city before it was obliterated with fire and brimstone from heaven. When Lot's wife disobeyed the angel's instructions and looked back, she turned into a pillar of salt. What a way to end a characterless life!

Lot's sad, shameful story isn't over. Soul sickness ran rampant in the family. Seeing the smoking remnants of what had been their home, Lot's daughters decided there were no men left to become their husbands and the fathers of their children. They got their father drunk, had sexual relations with him, and became pregnant. Their sons, Moab and Ammon, were thorns in the side of Israel throughout the generations.

Three lapses of godly character punctuate this tragic scenario.

First, Lot erred in selfishly choosing for himself. A man of godly character would have let God choose for him.

Second, when Lot moved his tent away from righteous Abram, he moved it toward wicked Sodom. Lot wasn't careful to watch where he pitched his tent. The power of association came into full play. He distanced himself from godly influence until he finally camped among the ungodly. What a terrible trade off — ungodliness for godliness, character for a bunch of characters.

Third, his wife and daughters did what he did. They disobeyed God, behaved shamefully, and lost everything the Lord had promised would be theirs if they kept faith and covenant with Him. What a sad legacy Lot passed on to his family and heirs.

The only reason the Lord spared Lot from the fiery destruction of Sodom was because of His compassion. If it hadn't been for his faithful uncle, Lot would have been doomed with Sodom. Why? No character. Influence comes through association. Where we spend our time and who we spend it with influences us for good or bad. It can determine our success or failure.

Lot willfully took his eyes off God and godly Abram and set his affection on ungodly Sodom and its wicked people. Then, he became like them. As a holy, righteous and just God, God's only recourse to Sodom and Lot's abominable and morally destitute behavior was to destroy them.

Lot was a character but Abram, who became Abraham, possessed character. Abraham let God choose for Him (13:15), while Lot chose for himself. Abraham saw with his spiritual eyes and was covenant motivated, not carnally motivated. Abraham moved his tent too (13:18), but he pitched it *in Hebron, and built an altar to the Lord there.*

The Bible refers to Lot as righteous (2 Peter 2:7) only because of his association with Abram. Lot lost not only the well-watered valley of the Jordan, he lost his character on the way to Sodom. He lost everything because he didn't spend time with (wait on) God. Instead, he spent his time with the wicked and reaped an unrighteous reputation.

While Lot hung out with wicked men, Abraham hung out with God. His focus was on worship, while Lot focused on well-watered valleys. Because Abram proved faithful in character and conduct, he ended up possessing and enjoying the bounty Lot lost!

Abraham developed godly character because he chose to put his faith in

God's promises. He pitched his tent with the righteous. He made the right decisions when faced with moral challenges. Above all, he waited on God continually. He was an altar builder in whom God built godly character.

Association with Hebron and good people brought Abraham the presence and help of God. Abraham is remembered in Scripture as the faithful *friend of God* (James 2:23). What a holy honor to be called God's friend! Read Hebrews 11:8-19 and Romans 4 as well as Genesis 12-22 and rejoice in the glowing reports of approval the Lord bestowed on Abraham, a man of righteous character.

Abraham is a great hero of the faith because he was brave enough to stand with God longer than Lot. Abraham's convictions made him a courageous character the Lord blessed.

Abraham's example teaches us 1) to wait on God; 2) to trust Him to perform what He has promised; and 3) the Lord rewards godly character.

We look at Abraham and Lot's lifestyles from a distance. What about our own character? Who is looking at our lives?

Henry Martyn wrote in his journal, "Let me be taught that the first great business on earth is the sanctification of my own soul." What is sanctification? It's the maturing, perfecting process of faith that results in Christ-like character. Sanctification comes from waiting on the Lord. Characters become men and women of character in the waiting places.

Character formation involves subtle little things. Choices. Decisions. Influence. Everyday stuff. Where we pitch our tents, who we associate with, and moral decisions we make determine our character. Daily living is the great revealer of character, or lack of it.

God is still looking for good men and women. Are you one of them He can use to show this sad and hurting world that godly character is what He blesses? Sign up today and join God's team.

Choose having character over being a character.

Chapter 7
God's Waiting Rooms

Almost all of us can identify with rooms that had one purpose — waiting. They're places and times when patience can be stretched to the limits. Sometimes the wait was good. Sometimes it wasn't. Whichever the case, we're all personally acquainted with waiting rooms. Whether we enjoy waiting in them or not, they're part of the fabric of the human experience,

I read a statement years ago and it has stuck with me over the years: The true measure of a man is the height of his ideals, the breadth of his sympathy, the depth of his convictions, and the length of his patience.

While its source is unknown, these outstanding words of insight challenge us to evaluate our lives in these four vital areas. I am especially challenged with "the length of his patience." Who isn't, I guess. Patience isn't likely to be named as the most enduring or endearing characteristic of many of us.

Waiting rooms are all about patience. Some with a capital "P." They can become excruciating experiences for the impatient of spirit.

A number of things are common to the typical waiting room scenario.

1. We have to sit and wait. The situation, usually out of our control, places us in the extremely uncomfortable position of being able to do absolutely nothing but sit and wait for something to happen.

2. Worry walks in. We must be vigilant and put up a valiant fight against anxiety as it intrudes into our emotional space in the midst of a crisis.

3. Answers to hard questions are not readily available nor easily accessible when we're pondering life and what is, or is not, happening. We sense a profound need to figure this thing out, or fix it. But the figures don't always add up and the fixes don't come easily.

4. Emotions run the gamut. From patience to impatience, hope to hopelessness, optimism to pessimism, faith to doubt, peace to fear, confidence to despair. Our moods can swing like a gigantic pendulum, from one end of the emotional spectrum to the other.

5. We usually have to wait with other people. Everybody is waiting, often not sure what to say or do. Just waiting. The situation can become pretty tense sitting with a group of stressed out loved ones.

6. We have to depend on someone else to bring us some news, whether good or bad. We're at the complete mercy of the messenger. Many of us know how it feels in the pit of our stomachs when the bearer of news steps through the door and asks to speak with us for a moment.

7. Waiting contains within itself the inherent potential to bring out the worst in people. Pressure builds and patience wanes. It's the perfect setting for frustrated responses to a situation that eludes our ability to control it. Negative reactions instead of positive responses often carry the day in waiting rooms.

8. Waiting introduces a wide range of "what ifs" into our thinking. We can what if ourselves into an emotional frenzy if we aren't careful. The enemy of our faith, the devil, loves to attack us with the fiery darts of doubt and despair. He comes to steal our hope in the quiet, reflective moments of solitude and silence that characterize waiting places.

9. Waiting rooms have a subtle way of showing us how utterly inadequate we are in and of ourselves in some situations. We think we can handle anything. Then a waiting room experience rattles our confidence. Facing our human frailty head on reduces us to feeling helpless, and dependent on the assistance of others. We must come to grips in the waiting room with our own immortality and our need for interdependency upon God, family members, friends and even strangers.

10. Waiting rooms have the capacity to pull families apart or draw them together. Crisis often brings out the love relatives have for each other, bonding them together even stronger. Or, the crisis reveals their lack of genuine affection and commitment to each other, causing them to distance themselves from one another in the midst of their personal pain. Sometimes even close-knit families

can treat each other badly after a long haul in a waiting room. Waiting experiences make or break families in times of crisis.

11. Most waiting rooms are usually located in isolated places. Think about all the places you have waited. Generally waiting rooms reflect a somber, subdued atmosphere, bordering on emotionally eerie while people wait for whatever it is. The settings are strikingly similar. Whether an automobile service area, emergency room, doctor's office, police station while waiting for a missing person's report, social security check line at the department of human services, a storm shelter during a tornado warning, the birth of that new baby in the wee hours of a long, labor filled night, a courtroom, the results of a surgical biopsy or waiting somewhere for something else, these places have an atmosphere all their own.

These experiences require patience if we are to successfully walk away from them. An important key to making them successes lies in realizing God, not man, ordains life's waiting rooms. Our perspective on patience shifts dramatically when we recognize that God appoints the patience-stretching scenarios in our lives.

Patience is a virtue that carries a lot of wait! He also meets with us in the waiting places.

Throughout the Bible, the Spirit of the Lord led both Old and New Testament people to places of waiting where God met with them and they matured in the midst of the pressures and trials they endured. It is what transformed them into the men and women of God we admire.

Waiting rooms can become special places for Christians if we acknowledge that they are God's appointments for us and that our Heavenly Father will work with us in those rooms for our good.

When we wait on God in *His* rooms, the Spirit searches our souls, pinpoints problems and supplies solutions. A divine/human partnership during times of life-crisis management is utterly unbeatable…if we accept the experiences as part of the patience-perfecting process God has planned for those who love Him and want to be like Him.

Have you ever seriously considered that God is behind your waiting room doors? Emergency rooms, counseling centers, spiritual wilderness experiences, being sidelined for a time from "normal living," life passages that require waiting (marriage, birth of children, death of loved ones etc.), crisis, crossroads, transition times are all rooms where God waits to assist us through the changing seasons of life.

God loves us. He is there and He cares. He patiently awaits our recognition of His presence so He can come to our aid to provide the grace, power, and patience we need to overcome and fulfill His promises.

James 5:7-8 exhorts us to be patient as we wait for Jesus to return.

> *Be patient, brethren, until the coming of the Lord. The farmer waits for the precious produce of the soil, being patient about it, until it gets the early and late rains. You too be patient, strengthen your hearts, for the coming of the Lord is near.*

I grew up in an urban setting, so some would consider me a city slicker. My hometown was surrounded by wheat fields, hay fields, and apple orchards. I knew just enough about farming to know I didn't ever want to be a farmer.

Do you realize how patient farmers have to be? Year in year out, season after season, crop after crop, they are at the mercy of many uncontrollable variables. Plant-scorching heat or early frosts; crop-choking weeds; invading hordes of field-stripping insects; uninvited varmints; market fluctuations; supply and demand; governmental regulations; taxes; machinery and equipment; drought, wildfires, tornadoes, hurricanes, floods, freezes, and who knows what else try the patience of the farmer more than once during a typical growing season.

I do know one thing about farming. Seeds need rain. And it doesn't rain until it rains! Farmers wait and wait for that tiny seed to sprout and break through the surface of the soil. I'm certain if I were a farmer I would be outside digging around in the dirt, coaxing those seeds with all my powers of persuasion if they weren't coming along as fast as I thought they should.)

Farmers wait more as the tender sprouts shoot up to stand tall and finally form whatever that particular plant is going to produce. The farmer waits on the process God built into the seeds, hoping, praying and laboring to keep anything from aborting the anticipated harvest. Finally, the farmer waits again for the right harvesting window. Farmers must wait until the crop is ripe. Just right. But they can't wait too long or it will become overripe or even rot in the field.

Farmers. Patient souls indeed! That's why God uses them as an example for us. Note the farmer waits. What do they wait for? The precious produce of the soil. Farmers work, and watch and wait for the fruit of their labors. They are painstakingly patient about farming. They look for the seasonal rains that even their favorite weathercasters can't guarantee will arrive. Farmers, by the very nature of their profession, have to trust nature to do its thing if they're to harvest a plentiful and profitable crop.

In like manner, as believers we have to trust God to do His thing. We have to be patient with the processes He has put in place if we're to harvest the fruit of godliness as we wait for the glorious return of our blessed Lord and Savior Jesus Christ!

Waiting is a process. Farmers don't reap mature crops overnight. They can't control the elements or environment. Farming demands long hours and hard work to cultivate a bountiful crop, Farmers live and labor for the day their crops are safe and securely harvested! The harvest is what farming is all about. Patient farmers know that in time, grass becomes milk!

Just as farming is a process, patience is a process. Eugene Peterson once wrote: The person who looks for quick results in the seed planting of well-doing will be disappointed. If I want potatoes for dinner tomorrow, it will do me little good to plant them in my garden tonight. There are long stretches of darkness and invisibility and silence that separate planting and reaping.

During the stretches of waiting, there is cultivation, and weeding and nurturing and planting still other seeds.

Patience is a similar process. It isn't a single experience or event. The fruit of patience isn't produced overnight, either. If we want enjoy the fruit, we have to participate in the process. That's the rule in both the natural and spiritual worlds. God designed it to work that way.

According to the Word of God, what exactly is patience? If we are to benefit from and reap the blessings of the patience process, we better know what the bull's-eye we're aiming for looks like.

First, let's consider a few of man's quotes about patience.
- Patience is a virtue that carries a lot of wait.
- Patience is like a mosquito sitting on the bed of an anemic person waiting for a blood transfusion.

- Patience is the ability to keep your motor idling when you feel like stripping your gears.
- Patience is a quality you admire in the driver behind you but scorn in the one ahead.
- This would be a wonderful world if men showed as much patience in all things as they do in waiting for a fish to bite.
- You never realize just how patient you can be until the fellow who is arguing with you is your boss.
- True patience means waiting without worrying.
- Patience is the ability to count down without blasting off.
- Patience is the ability to remain silent and hungry while everybody else in the restaurant gets served.
- Patience is accepting a difficult situation without giving God a deadline to remove it.
- Patience is a virtue. Possess it if you can. Seldom in a woman, never in a man! (And all the women said AMEN!)

Clever thoughts, huh! But we can't build our lives on clever sayings. To be biblically successful, we must base our thinking and actions on the Scriptures. We learned in the previous chapter that patience perfects Christian character (Romans 5:1-5 and James 1:1-3).

The following additional passages give us God's perspective on patience. They are all author's paraphrase. Try reading them yourself in several Bible versions.

- *The seed in the good soil, these are the ones who have heard the Word in an honest and good heart; and hold it fast; and bear fruit with patience.* (Luke 8:15)
- *You have need of patience, that, after having done the will of God, you might receive the promise.* (Hebrews 10:36)
- *Better is the end of a matter than it's beginning; patience of spirit is better than arrogance of spirit.* (Ecclesiastes 7:8)
- *Rejoicing in hope; patient in tribulation; continuing constantly in prayer.* (Romans 12:12)

- *Older men are to be temperate, dignified, sensible, sound in faith, in love, in patience.* (Titus 2:2)
- *Let patience have her perfect work, that you may perfect and complete, lacking in nothing.* (James 1:4)
- *As those who have been chosen of God, holy and beloved, put on a heart of compassion, kindness, humility, gentleness and patience.....* (Colossians 3:12).
- *I, therefore, the prisoner of the Lord, entreat you to walk in a manner worthy of the calling with which you have been called, with all humility and gentleness, with patience, showing forbearance to one another in love....* (Ephesians 4:1-2).
- *Now may the God who gives patience and encouragement grant you to be of the same mind with one another according to Christ Jesus.* (Romans 15:5)
- *I waited patiently for the Lord; and He inclined to me and heard my cry.* (Psalm 40:1)

These verses make three things plain: God is the source of patience. He wants us to have it. We can receive it by looking to Him and allowing Him to develop a persevering spirit in us through the patience-producing process. When it comes to patience, if we become anxious or in a hurry and "pluck the blossoms," we must do without the fruit. It's a simple law of spiritual life: God makes a promise, faith believes it, hope anticipates it, and patience quietly and confidently waits for it!

Sadly, I have known many people who have missed out on enjoying the fruit of patience because they misunderstood what it means to be patient. Misconceptions abound concerning what a patient spirit is. Some people think being patient means to be passive, inactive, immobile, just hanging out waiting for whatever to happen. The "couch potato" mindset fits here. In other words, to be patient, just don't do anything. Just hang out and hope for something to happen. Thinking about the hefty population of couch potatoes in our country, these people who get credit for being patient are, in actuality, just too lazy to start anything!

Then there are people who view patience as something beyond their capability. They see themselves as helpless pawns on the chessboard of life, subject to the whims and moves of external forces. For them, patience is riding out whatever comes their way, hoping to hold on, stay above water, and not drown in the process. They have a victim mentality: Life happens. Nothing I can do about it, so I'll just do my best to get by, survive, and get through the trials of life some way or another.

This philosophy is not a proactive stance to living. It's a reactive approach. When patience- producing situations enter these people's lives, they think all they can do is lie down, cover their heads, ride out the storm and hope for the best! Large numbers of people in our society think and live like this…pitiful, self-appointed victims who don't have a clue how to overcome life's trials and live victoriously!

William Penn said patience and diligence, like faith, remove mountains. No couch potato or victim mentality there. This man understood that life is about removing mountains, not being buried or blocked by them. He knew that just as faith is an active response to life's challenges, so is patience. To exude patience requires us to take action. To be patient is to be proactive (take action). We must remain diligent to positively respond to the challenges confronting us and testing our character. Penn knew that the secret of patience is to do something else in the meantime!

Handley Moule's definition of patience is worth meditating on: An enduring, unwearable spirit which knows how to outlast pain and provocation with a strength that is learned at Jesus's feet.

Read it again and let your mind feast upon it. Can you imagine if we lived like this? We, and everyone who has anything to do with us, would rejoice!

To withstand pressures successfully, it helps to know what the Bible says about how to take action when trials test us.

Surveying and studying the whole range of scriptures regarding the subject of patience, we find that patience is an attitude that manifests itself in certain types of actions. In the original language of the Bible patience means to remain under, an abiding under, to abide, to endure under great stress, to be long tempered, to suffer long, to bear pains or trials calmly or without complaint; manifesting forbearance under provocation or strain, not hasty or impetuous, steadfast despite opposition, difficulty, or adversity; the ability or willingness to bear; staying put and standing fast when you would like to run away. Patience is a strong, powerful concept that, when put into practice, enables us to stand firm and stand successfully when life puts our character to the test.

As an example of remaining under, staying put, and standing fast when you want to run away, James reminds us of Job.

> *As an example, brethren, of suffering and patience, take the prophets who spoke in the name of the Lord. Behold, we count those blessed who endured. You have heard of the endurance (patience KJV) of Job and have seen the outcome of the Lord's dealings, that the Lord is full of compassion and is merciful .*
>
> James 5:10-11

If anybody ever went through the fire, Job did. God gave Satan permission to test Job in every major area of his life (Job 1-2). When all hell broke loose, Job didn't run to his couch, grab his blanket, and cry, "Woe is me!" Experiencing tremendous personal pressure many good people would have buckled under, Job stood his ground. He abided under the shadow of the Almighty. Though tested to the max, Job held on to his faith, actively seeking God, actively confessing his belief, and actively trusting the Lord to deliver, vindicate, and restore his life.

The Lord did restore Job (Job 42). Why? Job didn't yield to impatience. By faith, he hung in there during the patience-perfecting process, not as a passive bystander, but as an active player who trusted in His God to perform what He had promised. Job's patient spirit carried the day when it looked like his good days were history.

Patience is trusting God. Impatience is trusting yourself. We quickly get into trouble when we decide to sidestep the Lord — because we think He isn't moving quickly enough — and take the reins of life into our own hands. Depending on our ability, instead of His, to solve our problems only gets us what we can do. Compared to what Almighty God can do, that doesn't amount to very much.

I'm grateful that the Bible contains illustrations of real people who chose to have God solve their problems and meet their needs instead of trying to do it themselves.

After Jesus' resurrection, He gave specific directions to His followers. In Acts 1:4-8 we read the orders the Lord gave to those who would build His church:

> *Gathering them together, He commanded them not to leave Jerusalem, but to wait for what the Father had promised, "Which," He said, "you heard of from Me; for John baptized with water, but you shall be baptized with the Holy Spirit not many days from now." So when they had come together, they were asking Him, saying, "Lord, is it at this time that You are restoring the kingdom to Israel?" He said to them, "It is not for you to know times or epochs which the Father has fixed by His own authority; but you shall receive power [spiritual dynamite!] when the Holy Spirit has come upon you; and you shall be My witnesses both in Jerusalem, and in all Judea, and Samaria; and even to the remotest part of the earth."*

Jesus commanded His followers to wait —there's that word again — for the promise of the Holy Spirit He had made to them earlier (Luke 24:29). He told them they would be baptized with the Holy Spirit and fire. Spiritual power for worldwide witnessing for Christ would be theirs when they received the Holy Spirit.

To receive the Holy Spirit, the disciples of Christ had to take positive action: Get up and go to the appointed upper room in Jerusalem…and wait. God's waiting room!

One hundred-twenty faithful followers of Jesus did what He told them to do. They went to the upper room and waited for 10 days. That's quite a while to wait when you don't even know exactly what it is you're waiting for.

The Word says they were *all with one mind…continually devoting themselves to prayer…* (Acts 1:14). They were patient, waiting together for the Promise of the Father to fall upon them. Waiting, standing fast, expecting God to perform what He had promised.

While Jerusalem went about its business, while the religious powers tried to track down the Master's followers and harass them, while the disciples huddled in that little room, anticipating to receive from God, in His time, the Spirit came! The day of Pentecost dawned, and the Spirit-filled church was born! (Acts 2:1-4) Each believer who patiently waited for the promise of the Father received the Holy Spirit and became a powerful witness for the Lord.

What would have happened if the believers in that upper room had decided after eight and a half days that they'd been patient enough? They would have missed the baptism of the Holy Spirit and the fire of God that the Lord wanted them to have. No patience, no Pentecost. No infilling with the Holy Spirit. No power. No successful witnessing.

Thank God they were obedient and patient. They left in the power of the Spirit and spiritually *turned their world upside down* for Christ (Acts 17:6).

Luke 21:19 tells us Jesus said, *"In your patience, possess your souls"* (KJV). The writer of Hebrews exhorted us, *"Let us run with patience the race that is set before us..."* (12:1). These two verses make it clear that success in life depends on possessing patience and running patiently through life.

If you're in a waiting place just now, don't despise it. You can find God in His waiting room. Be patient. Invite and allow Him to meet your needs as you wait on Him.

Chapter 8
God's Timing Is Everything

One of my strongest desires was to provide a Roll-owned roof over our heads where we could live, love, grow, and enjoy the blessings of family life. Our private little nest. A secure, restful refuge from the stresses of this world.

When Jo Ann and I married in 1974 we were working and preparing for full-time Christian ministry. With years of expensive education before us, the first commitment we made was to finish college and seminary training debt free. While I prepared to be a pastor we lived in rented apartments, duplexes, and a cozy, one-story, ranch style house. We disciplined ourselves, labored diligently, and with God's gracious hand of provision, we did indeed graduate owing no man anything!

As a diversion from the pressures of studies and the demands of theological training, we regularly hopped in the car and drove through the residential areas looking at homes in the towns where we lived. Our financial resources were limited, so home purchase was out reach. But we looked anyway, checking every open house within reasonable driving range.

On numerous occasions, when we were walking through a new home that I could tell Jo Ann really liked, I wanted so much to say, "Honey, you want it, it's yours!" Time after time, house after house, the desire to bless my wife with her own nest increased. Nevertheless, no matter how passionate I felt about the matter, the means to make her dream come true were not in hand.

The first church we pastored was a small, Midwest congregation. The church provided a parsonage; salary and benefits covered monthly expenses. The income didn't allow us to save for a down payment for a home; but we didn't get discouraged. We worked hard and faithfully ministered God's restoring love to the hearts of hurting people. And we kept looking.

We'd been married 10 years when we took a vacation to San Diego, California. We toured the sites, spent time with relatives, and you guessed it, snuck out to look at houses. We stumbled upon a subdivision that pulled on our hearts like a gigantic magnet. The new homes were spacious and luxurious. Everything about them appealed to our senses and left us fantasizing about moving from the Midwest and heading for California as soon we could pack our bags!

Part 1: About Waiting

I remember as if it were just yesterday, sitting on the plush carpet of one home and joining hands to pray together. We rejoiced and thanked God for His care for us. Then we asked Him to grant us the opportunity to own a beautiful home like this when the time was right. We left excited, looking forward to the day when we would become proud homeowners.

Five years passed. Two children and a Beagle puppy made us a family. The church kept growing. Responsibilities increased. Life moved right along. Friends and associates were now moving into newer, larger homes. We still resided in the church-owned house, hoping even more for the day to arrive when our dream of owning our own home would become reality.

After 15 years of dreaming, praying, and hoping, I began to think time was running out on my dream. At one point, we took steps toward home ownership only to have the deal that looked so good and seemed so do-able fall through, leaving us with nothing but a nightmare of unfulfilled desire.

Time was a big deal to me. I had set a personal goal to present my family with a house by age 35. I was now 37. So much for my goal! It had blipped off the screen of my personal plans. There didn't seem to be any way in the natural that I could step into home ownership now or in the near future, either. I must admit that I was seriously tempted to give up on our dream, wondering if God cared about our heart's desire to have our own home.

Over the next two years our family went through a traumatic resignation from my pastorate, relocation to two different cities, and a healing and restoration process that tested our mettle to the max. Our income became sporadic. Home ownership appeared to be completely and finally out of reach.

But God had a surprise in store for us! Knowing that I would be sidelined from organized ministry while He renewed my spirit, restored my dreams, and rekindled my passion for fulfilling His vision for my life, my Heavenly Father did for me what I couldn't do for myself. He provided us with our dream home.

After 17 years of waiting, through a series of events that were nothing short of miraculous, we built a beautiful home. To top it off, 17 months after taking possession of our house, our mortgage was paid off! Supernatural intervention and provision placed in our hands the deed to a debt-free dream house.

God had a perfect plan for providing our family with a home of our own. I had worried about time running out on my dream while God was working step by step on our behalf to fulfill His plan… at exactly the right time.

I learned something very important through those 17 years. When you look to the Lord and trust Him, dreams do come true! God is good, gracious and generous. He does grant us the desires of our heart when they line up with His Word: *Delight yourself in the Lord, and He will give you the desires of your heart*(Psalm 37:4). And most important of all, I have come to understand that He fulfills His will for us according to His time, not ours! Psalm 31:15 declares that *our times are in His hands.* Not our hands. His hands. And His hands are much bigger and stronger than ours!

Life comes down to time and timing. Man cares about time; God cares about timing.

We place clocks in convenient and conspicuous locations around the house. We wear a wide variety of wristwatches, from Mickey Mouse to Rolex; but if we don't like to wear watches, no problem…our cell phones can tell us exactly what the time is.

The current time is digitally displayed on our computer screens, in the corners of our televisions, and on bank marquees. Office phone systems display the time on a screen and even record the amount of time spent on a conversation. Every New Year's Eve millions of Americans count the seconds down with a gigantic clock in New York City's Times Square.

Alarms abruptly arouse us from sleep so we won't be late for work. Travelers scan airport arrival/departure monitors seeking flight information for the reassuring words "On time." We race through traffic to claim our seats before entertainment and sporting events begin. We wonder if we can manage to add an activity into our already over-busy schedules. We're concerned with how long things will take.

We habitually use phrases like "on time," "behind time," "ahead of time," "out of time," "anybody have the time," etc.

The pop/rock group Chicago enjoyed their musical heyday in the 70s. The title of one of their hits asked a question: "Does Anybody Really Know What Time It Is?" The reply to that question was another question: "Does anybody really care?"

I'm not sure about them, but I know the answer to both questions. God knows what time it is. Our Creator really cares about us and what we do with the time He gives us.

All people, especially Christians, should be properly concerned with time. Management consultant Peter Drucker said, "Time is the scarcest resource, and unless it is managed, nothing else can be managed."

Management is what stewardship is all about. Man is a steward (manager) of all God (the owner of everything) has entrusted to his care. Time management is at the top of the list of our stewardship responsibilities. Time indeed flies. Once time has passed, it is gone. That's why it's important that we manage it well.

In Ephesians 5:15-16 the Bible states: *Be careful how you walk, not as unwise men, but as wise, making the most of your time, because the days are evil.* People who believe in the Lord and choose to look to His Word for instructions for living their lives are exhorted here to redeem (recover possession or ownership of) their time, use it well, and not waste it. Why? Because the days we live in are evil. For Christians a lot of Kingdom work remains before Jesus returns to take His children home.

Christians who take the gift of time for granted and squander it on things that don't really matter in the long run lack wisdom because they don't see time as the Lord does. From God's perspective, time is opportunity. With time come people, events, and experiences…opportunities within divinely established time frames to witness for Christ and make an eternal difference in the lives of people for whom Jesus died.

If Christians miss witnessing opportunities because they mismanage and even waste time, what will happen to those who need the message we have to share? The next time you're sitting around somewhere watching the clock tick the seconds away, ask this question, "Lord, what can I be doing right now to make the most of this time for Your glory and the good of someone near me who needs to know about Your love?"

Believe it or not, there is plenty of time to do what God has called us to do. First Thessalonians 5:24 tells us *faithful is He who calls you, and He also will bring it to pass.* Note the emphasis on God doing the calling and God bringing the call to completion. The Lord always finishes what He begins. God is a faithful God who provides all the time we need to carry out what He has called us to do. Count on it… if we manage our time according to scriptural principles we have all the time we need to fulfill His will.

Understanding the principle of timing is a primary component to successful living. Believers and unbelievers alike habitually use the phrase "timing is everything," but few really know how timing operates. We can possess all the time in the world, but if we don't understand, appreciate, and respect timing we'll just end up with a lot of unprofitable time on our hands.

Counting time is not nearly as important as making time count! And timing is what makes time productive.

One NBA divisional playoff game on television had me sitting on the edge of the family room sofa. The score had see-sawed back and forth for four quarters.. This contest was so close neither team had led the game by more than a handful of points. The lead had changed hands so often it turned into a real barnburner of a ballgame. With only eleven seconds left on the clock, the visiting team drilled the basket with a magnificent shot from outside the three-point arc. The bucket put the team ahead by one point. The crowd was stunned into silence. The home team's captain hurriedly called a time out. The arena clock stopped at one second remaining in regulation play.

Time-out over, players lined up in their assigned positions. The referee blew his whistle.
A forward tossed the ball high into the air toward the home team's goal. As the ball spun toward the hoop, a center met it right over the rim. The moment his hands touched the ball, the clock started.

One tick. Then the buzzer sounded. As it did, the ball slammed through the net! Game over. Home team wins by one. A come-from-behind-victory won because of what basketball purists call the "Alley-oop".... a timing play!

Time wasn't the key factor in the win. One second is only one second — too little time to mount a full-scale strategy. But in that single second two players were in sync for one perfectly-timed play, and timing proved to be everything.

God's timing is everything. When and how things happen do matter to Him.

Scripture has much to say about the subjects of time and timing. Seven time-tested principles from God's Word regarding time and timing will radically change your life for the better if you will study them and apply them to your daily life.

God's Time Is Not Always My Time

The way God keeps time is not the same as the way we keep time. The Lord of the universe doesn't set His watch by the official Greenwich Mean Time. God set the standard for marking time and put into motion how time works. Man only discovered time and how to make it work for him; the Creator of time revealed it to His creation through the process of scientific discovery. God stands above and beyond time as we know it, operating out of an eternal realm that isn't measured in seconds, minutes, hours, days, months or years as we know them.

In 2 Peter 3:8 the Bible tells us: *Do not let this one fact escape your notice, beloved, that with the Lord one day is like a thousand years, and a thousand years like one day.* This verse tells us that God's days last 1,000 years (and we think we have put in some long days!). That's a long, long day in anybody's book. A day being 1,000 years, and 1,000 years being a day is difficult to comprehend because we're so locked into one day consisting of 24 hours.

Looking at those numbers, is it any wonder we become frustrated and stressed over periods of time that seem so critical to us but aren't to God?

I've been associated with a few people who literally plan their days in quarter hour increments. These time conscious people pencil in an appointment, activity, or event for every 15 minutes that tick by, and if something significant and productive doesn't transpire in that block of time, they spin into confusion and chaos!

We get too uptight about time. We think God is on our timetable. But the truth of the matter is, we're on His. And His is a big picture, time/space continuum that encompasses not only our short lifespans, but all of eternity. The way God sees time and the way we see time are very different. He moves in millennia and predetermined dispensations, major movements and vast moments of time that serve His eternal purposes. Think about it. The expanse of the universe He created is so immense that we have to measure distances in light years (light travels at the speed of 186,000 miles per second!)

If we're to succeed in life, we need to concede that God's time and our time aren't the same; our times are in His hands (Psalm 30:15); there is a time for everything under the sun (Ecclesiastes 3:1-11); and God's will and plans for our lives are ticking according to His clock, not ours!

What does that mean for us? It means we need to relax and trust that God's time is far superior to ours. It is above, beyond and behind what we see played out on this time bound planet of ours. God is always working in the supernatural and moving into the natural where we live…according to His time, not ours. We will spare ourselves a lot of grief, spend a lot less money on antacids, and frustrate fewer people if we would only recognize that His time is not always our time. His time is not only beyond ours, but is better, too!

God's Time Is the Right Time

While I was attending college I thought I had fallen in love. But before I could pop the question, she became interested in someone else.

Through my romantic disappointment, I received Jesus Christ as my personal Lord and Savior. He turned my life around and gave me hope of a great future following His plan for my life. God's first step was for me to enlist in the United States Navy. The Vietnam War was in full swing. My number wasn't called in the draft lottery. But as a newly born-again Christian, I knew in my heart I was to go south to San Diego and boot camp. The war was unpopular. My closest friends thought I was crazy. But I followed the Spirit's leading to the best of my ability as a young Christian.

I was still reeling a little bit from my heartbreak when I met Alice. Alice was a fine Christian. We went out a few times and enjoyed being together, but we both knew our relationship was only going to be a friendship.

Becoming a Christian doesn't mean you lose your interest in the fairer gender. It means you should look at them differently…with a purer heart and more honorable intentions.

I decided to focus my energy on getting to know the Lord better and pursuing my recently received call to preach the Good News of Jesus Christ. I put finding the right Christian mate on the back burner for the time being.

I lived in a house with several other Christian guys. My roommate was dating a nice young woman who "had a friend." So they plotted to get us to go on a blind date. I had told myself I'd never go out with someone I hadn't seen. But I did, and the very night I met Jo Ann, I knew she was the one God had prepared for me. We were engaged in six weeks, married seven months later, and have been happily married for nearly four decades.

When we decided to go on that first date, neither of us was interested in dating. We almost didn't go out. It was a Wednesday and we both wanted to go to our own church's midweek meetings. Both of us had just broken up with other people. We really didn't care much about starting up romantically with anybody else. But God's plan and timing was in motion for two young Christians who loved Him and wanted to marry according to His will.

We marvel at the providential process that brought us together. God's time and timing directed our paths to become husband and wife. Who else but God could bring two people together who had lived 1,500 miles apart all of their lives, grown up in different family settings, were of different religious backgrounds but found themselves in San Diego courtesy of Uncle Sam!

Jo Ann was a Navy brat. Her father had served in the military for over 20 years. She had declared often and emphatically to anyone who would listen that she would never marry a sailor or a preacher.

She got both in me. Doesn't the Lord have a delightful sense of humor!

God's time is the right time. Neither of us could have orchestrated such a match. At the right time, His time, God brought us together. He knew all along who, what, where, when, why and how Steve and Jo Ann would become Mr. and Mrs. I'm so glad He knew what He was doing!

As I mature in my understanding of how my Heavenly Father operates I have come to appreciate 1 Peter 5:5-7. Peter penned these words about attitude and God's response to the way we choose to live.

> *You younger men, likewise, be subject to your elders; and all of you, clothe yourselves with humility toward one another, for* GOD IS OPPOSED TO THE PROUD, BUT GIVES GRACE TO THE HUMBLE. *Therefore, humble yourselves under the mighty hand of God, that He may exalt you at the proper time, casting all your anxiety upon Him, because He cares for you.*

The point of this passage is that in God's Kingdom, pride is out and humility is in. God is against the proud, and that's not a good position to find yourself in. The Lord does extend grace (unmerited favor) to the humble (those who are not arrogant, full of pride and stuck on themselves). God works on behalf of the humble, exalting, elevating, promoting, moving them ahead at the proper time. God's part is to exalt. Our part is to humble ourselves. It's our responsibility to clothe ourselves with humility toward one another. God and others don't make us humble. We must humble ourselves and dress ourselves in humility each day if we expect the Lord to exalt us at the right time.

Proud people are arrogant. They exalt themselves above others, and end up being opposed and humbled by God. The proud trust in themselves; the humble trust in the Lord. Proud or humble, exalted or abased (KJV), we choose.

Because God sees the big picture, He knows when the right time is for exalting His humble servants. Note Peter addressed the younger men. The young struggle most with pride. Arrogant egos have tripped up more than one good man in the past few millennia. If we will practice humility, the Lord will take care of our advancement in life at the proper time.

Proper timing is everything with God.

- *When the fullness of time came, God sent forth His Son, born of a woman, born under the Law.* Galatians 4:4
- *It came about in due time....* 1 Samuel 1:20 (regarding Samuel's birth)
- *He had sent a man ahead of them— Joseph, who was sold as a slave....Until the time his prediction came true, the word of the LORD tested him.* Psalm 105:19 HCSB
- *The eyes of all look to You, and You give them their food in due time.* Psalm 145:15
- *While we were still helpless, at the right time Christ died for the ungodly.* Romans 5:6
- *Let us not lose heart in doing good, for in due time, we shall reap if we do not grow weary.* Galatians 6:9
- *...until the appearing of our Lord Jesus Christ, which He will bring about at the proper time.* 1 Timothy 6:14-15 (the Apostle Paul to young Timothy)

The terms *proper time, in due season, in due time, the fullness of time,* and *at the right time* all describe God's time as being the right time.

Pastor Robert Schuller clarifies the concept this way:

When the idea is not right, God says "NO!"
When the time is not right God says "SLOW"
When you are not right God says "GROW"
When everything is right God says "GO!"

I don't know about you, but I like to GO! When everything is right, including the timing, the Lord gives us His green light. Throughout the Bible, men and women of faith moved ahead (were exalted) when they humbled themselves, believed God, and trusted Him for the timing of the important events in their lives.

May we never forget that proud people walk without God, while humble people walk with God. Walking with God involves waiting on Him, as we will see in the next chapter. If we choose not to wait, we'll miss His proper timing for our lives. If we choose to wait, His time (the right time) becomes our time! God is the right One, and His time is the right time if we want to enjoy the richest rewards and benefits of life.

God's Timing Is Always Purposeful

The God of the Bible is purposeful in everything He does. If He runs His Kingdom according to a rule of right timing, then there must be some reasons for proper timing.

Proverbs 16:4 declares: *The Lord has made everything for its own purpose, even the wicked for the day of evil.* Solomon also wrote in Ecclesiastes: *There is an appointed time for everything. And there is a time for every event under heaven* (3:1)....*He has made everything appropriate in it's time* (3:11). Scripture is clear. All events have a place and a purposeful part to play in God's appointed time (the time He has deemed appropriate and proper).

Ecclesiastes 8:5-6 holds another witness from the Word to God's purposefulness in His timing of life. The writer is exhorting the man who would be wise to obey the rulers in authority over him: *He who keeps a royal command experiences no trouble, for a wise heart knows the proper time and procedure. For there is a proper time and procedure for every delight, though a man's trouble is heavy upon him.*

The wise heart understands that if, in the human realm, there is procedure, proper timing and purpose, how much more so these things apply when we move them from the realm of earthly kings to the rulership of the King of Kings and Lord of Lords! The King of Creation rules and runs His created and redeemed universe on the basis of purpose, procedures, and proper timing.

Therefore, if we want to be successful we must come to grips with and settle in our spirits once and for all that there is divine purpose behind the timing process that so often frustrates us. If we would be convinced that God is working out His perfect will (purpose and plan) for us via the time and events we live through, then maybe, just maybe. we would relax a little and let Him be God and perform His promises for us.

You may be wondering what God's purposes are behind His timing. Through His timing process (remember, timing is everything) God accomplishes the following:

- He glorifies Himself as He comes through at just the right time.
- He defeats the devil in the most decisive manner.
- He builds our faith and perfects our character.
- He gets the attention of the unsaved, causing them to consider Him and seek Him.
- He teaches timeless truths about His eternal Kingdom.
- He brings tremendous blessings to those who trust in Him.

That's a pretty good list for starters, isn't it? The prophet Isaiah learned through his personal experience dealing with a disobedient nation to appreciate God's timing and purposefulness. He succinctly summarized this whole business of divine purpose through timing:

> *Declaring the end from the beginning, and from ancient times things which have not been done, saying, "My purpose will be established, and I will accomplish all My good pleasure;" calling a bird of prey from the east, the man of my purpose from a far country. Truly I have spoken; truly I will bring it to pass. I have planned it, surely I will do it.*
> Isaiah 46:10-11

Did you understand what God said through His prophet? He said regarding Israel that He had a purpose and it would be established. Because He had spoken it, it would indeed come to pass. He had planned it, and He would carry out His plans.

God raised up a nation to capture Israel and humble her. Israel's Assyrian captivity was all about God's timing. Israel would repent and be restored to the

Lord, and God's ultimate purpose to redeem and restore his erring children to Himself would be fulfilled at the right time.

Are you in the middle of a timing process that has you waiting for God to break through? Do you find yourself worrying, wondering, whining, or becoming weary with it all? Maybe you feel like the author of Psalm 69:3: *I am weary with my crying; my throat is parched; my eyes fail while I wait for my God.* If this describes you, it's time for you to humble yourself before God. Confess your doubts and stop spinning your spiritual wheels. Start trusting Him. Begin to speak your faith that God has a purpose in all that you are experiencing… and it's good!

God's Timing Is Perfect — He's Always on Time

One of my favorite pastimes is to sit on the couch in my study, sip a diet Pepsi, and soak up a good book. I thoroughly enjoy reading the biographies and autobiographies of outstanding men and women, especially people of faith.

George Müller is one of those godly men whose faith has inspired me to take God at His Word. Müller established and administrated Christian orphanages in England in the 1800's. His is an amazing story about a man who trusted God to meet his needs — right down to the very moment something needed to be met. In his personal journal he recorded many instances when he was praying for that day's food for the children. Because of personal conviction, he refused to solicit any help. He chose instead to depend totally on God to provide for the daily needs of the children.

On one occasion even though the orphanage pantry was empty, Müller had the hungry orphans sitting at their assigned places at the dining tables, waiting to be served their meal. At that very moment, a farmer's wagon broke down right in front of the orphanage. Not able to move his vegetables, produce, and poultry to market, the farmer donated the food to Müller's orphanage. On another occasion while Müller was literally saying grace and thanking God for the meal that was coming, someone knocked on the orphanage door…and the local baker delivered more than enough food to fill the stomachs of the hungry children. A second knock was the milkman.

George Müller never asked anyone but God for anything, yet in his journals he recorded over 50,000 answers to prayers. Talk about a man of faith! How many of us could live like that?

God's Timing Is Everything

Perfect timing. Not too soon, not too late. Right on time. In the margin next to Psalm 37:23 in George Müller's Bible, this simple man of tremendous practical faith wrote, "The steps of a good man are ordered by the Lord….and so are his stops!"

Waiting on the Lord necessitates an acknowledgement on our part of the principle that God is always on time. Our Heavenly Father is never early. Never late. Always, perfectly on time.

Moses delivered Israel from Egyptian bondage. But the first time he tried he failed because it wasn't God's time. Exodus chapter 4 shows us that Moses killed an Egyptian and tried to cover it up. He was found out, and fled for his life. Because his heart overruled his head, Moses got ahead of God's deliverance plan. He spent the next 40 years on the backside of an unforgiving desert getting to know God. Jehovah God had a perfect plan for delivering Israel from Pharaoh. God knew exactly when He would execute it. The timing wasn't right for the Exodus until Moses, the agent of deliverance, was prepared. Exodus 4:19 reads, *Now the* LORD *said to Moses in Midian, "Go back to Egypt, for all the men who were seeking your life are dead."* Moses received God's go ahead because he was ready spiritually and no one was looking to kill him anymore. It was the right time, the perfect time. God had prepared everything and everyone and everything — Moses, Aaron, the people, Pharaoh, the rod, and the plagues — for the great Exodus.

Exodus 12:41 tells us *at the end of four hundred and thirty years,* **to the very day**, *all the hosts of the* LORD *went out from the land of Egypt.* Exactly 430 years earlier the Lord had revealed to Joseph when the children of God would be delivered from Egyptian bondage. The Lord led them out on the *very day*. That's perfect timing, right down to the day, after more than four centuries!

We're not done yet. As we study the Hebrews' exit from Egypt, and Pharaoh's hot pursuit, we see perfect timing written all over the Red Sea miracle. The charging chariots bearing down on them; the cloud and pillar of fire moving to a divinely designated protective position between Israel and Pharaoh's avenging army; the seemingly impassable sea; the water parting early enough and long enough for every single child of God to cross on dry ground; the collapse of the wall of water, exactly when the Egyptian chariots and soldiers were in the middle of the channel, right where they would all drown. Not one Egyptian soldier escaped. If the Lord had been late in separating the sea,

Israel would have been massacred. If He had been too early, the Egyptian army wouldn't have died.

The Exodus event and Israel's divine deliverance at the hands of Moses were perfectly timed. Not by chance, not coincidentally, but at precisely the right time.

In the New Testament, soon after James had been put to death by the sword, Herod had Peter imprisoned. We read in Acts 12:5-7:

> *Peter was kept in the prison, but prayer for him was being made fervently by the church to God.* **On the very night** *when Herod was about to bring him forward, Peter was sleeping between two soldiers, bound with two chains, and guards in front of the door were watching over the prison. And behold, an angel of the Lord suddenly appeared, and a light shone in the cell; and he struck Peter's side and woke him up, saying, "Get up quickly." And his chains fell off his hands.*

Note specifically the phrase "on the very night." That night Herod was going to behead Peter too, but at the perfect moment, before Herod could carry out his plans, the angel of the Lord arrived, woke Peter up, and the Apostle walked out of the heavily-guarded prison unharmed.

Faith, demonstrated by the church's fervent prayer on behalf of Peter, brought deliverance to Peter.

Perfect timing once again. God knew the exact moment to spring Peter from prison. He knew the perfect time when He would get the glory, Herod would be disturbed, the church would be blessed and encouraged by receiving a tremendous answer to prayer, and the community would witness a miracle of supernatural intervention they could not explain away. God was on perfectly time for Peter.

Let's look at a few other biblical examples of God's perfect timing:

- Jericho's walls came tumbling down on the thirteenth lap, when Israel shouted…just as Joshua had been told they would. (Joshua 6)
- The prophet Elijah and the widow from Zarephath were both provided food at just the right moment. (1 Kings 17)

- Elisha performed the miracle of the oil, filling the pots to pay for the debt of the widow woman just before the creditors would come to enslave her sons. (2 Kings 4)
- Jesus produced a coin for Peter when the taxes needed to be paid.
- The Lord arrived at Mary and Martha's home and raised Lazarus from the dead (John 11). Lazarus had been dead four days when Jesus commanded him to come forth — a resurrection miracle that left no doubt who Jesus was and what He could do. The whole town came out to see what had happened at that tomb.

You can't study the Bible and not see God's perfect timing operating in the lives of His people. Almighty God still always works His divine plan for the right people, in the right way, at the right time, for the right reasons. Perfect purpose and perfect timing. What a great and awesome God we serve!

God's Greatest Works for Us Take Time

We discussed the topic of greatness, waiting and time at length earlier. But it's important that we remember that the Lord's finest and most lasting work happens over time. And time involves timing.

One day in 1986, I announced to my secretary that I was going to write a book. I wanted to write and I believed I had the ability to communicate clearly via the pen (now word processor software) and the printed page. I felt certain that I could write a book.

My grandfather, who had been a minister, had been published. While I was growing up, he encouraged me to put my thoughts on paper. I think he hoped that his writing gift would be passed on to me.

Time and years passed while I kept thinking about that book I was going to write. A friend who is an author told me that being successful as a writer requires two things: 1) Have something to say, 2) say it well.

Ten years after I announced I was going to be a published author, my first book was released. What took so long? Had I been lazy? Hardly! I'm a hard working, self-motivated individual. Maybe I didn't have anything to say?

The issue was timing. I had a lot to say, but hadn't written it down. During that decade of waiting to write, the Spirit of the Lord did some perfecting on my character. I gained some maturity, experience, and wisdom I didn't have in 1986. I remember well in October of 1994 while praying in the woods behind our house one evening when the Spirit whispered to my spirit, "Steve, start writing your book now. Title it *Holy Burnout*." I obeyed, put my nose to the grindstone, and *Holy Burnout* was published two years later. I know in my heart that any time earlier than 1996 wouldn't have been the right time. The proper time, the perfect time, the time where the Lord could bring the most glory to Himself through my restoration story was 1996, not 1986.

David wrote in Psalm 37:34: *Wait for the Lord and keep His way, and He will exalt you to inherit the land; when the wicked are cut off, you will see it.* If we'll wait, when the time is right (perfect), the Lord will take care of His kids!

SUCCESS OCCURS WHEN PREPARATION MEETS OPPORTUNITY

Often people miss opportunities because they aren't prepared for them. Opportunity knocks, but nobody's home to answer the door. Many people want the perks but few are willing to wait and pay the price of preparation.

A young man once came to me seeking advice about his future. He was having trouble discerning the direction he should take for a career path. I asked what his dream was, what he really desired to do in life. After he shared his passion with me I said, "That's great. Now, what are you doing right now to prepare yourself for the day when God opens the doors to your dreams?" He replied, "Not much. I sort of thought the Lord just drops the dream on you and opens doors and we walk through them."

No wonder he was struggling with purpose and direction! Time is opportunity for preparation for future fulfillment of our God-given dreams. When we use our time wisely, the time will come when preparation pays off (timing). Training, schooling, mentoring, apprenticeships, internships, etc. prepare us for our moment in the sun (or should I say Son!). Examine the lives of the men and women of the Bible and you will discover that every one of them went through phases of preparation before they experienced the fulfillment of their divinely inspired dreams. They waited well, prepared, and were ready to fulfill their role when the Lord called them.

There is no success in God's Kingdom without preparation. And there is no preparation without the passage of time.

We Learn Timing by Waiting on the Lord

During a period of significant transition in my life, as I sought the Lord's will and direction for me, my family, and my ministry, the Holy Spirit directed me to Isaiah 30:21: *Your ears will hear a word behind you, "This is the way, walk in it," whenever you turn to the right, or to the left.*

Isn't that a great verse! God says He will speak to us and reveal to us the way to walk — as specifically as whether to turn right or left. I need that kind of guidance, and so do you.

To hear that word we have to actively wait for it. Get alone with the Lord. Put in the time before Him. Then we will know the timing for turning this way or that way in life. Waiting puts us in sync with God's timing, while impatience and unwillingness to wait on Him takes us out of His timing.

In the next chapter, we'll lay out practical ways to wait on the Lord so we can hear His voice and follow His directions. Whether we call it spiritual sense, hunch, sensitivity, or knowing, that sense of "I know that I know that I know that I know," comes from waiting on the Lord. That's certainly more than insight, more than intuition. It's inspiration. Put perspiration (work and preparation) together with inspiration (word and spiritual power), and over time God produces a winner!

Every so often, I reread a journal I wrote during my restoration process. One entry is a fitting closing for this chapter. I wrote a simple modern life illustration:

> Jo Ann cooked some hamburgers. They were as tasty as usual. She times them to seven minutes on one side, then seven on the other. Perfectly cooked, juicy, just right. The second batch was still on the grill. The kids were hollering, "Hurry up hamburgers, we're hungry!" I chuckled and then told them we couldn't hurry them up. If we did, they wouldn't cook properly and wouldn't taste just right. Hamburgers have to be fully cooked to taste really good.
>
> The Lord said to me, "Steve, you're like those hamburgers. You're on my grill. The Holy Spirit (fire) is cooking you. You're being grilled to perfection. Not quite done yet. I know you're hungry to go and preach and fulfill your call. Wait just a little

longer. Then you'll be good and tasty, useful to Me. Stay on my grill. Let the Holy Spirit complete His work in you. Soon you'll be completely cooked (healed and restored). Spiritually mature. Good and juicy. When you're completely cooked according to My timer, then I will use you in ways you never imagined possible."

Glory to God! I'm seeing that analogy unfold before my eyes. I'm seeing and doing things I only dreamed of before. Why? Timing. Time spent waiting is never wasted time when God is in it. We wait with confidence for God to meet our needs because timing is everything in His Kingdom.

God's Help Sure
God's help is always sure,
   His methods seldom guessed;
Delay will make our pleasure pure,
   Surprise will give it zest.

His wisdom is sublime,
   His heart profoundly kind;
God never is before his time,
   And never is behind.
   Rev. Thomas Toke Lynch[3]

WAIT TRAINING

CHAPTER 9
WAIT TRAINING 101

WHAT WAIT TRAINING IS

If you go to any gym or health club, you'll notice they offer beginner and advanced programs and classes. Exercises for novices are different than those for the more experienced and skilled. Advanced exercise routines build upon the basics taught in beginning courses.

Faith builders, like body builders, have to begin with the basics. When they master the elementary routines, then they can move up to the advanced level to learn the exercises that will really produce the results they desire.

Many believers in Christ readily acknowledge that they need to wait on Him. But sadly they simply don't know how. They need to be shown how to come before the Lord to learn from Him.

To want to wait and to actually wait on God are two very different things. To walk with the Lord, we must wait on the Lord.

If we're to be successful Christians, we must move from desire and theory to action and the actual practice of the disciplines that develop godly character. Because waiting demands discipline, we must train ourselves in the spiritual skill of waiting on God.

So let's go to work in God's workout room. First, we will discuss Wait Training 101, spiritual exercises and disciplines for beginners. We'll devote this chapter to learning the "how to's" of waiting on the Lord. Then, in the next chapter, we'll lay out Advanced Wait Training, waiting practices for the more experienced in the faith.

Waiting demands discipline and good old-fashioned hard work, because there are no shortcuts to holiness or heaven.

As a high school sophomore, I really wanted to play football. When the tryouts for the varsity team were held I was trying my hardest to impress the coaches when the head coach looked over my 5' 5", 130 lb. body and said, "Roll, if you want to play ball for me and escape serious injury, maiming or maybe even death, you're going to have to grow some muscles and put on some bulk."

Off I went to the gym for weight training. At first, I thought weight training would be fun. I bench pressed myself silly; ran the stadium stairs with weights attached to my ankles; and hoisted barbells over my head, behind my neck, and past my scrawny shoulders innumerable times. Military presses, clean and jerks, curls, reverse curls, deep knee bends and stomach crunches kept the lactic acid burning my stressed muscles. Only God knows how many push ups, squat thrusts, and sit ups I groaned my way through!

After a few weeks, I began to notice results. My strength increased. I felt more solid. I was no longer a 130-pound weakling. I had become a lean, mean, 140-pound football-playing machine. At least I thought so!

Still uncertain if I could take a hit and because of my size (or lack of it), the coach decided the only place for me was at running back. I wasn't very swift of foot, so I ended up on the third string squad. I practiced a lot, but played in games very little. As a ball carrier I wound up bruised and battered because I was so small in stature compared to the defensive linemen and linebackers. I wore a lot of black and blue along with our red and white uniforms. Sprained ankles, jammed fingers, bruised ribs, and generous quantities of Ben Gay each night after practice, left me questioning how realistic my dreams were of having a successful career in the NFL.

Before the end of the season, I cheerfully exchanged my helmet and pads for a set of car keys. I'd concluded that for me it was certainly safer and a lot more fun to sit with a pretty girl in the stands and watch the games. So much for my football fantasy and dream of dethroning Mr. Universe!

Though my weightlifting days were short lived, I did learn some things about building muscles.

1. Muscles don't build themselves. They must be exercised and used to become larger and stronger. Muscles have to be stretched and torn to grow. The force of weights against the muscle tissue tears them, and in the tearing and repairing process, growth results.

2. Weight training and muscle building for the purpose of increasing strength requires repetition. — set after set of 10 to 15 repetitions of an exercise faithfully performed every other day for weeks, months or even years (depending how big and

strong you want to become) produces muscles. Weights must be lifted over, and over, and over again for maximum benefit.

3. Some exercises are designed to build nothing but bulk, (the bulging biceps) while others produce body tone (shape, form, lines and curves…the stuff we like to admire in the mirror).

4. Weight training requires some basic knowledge of how your body works and how you can get the most out of it through physical exercise. Understanding what you're doing and why you're doing it helps immensely in the doing of it.

5. Though basic in principles weight training is highly individualistic. Because of God-given differences in body build, some weight lifters are featherweights while others are heavyweights. How much you lift is not the issue. How well you do it is.

6. Weight training takes time. Body builders and exercise enthusiasts must take time and make time to workout if they expect to see results.

7. There are various levels of body building training. Beginner, intermediate and advanced weight training programs offer progressive steps to a slim and trim physique.

8. Building muscle requires a disciplined and diligent commitment to the process of weight training. Some people get motivated and enthusiastic for a couple of weeks after they join a fitness club. Then, when the pain and soreness sets in, they drop out with nothing to show but a long-term payment schedule for use of a club they no longer make use of. Those who stick with their programs whether they feel like it or not have something worthwhile to show for their investment of time, energy, and money — enjoying the rewards of a strong, attractive, healthy body.

SPIRITUAL WAIT TRAINING

Spiritual muscles, much like physical muscles, must be exercised if they are to grow and be useful. Faith is like a muscle. It must be stretched and strengthened to be most effective. Recall what James said about the faith-testing and character-developing process:

> *Consider it all joy, my brethren, when you encounter various trials, knowing that the testing of your faith [pressures that come against you] produces endurance [the ability to stand firm and steadfast]. And let endurance have its perfect result, so that you may be perfect and complete, lacking in nothing.*

Faith doesn't grow by itself. It is every believer's personal responsibility to nurture and mature in their faith.

Wait training (waiting on/for the Lord to learn from Him) builds our faith up so it can withstand the attacks of the evil one and the wearing-down effects of the unbelieving world in which we live.

In Ephesians 4:11-16 Paul wrote the goal of individual Christian living.

> *He gave some as apostles, and some as prophets, and some as evangelists, and some as pastors and teachers, for the equipping of the saints for the work of service, to the building up of the body of Christ; until we all attain to the unity of the faith, and of the knowledge of the Son of God, to a mature man, to the measure of the stature which belongs to the fullness of Christ. As a result, we are no longer to be children, tossed here and there by waves, and carried about by every wind of doctrine, by the trickery of men, by craftiness in deceitful scheming; but speaking the truth in love, we are to grow up in all aspects into Him who is the head, even Christ, from whom the whole body, being fitted and held together by what every joint supplies, according to the proper working of each individual part, causes the growth of the body for the building up of itself in love.*

Faith grows under pressure. When we exercise our faith regularly, daily, our faith grows stronger. As the weight of this world's temptations press in on us and tear away at the very fabric of our belief, we must repeat over and over the things God has established that build belief and mature believers. We have to keep our *shield of faith* (Ephesians 6:16) up and in its protective position in order to *extinguish all the flaming missiles of the evil one.*

Just as no one else can work out and build your muscles for you, no other believer can exercise your faith, hold your shield of faith, and battle the devil for you.

Wait training is personal. God and you. Faith isn't automatic. It isn't made perfect overnight. Because it takes time and effort to build our faith, we have to make time for faith development. Stable, steady, strong faith requires effort, and effort requires time. Hebrews 11 records and rehearses the lives of great men and women of God who made faith their first priority. The phrase *by faith* is used each time an inductee into God's Hall of Fame of Faith is introduced. In verse 39, they all are honored with a fitting epitaph for heroes of faith: *All these having gained approval through their faith....* God approved these spiritual heroes because of their faith.

Our faith is strengthened and built up over time as we journey through this life and trust God to meet our needs each day. Our personal faith will be as strong as we want it to be.

If body builders want bigger and stronger muscles, they put in more time on the equipment. If we want to stand up, stand firm, and stand out as people of faith, we must put in time with God, who strengthens our faith. In life if you give a little, you get a little; if you give a lot, you get a lot. Simple, isn't it? We do indeed reap what we sow. (See Galatians 6:7-8.) When it comes to developing faith, little effort equals little faith while lots of effort equals a lot of faith.

Having faith that grows and matures requires an uncompromising commitment to do whatever it takes to become the kind of person God can count on. Committed people of faith move mountains. (See Mark 11:22-26.) In the same way as sporadic, minimal effort and inconsistent workouts build little physical muscle, occasional, undisciplined spiritual exercises produce little spiritual fruit. We have to work our faith for faith to work! As Paul wrote in Philippians 2:12-13, we have to work out what God has worked in.

> *My beloved, just as you have always obeyed, not as in my presence only, but now much more in my absence, work out your salvation with fear and trembling; for it is God who is at work in you, both to will and to work for His good pleasure.*

God, by His grace and through the Holy Spirit, works in us to desire and to do His will. It is our personal responsibility to work out the salvation (our faith walk) that the Lord Jesus has provided for us. "Fear and trembling" means that we respect and love Him and what He has done for us so much we take His call on our lives very seriously. Working *out* what God has worked *in* happens every day as we wait on the Lord and walk by faith.

A first grader had his explanation for the fire at his school: "I knew it was going to happen," he told his parents, "because we've been practicing for it all year!" Fire drills are regularly conducted so students can be protected from injury in the event of a real fire. Practice, practice, and more practice prepares children for getting out of harm's way if the fire alarm sounds. Practice can make the difference between life and death.

In a similar manner, faith must be practiced to be effective. God's children need to regularly participate in certain spiritual drills if we are to withstand the fiery trials that come our way. It's called waiting on the Lord. If we will diligently wait on Him, we can be certain that we will stand firm when trials come crashing into our lives. If we will practice the disciplines that produce holiness, we will be able to persevere and produce the fruit of Christ-like character that causes us to triumph over life's trials.

One verse of Scripture that meant a lot to me during my spiritual rebuilding process is found in Isaiah 58:11:

> *The* L*ORD* *will continually guide you, and satisfy your desire in scorched places, and give strength to your bones; and you will be like a watered garden, and like a spring of water whose waters do not fail.*

Isn't that a marvelous verse? Life can drain us dry, but the Lord promises to guide us, satisfy us, and strengthen us continually if we're careful to wait on His renewal and refreshment. In the process of allowing God to perform His work in us in these ways, we become watered gardens who never run out of water.

Dig a spiritual well that taps into the river of life so you can draw from it in the days ahead. Remember that God said in His Word: Out of your innermost being will flow rivers of living water. (John 7:37-39.) Concentrate on building your faith as you spend time with God. Dig deep into His Word and He will show you how to be a person who walks by faith, not by sight. He will guide you every step of the way, strengthen your bones (spiritual muscles), and satisfy (fulfill and bring to pass) the godly desires that burn in your heart.

God assures us that when life seems to be out of control He is in control, continually directing our paths, empowering us, and faithfully fulfilling the promises He has made. Our responsibility is to wait on Him and follow His leading.

BEGINNING SPIRITUAL WAIT TRAINING

Five basic spiritual exercises are necessary to begin building the new believer's faith.

HAVE AN ATTITUDE OF EXPECTANCY

Our conduct is influenced not by our experience, but by our expectations. We really do get what we expect in life. Expectations have to do with attitude. Waiting on the Lord requires a positive attitude of expectancy if we are to receive anything from God.

Many good people who love God go through the motions of waiting before the Lord, but they don't really expect to hear from Him. So, guess what? They don't. Why? They approach God out of duty, or desperation, but not out of an attitude of devotion and delight that expects to be blessed.

The prophet Micah had the right attitude about waiting for the Lord: *As for me, I will watch expectantly for the LORD; I will wait for the God of my salvation. My God will hear me.* (Micah 7:7)

The prophet chose to wait for God and watch expectantly for Him. Micah made the personal choice to look to the Lord to meet His needs, whether others did or didn't. He expected the Lord to come through for him because he knew the God of his salvation would hear him. So he watched for Him with an attitude of expectation.

The word translated *watch* means "to stay in place, in expectation of, to await, to look forward expectantly."[4] To *expect* means to "look forward to, to anticipate, to consider probable or certain, reasonable, due, or necessary, to wait."[5]

For Christians waiting on the Lord that involves expecting Him to do something on our behalf. The psalmist wrote in Psalm 62:5, *My soul, wait in silence for God only, for my hope [expectation] is from Him.*

David's hopes (expectations) were grounded in God. He looked to God, and God alone, to care for his needs.

Those who wait for the Lord expect Him to show up and do His thing!

When we study the word *wait* in the Bible, it always carries with it the idea of expectation. *Vine's Expository Dictionary of New Testament Words* depicts the word *wait* as an expression of "eager and strong expectation, an eager looking for or looking to."⁶

The following selected Scriptures are representative of the word *wait* that in Bible usage denotes expectancy.

- *There was a man in Jerusalem whose name was Simeon; and this man was righteous and devout, looking for the consolation of Israel. Luke 2:25*

- *There is in Jerusalem by the sheep gate a pool, which is called in Hebrew Bethesda, having five porticoes. In these lay a multitude of those who were sick, blind, lame, and withered, [waiting for the moving of the waters; for an angel of the Lord went down at certain seasons into the pool and stirred up the water; whoever then first, after the stirring up of the water, stepped in was made well from whatever disease with which he was afflicted.] John 5:3-4*

- *As Jesus returned, the people welcomed Him, for they had all been waiting for Him. Luke 8:40*

- *Cornelius was waiting for them and had called together his relatives and friends. Acts 10:24*

- *The anxious longing of the creation waits eagerly for the revealing of the sons of God. Romans 8:19*

- *So Christ also, having been offered once to bear the sins of many, will appear a second time for salvation without reference to sin, to those who eagerly await Him. Hebrews 9:28*

The spirit of expectancy is the common theme running through these verses. It won't do us any good to wait on the Lord if we don't expect anything from the meeting. It's that simple: *You will know that I am the* Lord; *those who hopefully [expectantly] wait for Me will not be put to shame.* When we come into God's presence with an attitude of expectancy, the time we spend waiting is never wasted.

I enjoy meeting with Jesus because He always shows up and cares for my needs. He taught me from the very beginning of our relationship to come to Him like a son who expects his father to give him what he asks for.

When my son was a teenager, he had this expectation thing all figured out. He had no problem at all approaching boldly and asking me for money. If it was a legitimate need, he knew that because his dad loves him and delights in providing for him the odds were pretty good that he would get what he asked for. He came unashamedly and unhesitatingly into my presence expecting to walk away with what he needed…and he usually got what he expected!

Don't forget what Matthew 7:7-11 tells us Jesus said about God's willingness to give good things to those who expect Him to.

> "I say to you, ask, and it shall be given to you; seek, and you will find; knock, and it will be opened to you. For everyone who asks receives, and he who seeks, finds, and to him who knocks it will be opened. Or what man is there among you who, when his son asks for a loaf, will give him a stone? Or if he asks for a fish, will your Father who is in heaven give what is good to those who ask Him!"

Is your attitude toward waiting on the Lord positive or negative — expectant and hopeful, or doubtful and hopeless?

Faith expects God to act. Waiting is an act of faith that expects God to do something.

The place to begin building your faith is in your mind. You have to believe and expect the Lord to meet with you and meet your needs. It's an attitude. Maybe it's time to check your attitude and see if it lines up with the Bible's attitude toward waiting. If you do a Scripture search along the lines of how to wait well on God, you'll find the following adverbs attached to the verb *wait*. They clearly convey this principle that we must have an attitude of expectancy if we expect God to act.

Patiently	Psalm 37:7
Hopefully	Isaiah 49:23
Courageously	Psalm 27:14
Silently	Psalm 62:1
Faithfully	Hebrews 10:23
Honestly	Psalm 25:21

Joyfully	Psalm 59:16
Wholeheartedly	Psalm 119:10
Obediently	Romans 4
Reverently	Psalm 147:11

How does your attitude measure up to this list? In these verses those who were waiting looked to the Lord to provide whatever they needed to live victoriously. They waited well and received great rewards because they expected God to perform what He had promised.

The first discipline in spiritual exercise is mental. You have to train yourself to expect to receive from the Lord when you meet with Him. You will not do that naturally. Your thought process has to be spiritually renewed (See Romans 12:1-2.). You have to train yourself to have an attitude of expectancy toward the Lord.

Check your attitude. Do you expect to receive from the Lord when you go to Him? Do you really?

Have an Attitude of Quietness

Ecclesiastes 3:7 tells us there is *a time to be silent, and a time to speak*. By this, the wisdom writer means there are seasons for talking and seasons for being quiet; times for speaking and making some noise, and times for silence and listening. This verse has to do primarily with personal relationships (interaction between people), but there is a broader context — life itself. We experience active seasons as well as inactive seasons while journeying through life. Both are necessary for balanced, successful living.

But modern man has strayed from this balanced approach to life. Our society has tipped the scales heavily to one side of the speaking/silence balance. We are horribly, unhealthily out of balance when it comes to a time for silence. We live in an age that is long on noise and short on quiet. Everyone loves to speak, but few seek to be silent and listen. Most of us clamor for activity, while very few of us search for solitude — secluded places — the state of being alone, where silence is so pervasive that it's almost deafening.

Søren Kierkegaard once wrote, "If I were a doctor and were asked for my advice, I should reply: 'Create silence.'" That's good advice in an age when silence is no longer golden. Quietness isn't even silver anymore! It's almost non-existent in these times when success is measured by action and activity fueled by a frantic, hectic pace to produce results we hope will somehow satisfy the longing of our hearts and the hunger of our spirits.

Blaise Pascal said, "I have often said that the sole cause of man's unhappiness is that he does not know how to stay quietly in his room." How true! We've become a restless society that has lost sight of the value of being quiet and resting in the Lord.

In Isaiah 30:15 we read: *The Lord God, the Holy One of Israel, has said; "In repentance and rest you shall be saved. In quietness and trust (confidence) is your strength, but you were not willing."* Talk about hitting 21st Century America right between her spiritual eyes. Salvation and strength, according to the Lord, come from repentance, rest, quietness and trust. We're invited to do these healthy things. But as in Bible days, we are not willing. Is it any wonder then that an unrepentant, restless, cynical culture such as ours is on the verge of burnout and collapse? We're reaping the curses associated with behavior that disobeys the Lord and refuses to wait on Him and find rest in His Word.

This pointed and important question will help you determine the state of your personal spiritual health: When is the last time you got alone, turned off everything that makes sound, and sat still and quiet, peacefully, soaking up the silence? Be honest. How long has it been since you experienced solitude?

Solitude (being alone with God in a quiet place) is powerful. It produces health, happiness and holiness because when we get away to a secluded, noiseless place, we can focus spiritually.

Many people's spirits are out of focus because they forsake solitude. They avoid silence like a communicable disease.

Jesus knew the value of being spiritually focused. In Mark 1:35 we read: *In the early morning, while it was still dark, Jesus got up, left the house, and went away to a secluded place, and was praying there.*

In this brief verse, the Lord Jesus gave us a great pattern for waiting on God. Note how Jesus got up by Himself and while the others were sleeping, went to a lonely place. He went out to pray. By Himself. Away from others. Why alone and away? No distractions. Solitude is getting away and getting alone with God. That's the key to solitude: alone and apart. We can't experience stillness before the Lord in the middle of a group people and in places we usually associate with activity and busyness.

To be effective, faith must be focused. In John 3:34, the New Testament declares and demonstrates that Jesus, as God's Son, had the Spirit without measure (limit). If anybody was spiritually focused and exercised perfect faith, it was Jesus. The Lord possessed and practiced an unlimited and unhindered trust in the Father. Yet, He stole away to secluded places to be alone with Him. Why? He got away to solitary places to maintain focus on His relationship with the Father. Renewal, refreshment, restoration, direction, guidance, instruction and prayer awaited Him there.

Jesus regularly slipped away to meet with the Father as the disciples slept. In the lonely, stillness of the early morning, Jesus could wait on the Father without His followers asking Him questions; the sick seeking a healing touch; or the crowds clamoring for another sermon. The Master's only undistracted time for fortifying His faith and renewing His spirit came when He got away from people and got alone with His Father in a secluded, quiet place.

If the Master required solitude to be successful in His ministry, how much more do we, His servants, need to seek solitude? The only way we can hear the still, small voice of God is to get quiet.

In 1 Kings 19 we read the story of Elijah. Burned out, discouraged and depressed he went to Mt. Horeb where the Lord sent a powerful wind, an earthquake, and fire. But God wasn't in any of those events. In verse 12 we see that God came to Elijah in a *gentle whisper* (also called a *gentle blowing* and *still small voice*).

The Lord wanted Elijah to realize he needed to settle down spiritually and listen for the quiet voice of the Spirit. Stillness puts us in a position to receive the Lord's ministry to us. When Elijah got still and quiet, God ministered to Him and gave Him specific directions for the next steps in his ministry (vv. 14-21).

Today many of us won't go anywhere without turning on a radio, CD player, MP3 player, cell phone, TV or something that produces noise and keeps our minds occupied.

Sound has its place. But when it comes to spiritual focus, silence is indeed golden.

How can we hear the still, small voice of the Lord when we allow our senses to be bombarded by iPods, surround-sound systems, and blaring televisions?

Even in many of our churches we keep the music playing at deafening levels and the activity going at fever pitch so we won't experience the dread diseases of our age — dead air.

In Psalm 4:4 David exhorts us: *Meditate in your heart upon your bed, and be still.* Contemplate, dwell upon, ponder, turn over, reflect upon the things of God in your heart. Cease the busy activity of the day and set your heart upon God. Meditation and stillness pave the way to hearing the voice of the Holy Spirit.

In Psalm 39:7 David reminds us of the purpose of waiting: *Now Lord, for what do I wait? My hope is in You.* We wait because our hope is in the One we steal away to meet with.

The benefits of solitude are dependent on this one inescapable fact: Being alone with God requires solitude. Like Jesus, we have to go to the places where we can meet with God without distraction.

It takes commitment, courage and love for God for us to regularly get away to spend time alone with our Lord. Solitude doesn't just happen. We have to seek it. We have to create it. We have to be intentional about spending some time with the Lord in a quiet place. For some of us that's not easy. Solitary places are lonely places, and for many of us, our nature balks at being alone. But the purpose of solitude is all about hearing from God. And what we need most is to hear from the Lord.

Spiritual refreshment and refinement occur in the solitary places where we set ourselves apart to wait upon our Heavenly Father. We can never realize the deep heartfelt joy, spiritual peace, and power that comes from going one on one with the Him until we set aside a special place to spend time alone with Him.

Your waiting place could be anywhere — a study or an isolated room in the attic or basement of your home; a mountaintop; a spot just outside your city limits; a beach; maybe a prayer place in the woods.

I've consistently slipped away to meet with the Lord in parks, woods, and forests near our home. I feel closest to my Creator when I commune with Him in the surroundings of His creation. For me, nature provides solitude that man in all of his sophistication simply cannot duplicate.

Ask the Lord where He would like you to meet with Him. Listen for and obey the leading of the Holy Spirit. He will draw you to that secret place where He is waiting to fellowship with you. Plan to meet there regularly with the Him.

If you're a night owl (evening person), rendezvous with God at the end of your day. If you are an early bird (morning person), start your day with the Lord. Whatever the best time of the day is for you, get away then to be with Jesus.

Alone and away is the secret of solitude. Running and walking with the Lord is contingent upon waiting on the Lord in quiet places. Follow the example of the great men and women of faith in the Bible. Slip away from the routine of life to meet privately with the Lord. In the solitary places you will find, as they did, the quiet, confident strength that only comes from sitting in the presence of God.

Apply the Bible to Everyday Life

Some books are for our information, others for our inspiration. The Bible is for our transformation. To build our faith muscles we must regularly feed our spirits upon God's Word because faith cannot grow apart from God's Word: *Faith comes by hearing and hearing by the Word of God* (Romans 10:17).

Evangelist D. L Moody personally experienced this. He once said, "I used to think I should close my Bible and pray for faith; but I came to see that it was in studying the Word that I was to get faith."

Getting alone and away with God and His Word prepares us for a life-changing encounter with our Heavenly Father. When we seek solitude and open the Word of God with an expectant attitude, we're in a position to be changed more into the likeness of Jesus. As James W. Alexander said, "The study of God's Word for the purpose of discovering God's will is the secret discipline which has formed the greatest character."

Matthew 4:4 tells us Jesus said, *"It is written, man shall not live on bread alone, but on every word that proceeds out of the mouth of God."* Centuries earlier Job declared, *"I have not departed from the command of His lips; I have treasured the words of His mouth more than my necessary food"* (Job 23:12).

And Paul, in his pastoral letters to Timothy, instructed the young Christian and future church leader concerning the importance of the Bible in the believer's life:

> *Be diligent (study, KJV) to present yourself approved to God as a workman who does not need to be ashamed, handling accurately the word of truth....* (2 Timothy 2:15)

All Scripture is inspired by God and profitable for teaching, for reproof, for correction, for training in righteousness; that the man of God may be adequate, equipped for every good work. (2 Timothy 3:16-17)

The emphasis here is on how God's Word profits our lives. In the original Greek language *theópneustos,* the word translated *inspired*, literally means "God-breathed." We understand therefore, that it came from the mouth of God. God-breathed and inspired by the Holy Spirit, the Bible teaches, reproves, corrects, and trains us in righteousness (right living) so that as God's men and women we will be fully equipped to walk by faith and fulfill the good works God has called us to accomplish. We can stand before the Lord as His approved and unashamed workers if we are diligent to study His Word and use it correctly in our daily lives.

There's a story about two lawyers who were close friends. Much to the amazement of one, the other became a Sunday School teacher. "Why?" he protested. "I'll bet you don't even know the Lord's Prayer." "Everybody knows that," the new teacher replied. "It's 'Now I lay me down to sleep.' " "You win," said the other admiringly. "I didn't know you knew so much about the Bible."

It's supposed to be just a cute story, but it contains more truth than some would like to admit. Many people want God to work in their lives, yet they have no idea how He works because they're ignorant of His Word. Because they don't know His Book, they don't know how and where to look for His help.

Think about this: Could someone become a good doctor without first studying his medical books? What lawyer could enter a courtroom, stand before a judge and jury, and argue his case without having spent considerable time studying and reviewing his law books? What good automobile mechanic would open the hood and start working on a car without first checking the latest technical manuals for the specifications and adjustments the automobile requires to perform efficiently? To be successful in any endeavor, we must regularly consult books, manuals, and guidelines for directions.

The Psalmist declared in Psalm 119:81-82: *My soul languishes for Your salvation; I wait for Your word. My eyes fail with longing for Your word....* David waited for God's Word. Why? It was His salvation. King David didn't need man's word. He needed to hear the Word of the Lord. So do we. We need to wait for His Word, longing (intensely desiring) to hear God speak to us in the secret waiting places. He speaks through His Word.

Psalm 119:165 tells us *those who love Your law have great peace, and nothing causes them to stumble.* What a tremendous verse! Great peace and stumble-proof living belongs to those who love God's Book!

David rejoiced and delighted in God's Word. Look what he wrote in Psalm 119:14, 16 about His love for the Scriptures: *I have rejoiced in the way of Your testimonies, as much as in all riches....I shall delight in Your statutes; I shall not forget Your Word.*

David enjoyed the Word of the Lord as much or more than all the worldly riches he could imagine. And he chose not to forget what Scripture has to say about life.

We believers need to be trained in righteousness, and spiritually equipped to fulfill our calling. We need correction from time to time. We need direction and a word from the Lord to go forward in our faith walk. To live a victorious and satisfying life in Christ, we need the strength and power that only God's Word can provide.

As the old saying goes: If a Christian's Bible is coming apart, it is an indication that he is fairly well put together. (In other words, if your Bible's falling apart, you probably aren't!)

For us to master the Bible, it first must master us. The very first time God called me to a solitary place to meet with Him, I took my Bible. Ever since that first appointment with the Lord, His Word has been my constant companion. I never go into any private place to meet with God without the Word. It's my spiritual manual for faithful and holy living that I must consult regularly to be successful in my Christian life.

I love the Word because the Lord speaks to me through it. The Word is my delight. I rejoice, as David did, in God's words because the Bible answers my questions, solves my problems, inspires and sharpens my spirit, stimulates my creativity, gives me wisdom, equips me for service, anoints me with power, defeats the devil, and strengthens me for spiritual warfare.

The bottom line is this: The Bible meets our every need! That's why we need to wait on the Lord with the Word of God open before us. God's Word provides the guidance and direction necessary for victorious Christian living.

The Scriptures weren't given to increase our knowledge, but to change our lives. Look at what the Bible has to say about itself when it comes to helping us navigate successfully through life.

- *Your Word is a lamp unto my feet, and a light unto my path.* Psalm 119:105
- *How can a young man keep his way pure? By keeping it according to Your Word.* Psalm 119:9
- *Your testimonies also are my delight; the are my counselors.* Psalm 119:24
- *This book of the law shall not depart from your mouth, but you shall meditate on it day and night, so that you may be careful to do according to all that is written in it; for then you will make your way prosperous, and then you will have success.* Joshua 1:8
- *By these He has granted to us His precious and magnificent promises, so that by them you may become partakers of the divine nature, having escaped the corruption that is in the world by lust.* 2 Peter 1:4
- *Jesus was saying to those Jews who had believed in Him, "If you continue in My word, then you are truly disciples of Mine; and you will know the truth, and the truth will make you free."* John 8:31-32

We need God's Word to escape the corruption of this world and enjoy the freedom and joy of the coming Kingdom. By getting alone and away with God and His Word we prepare for a life-changing encounter with our Heavenly Father.

I promised this book would be practical. I want to share some things I do when I wait on the Lord with my Bible in hand. I haven't perfected these spiritual disciplines, but I do my best to be consistent. I hope they will encourage you in your time with the Lord studying His Word.

Read the Word

Ask the Holy Spirit to direct you to the passages, or verses He wants you to focus on. Begin your time by clearing your mind of worldly thoughts and filling your head and heart with His Word. Read scripture silently and out loud. One of the reasons I like the woods for a meeting place with God is that I can read, speak, or shout the Word. I can be vocal and verbal and not bother anybody.

MEDITATE ON THE WORD

Be like a spiritual sponge: Soak up the Scriptures. Think about the truth. Mull it over. — What does this say? What does this mean? What is the Lord trying to say to me through this passage? How does it apply to my current life situation? Chew it over like a cow chews its cud. Reflect upon it. Let it sink into your spirit.

LISTEN FOR THE WORD

Get quiet and ask the Lord to speak to you. When we listen, He speaks. God will put a verse on your heart. Maybe it will be scripture you've memorized in the past. He might direct you to a specific place in the Bible.

RECEIVE THE WORD

God's Word doesn't do us any good if we don't receive it into our lives. Take the Word the Lord has revealed, thank Him for it, and apply it to your need. You must be humble and teachable enough to receive whatever the Holy Spirit sends. Ecclesiastes 4:13 is an insightful passage about receiving instruction: *A poor yet wise lad is better than an old and foolish king who no longer knows how to receive instruction.*

WRITE THE WORD

Take a pad and pen with you. Write out what God tells you. Writing things down is a great way to remember what God said to you. Seeing God's Word on paper drives it deeper into your mind and heart. Keep a personal spiritual journal. Record your waiting experiences in detail. You'll return to your writings in the future for encouragement, remembering and reflecting on what God gave you previously. You'll rejoice again in the adequacy and timeliness of His Word.

SPEAK THE WORD

There is power in the spoken Word. If you don't believe it, read Mark 11:22-24 and note the emphasis on "saying" when it comes to removing mountains by faith. "Say it" means to speak it with your mouth. Speak Scripture so God, angels, Satan, demons, and the world around you can hear it. The power contained in God's Word becomes activated when it's spoken. (See Genesis 1 and the numerous times the creation narrative tells us "God said," and something happened).

According to Ephesians 6:17 we are to take up *the sword of the Spirit, which is the word of God* as part of our spiritual armament against Satan. We wield the sword of God's Word effectively when we speak it! Speak the Word. Speak it boldly!

STAND ON THE WORD

Waiting on the Lord has nothing to do with feelings. It has everything to do with faith. No matter how we might feel emotionally while waiting before the Lord, we must choose spiritually to stand on our faith. Ephesians 6:10-20 tells us about the whole armor of God. Ephesians 6:10-12 describes the specific pieces of the armor we are to put on to resist the devil and his wicked schemes. Ephesians 6:13 tells us that once we've done all we know to do, we're to stand firm. What do we stand firm on? God's Word! We must plant our spiritual feet firmly on the Rock of God's Word and stand there. We can stand tall, unmoved, unwavering, fully confident that the Lord will perform what He has promised.

SHARE THE WORD

Try to tell somebody else what you learned from your time with the Lord. Be very discerning about who you share with and what you disclose to them. Not everyone can be trusted with spiritual truth and treasure. Seek God's wisdom in this area. But don't hoard your good news! Share it with those who appreciate God's Word and will be built up and encouraged by what God gave you.

WORK GOD'S WORD INTO YOUR EVERYDAY LIFE

God's Word is practical and applicable to every area of our lives. We need more than head knowledge when it comes to the truth. Ask God how to make the Word you have learned to come alive in your daily life. As His representative, you want people to see the Word (Jesus Christ) through your words and behavior.

Thank God for His Word

God has magnified His Word above all things. So should we. Be thankful for your Bible. Make it a habit to continually give thanks to God for His Word. Look at what David wrote in Psalm 138:1-2:

> *I will give You thanks with all my heart; I will sing praises to You before the gods. I will bow down before Your holy temple, and give thanks to Your name for Your lovingkindness and Your truth; for You have magnified Your Word according to all Your name.*

Waiting on God, and of God go together. You can't wait successfully without the Word and you can't study the Word successfully without waiting. Keep your Bible in hand when you slip away to meet with the Savior.

Someone with insight once said, "Study the Bible to be wise; believe it to be safe; practice it to be holy." That's good advice for those of us who want to mount up with wings as eagles and soar through life in the power of God.

The early church father Jerome wrote, "Ignorance of the Bible means ignorance of Christ." It isn't possible to know the Lord if you don't know of the Lord! Do you love God's Word? What does your Bible mean to you?

Make a Specific Appointment for Prayer

When we were children, my brothers and I rode a church bus to attend Sunday School each week. I'm grateful to my mother who, as a single parent, made sure we were exposed to Christian teaching. Yet, looking back over my formative years, I don't recall knowing anyone at church firsthand who was what old- timers would call a prayer warrior. I know we prayed at church. But as an impressionable young man who was hungry for spiritual truth, I wasn't personally connected with an elder Christian brother who could take me under his wing to teach and mentor me about prayer.

I knew my godly grandparents were prayer warriors. I always wondered why they talked so much about talking with God. But I didn't see them often enough to learn and benefit from their personal prayer experience.

Everything changed in my life at age 20 when I accepted Jesus as my personal Lord and Savior. Upon receiving Christ I immediately hungered and thirsted for the things of God. I developed an intense desire to learn how to pray. I longed with all my heart to find out how to talk with my newfound Father in heaven. So, I sought out my grandparents. My spiritually wise grandfather gave me a verse He called it God's telephone line: *Call to me and I will answer you, and I will tell you great and mighty things, which you do not know.* (Jeremiah 33:3)

This singular verse started me on a marvelous prayer journey that has continued to this day. I have made it a habit to call upon the Lord every day. When I call God He does what He says He will do. He answers and shows me wonderful things that I would have no way of knowing except from Him. It's so exciting to know that when I call, He will answer and tell me all about the great and mighty things of His Kingdom!

In the final analysis, prayer is an act of faith. People don't call upon a supreme being (God) unless they believe He exists. Each time I pray, I am exercising faith. I am believing and trusting that my Heavenly Father is there and that He cares about every aspect of my life. The more I pray, the more I realize and experience God's faithfulness. My faith is built when I see the Lord respond to my prayers.

Pastor A. C. Dixon used to say when we depend on our money, our teaching, our education, our preaching, we get what these can do and that is something. But when we depend upon prayer we see what God can do! And what all of us need most is what God can do!

I don't know you personally, but I know myself. And I know I need what God can do in my life.

Believing prayer brings the Almighty's presence and power into our circumstances. If we are strangers to prayer, then we are strangers to power. The mighty men and women of God in the Bible were people who prayed. If you use a concordance and study the prayer lives of the Bible characters, you'll find each one developed an intimate, personal relationship with God by communicating with Him through prayer.

Prayer in its simplest form is communion with God. We communicate with the Lord through prayer by talking, listening, praising, worshipping, requesting, interceding, confessing, professing, and giving thanks. Prayer is a two-way spiritual highway where we talk with God and He talks with us.

Prayer is our lifeline to God. The great tragedy of life is not unanswered prayer but unoffered prayer. The courageous church reformer Martin Luther said, "If I should neglect prayer but a single day, I should lose a great deal of the fire of faith!"

God's people are to be on fire spiritually. Christians are to be bold, flaming witnesses for the Kingdom, people of strong, passionate faith who gladly endure hardship and persevere through difficulties while sharing the Good News of Jesus Christ!

Prayer fans the flames of spiritual passion. Fire falls when we pray. On Mt. Carmel Elijah prayed and fire fell, consuming the altar doused with water (1 Kings 18). The fire of the Holy Spirit came upon the church at Pentecost when a faithful band of Christ's followers prayed (Acts 1-2). Jesus specifically instructed His disciples to wait in Jerusalem. They obeyed. They prayed while they waited and the fire of God fell. The disciples were baptized with the Holy Spirit and became bold witnesses of Christ.

"Call to Me and I will answer you, and I will tell you great and mighty things, which you do not know" is God's invitation to prayer. Jesus taught us that if we will ask, seek, and knock, we will receive, find, and have doors opened to us. (See Matthew 7:7-8.) He gave us what we call the Lord's Prayer (Matthew 6:9-13) as a guideline for how to pray. He also told His followers where to pray (Matthew 6:5-8). Take careful note of Jesus' instructions concerning the place and pattern of prayer.

> *"When you pray, you are not to be as the hypocrites; for they love to stand and pray in the synagogues and on the street corners so they may be seen of men. Truly I say to you, they have their reward in full. But you, when you pray, go into your inner room, close your door and pray to your Father who is in secret, and your Father who sees what is done in secret will repay you. And when you are praying, do not use meaningless repetition as the Gentiles do, for they suppose that they will be heard for their many words. So do not be like them; for your Father knows what you need before you ask Him."*

Religious people prayed in Jesus' day, but not properly or effectively. The Lord labeled them hypocrites because they prayed in public so men would notice them and hear their pious petitions. Jesus wasn't opposed to praying in public. He was opposed to hypocritical public prayers when the motive of the people praying was for others to observe them and think they were holy. Jesus not only condemned hypocritical prayer, He also blasted meaningless prayer…prayers full of vain religious words repeated in a ritualistic fashion. Praying spiritual sounding phrases intended to arouse God's attention is what purely religious people do. Jesus said the world's religious hypocrites pray this way; but not His followers.

Those who serve Christ go to a secret place alone and away, shut themselves in, and talk to their Father in simple, everyday language). Forget the religious mumbo jumbo! Your Heavenly Father sees you in the inner room, communes with you there and meets your needs. According to Matthew 6:8, 32, God knows what you need even before you ask. Amazing, isn't it?

The point of this teaching is clear: A Christian's richest reward comes from the Lord in the secret place of prayer.

The secret of praying is praying in secret. God and you, one on one, is what secret praying is all about. God, not man, rewards those who diligently seek Him in the secret place of the inner room. (See Hebrews 11:6.)

Our faith stretches and expands when we spend time waiting on the Lord in our secret place of prayer. We're to enter there often. The Bible says believers are to *pray without ceasing* (1 Thessalonians 5:17), be *devoted to prayer* (Romans 12:12) and *at all times…pray and not lose heart* (Luke 18:1). Because we live one day at a time, *waiting on God through prayer is to be a daily event.*

In the midst of the crisis of the Civil War, President Abraham Lincoln said, "I have been driven many times to my knees by the overwhelming conviction that I had nowhere else to go!"

If we're going to be great for God, there's only one place for us to go.....Call to Him and He will answer you and show you great and mighty things that you do not know.

Years ago while I was conducting a worship service in a nursing home, a white-haired man stooped with age, stood and quoted the following poem from memory.

The Difference

I got up early one morning and rushed right into the day.

I had so much to accomplish, I didn't take time to pray.

Problems just tumbled about me and heavier grew each task.

"Why doesn't God help me?" I wondered. He answered, "You didn't ask."

I wanted to see joy and beauty, but the day toiled on gray and bleak.

I wondered why God didn't show me. He said, "But you didn't seek."

I tried to come into God's presence; I used all my keys at the lock.

God gently and lovingly chided, "My child, you didn't knock."

I woke up early this morning and paused before entering the day;

I had so much to accomplish, that I had to take time to pray.

Grace L. Naessens[7]

What are you going to do with your busy day today? Why don't you get alone with God and pray!

Appreciate Your Relationship with Your Heavenly Father

The most important things in life are relationships. In fact, the Bible is a book about relationships. First is the vertical relationship between God and people. Second is a horizontal relationship — people to people.

The quality of our relationships with our Creator and His creation determines whether or not we are successful in life. Jesus stressed the importance of relationships when He gave us the two great commandments.

> *He said to them, "'You shall love the Lord your God with all your heart, and with all your soul, and with all your mind. This is the great and foremost commandment. The second is like it, 'You shall love your neighbor as yourself.' On these two commandments depend the whole Law and the Prophets."*
>
> Matthew 22:37-40

According to Jesus, everything in life hinges on loving God, loving our neighbors and loving ourselves.

Love requires a relationship. Our relationships with others will flow out of our relationship with God. When we love God and live right before Him, then we can love others and treat them right.

Waiting on God develops and deepens our personal relationship with the Lord. James 4:8 exhorts us: *"Draw near to God and He will draw near to you...."* Drawing close produces relationship. Isn't it great to know that if we will get close with God, He will come close to us! In Proverbs 3:32 we find these words about the kind of relationship God wants to have with His children.

> *The devious are an abomination to the LORD;*
> *but He is intimate with the upright.*

Webster defines *intimate* as "belonging to or characterizing one's deepest nature, marked by very close association, contact, or familiarity, marked by a warm friendship developing through long association."[8] So, according to Proverbs 3:32 God wants to have a very close, warm, friendship with us that gets closer and grows stronger over time. Maybe that's why in John 15:12-15, Jesus called His followers friends. Friendship implies relationship. Jesus Christ wants to have an intimate, friendship relationship with us!

Everything Jesus said about our relationship with Him flows from His relationship with the Father. John 17 records one of Christ's greatest prayers for the church. This chapter is a divine blueprint for the type of relationship we believers are to have with our Heavenly Father. After praying for the Church's protection, provision, and progress as God's witnesses in this world (vv. 1-21) the Lord spoke of the relationship His people are to have with Him.

> *The glory which You have given Me I have given to them, that they may be one, just as We are one; I in them, and You in Me, that they may be perfected in unity, so that the world may know that You sent Me, and loved them, even as You have loved Me.*
>
> vv. 22-23

Jesus prayed that we would be inseparable from God and one another. Why? So the unbelieving world would know that the Father loves us and He sent His Son to be the Savior of all mankind. Jesus wants us to have loving relationships with God, fellow Christians, and the non-Christian world.

To love God we have to know Him. In John 17:3, Jesus defined eternal life: *This is eternal life, that they may know You, the only true God, and Jesus Christ, whom*

You have sent. Eternal life is more than forgiveness of sin and spending eternity in heaven with Jesus. It's knowing (by experiencing a personal relationship with) our Heavenly Father and His Son Jesus.

Many Christians who come to me for consultation and counseling express a desire to get closer to God, to have a deeper relationship with Jesus. That's admirable. But when I ask them what they're doing to develop that relationship, what they do on a daily basis to draw close to the Lord, most are clueless about how to be intimate with Jesus.

Relationships aren't automatic. They have to be nurtured. Spiritual maturity and Christlikeness aren't produced by quoting a religious formula or getting zapped by the Spirit at some deeper life conference. We develop a deep, personal relationship with Jesus Christ over time as we take time to wait on Him. We wait on God because we love to meet with Jesus and get to know Him better!

Out of our relationship with Jesus flows revelation, inspiration, anointing, restoration, renewal, revival, fruitfulness, and victory. All of the blessings of God come from our relationship with the Lord. The Lord not only wants to be intimate with the righteous, He also wants to bless them:

> *The curse of the LORD is on the house of the wicked, but He blesses the dwelling of the righteous.*
>
> Proverbs 3:33

What would happen if you started approaching waiting on the Lord as an exciting opportunity to develop your personal relationship with Him instead of looking at waiting time as some dry, meaningless religious duty? You would move from boredom and frustration to blessing and fruitfulness!

The way you wait on the Lord is your choice. Job knew that, and made his choice about who he would seek: *As for me, I would seek God, and I would place my cause before God; Who does great and unsearchable things, wonders without number.* (Job 5:8-9)

What about you? What's your "but as for me" statement? Are you willing to seek God in an intimate relationship?

Don't hesitate to wait on the Lord. He's waiting for you to wait on Him so He can bless your life.

Chapter 10
Advanced Wait Training

To us God revealed them through the Spirit; for the Spirit searches all things, even deep things of God.

1 Corinthians 2:10

Let the heart of those who seek the Lord be glad. Seek the Lord and His strength; seek His face continually.

Psalm 105:3-4

One of the most exciting things about the Christian life is that it's dynamic…ever changing, never static for those who choose to mature in their relationship with Jesus Christ. Christians who are hungry for a deeper walk with Jesus can experience it.

In 1 Corinthians 2:10 the Apostle Paul wrote that the Holy Spirit searches out the deep things of God and then reveals them to us. The Lord has provided much more for His followers than a shallow, feel-good religious experience. Deeply satisfying spiritual life awaits those who wait on the Lord. Paul also told the Corinthian Christians that they could be changed from one level of glory to another as the Spirit worked in their lives.

> *The Lord is the Spirit, and where the Spirit of the Lord is, there is liberty. But we all, with unveiled face, beholding as in a mirror the glory of the Lord, are being transformed into the same image from glory to glory, just as from the Lord, the Spirit.*
>
> 2 Corinthians 3:17-18

Note that we *are being* transformed (continuous present tense) into the same image of Jesus. "Glory to glory" suggests progress. Christlikeness is achieved through a process of progressive steps or stages of maturity. The Holy Spirit is always at work in us if we give Him the freedom to be. The Christian is supposed to be advancing, maturing in his faith and looking more and more like Jesus every day.

Every born again believer begins his faith walk as a baby in Christ. In 1

Peter 2:2-3, referring to new Christians, Peter said, "*Like newborn babes, long for the pure milk of the word, that by it you may grow in respect to salvation, if you have tasted the kindness of the Lord.*" Like natural newborns, spiritual babies get their initial nourishment through milk — the pure milk of the Word of God. It provides the basic sustenance infant Christians need.

Children have to grow on milk before they can move on to solid food. But milk is for babies, not mature men and women of God; they need spiritual meat to grow strong in the Lord.

In Hebrews 5:12-14, the writer was telling the Hebrews they weren't as mature as they should have been:

> *Though by this time you ought to be teachers, you have need again for someone to teach you the elementary principles of the oracles of God, and you have come to need milk and not solid food. For everyone who partakes only of milk is not accustomed to the word of righteousness, for he is an infant. But solid food is for the mature, who because of practice have their senses trained to discern good and evil.*

In like manner, Paul rebuked his spiritual children at Corinth for not being spiritual adults. He accused them of remaining carnal (like people of the world), unable to eat solid spiritual food (1 Corinthians 3:1-3). By not growing and maturing spiritually, the carnal Corinthians were clearly missing the mark of God's will for their lives. Paul addressed their spiritual immaturity in the rest of his letter, correcting them and exhorting them to better Christian conduct.

In the last chapter, we discussed five basic spiritual exercises (holy disciplines) that when practiced regularly will strengthen a young believer's faith. When it comes to waiting on the Lord, these are the milk. They're foundational and absolutely essential for all who would walk by faith. In this chapter, we'll discuss the meat (solid food) that baby Christians are to advance to. These waiting exercises are for those who desire to progress from milk to meat. They're advanced spiritual exercises that build upon the basic disciplines.

Advanced exercises will assist us in having a deeper personal relationship with the Lord.

Praise

The most spiritually mature people I have met in life are the ones who have made it their personal practice to regularly praise the Lord. A depth of joy, peace and security radiates from these Christians. Their joy is contagious! You can learn much about Christian maturity by observing the devotional lives of those who know the power that comes from praising God.

God isn't glorified by our silence, our fears, our doubts, or our frustrations. He's glorified by our praise. Praise is simply giving God the glory due His name. Hebrews 13:15 exhorts us to regularly praise the Lord: *Through Him then, let us continually offer a sacrifice of praise to God, that is, the fruit of lips that give thanks to His name.* Praise is to be the fruit of the lips of God's children. Christians are to continually speak our Heavenly Father's praises and give thanks to Him. Why? Because He's worthy!

The Bible gives a sneak peek as to what is happening in heaven where high praise is the rule, not the exception.

> *I looked, and I heard the voice of many angels around the throne and the living creatures and the elders; and the number of them was myriads of myriads, and thousands of thousands, saying with a loud voice, "Worthy is the Lamb that was slain to receive power and riches and wisdom and might and honor and glory and blessing." And every created thing which is in heaven and on the earth and under the earth and on the sea, and all things in them, I heard saying, "To Him who sits on the throne, and to the Lamb, be blessing and honor and glory and dominion forever and ever." And the four living creatures kept saying, "Amen." And the elders fell down and worshiped.*
>
> Revelation 5:11-14

The heavenly host declares that the Lord is worthy to be praised and given glory due His name. When all who confess Christ arrive in heaven, they will join this holy chorus of praise to Almighty God.

According to Scripture, praise is the order of the day for all of God's creation. That's why in Psalm 150:6 the psalmist exhorts: *Let everything that has breath praise the* Lord. *Praise the* Lord*!*

In Psalm 86:8-10 David told us why we should praise God:

> *There is no one like You among the gods, O Lord, nor are there any works like Yours. All nations whom You have made shall come and worship before You, O Lord, and they shall glorify Your name. For You are great and do wondrous deeds; You alone are God.*

Simply put, there is no one like the God of the Bible, and no one has done the wonderful things He has done! We are to praise God and give glory to His holy name because of who He is and because of what He has done.

God's only Son came to the earth, lived, taught truth, suffered at the hands of spiritually blind men, died a horrific death on a Roman cross, and then rose from the dead in power and victory so that our sins could be forgiven and we could spend eternity in heaven with our Redeemer. That's worth praising Jesus for! The Lamb that was slain and Who now sits at the right hand of the Father deserves all the praise, glory and thanks we can give Him!

David wrote in Psalm 34:1-3:

> *I will bless the LORD at all times; His praise shall continually be in my mouth. My soul shall make its boast in the LORD; the humble will hear it and rejoice. O magnify the LORD with me, and let us exalt His name together.*

If you want to grow spiritually, praise the Lord often. Regular, continual praise — giving thanks to the Lord at all times — deepens our relationship with Him and strengthens our faith like nothing else can.

Praise has a liberating effect on our spirits. If we will start praising God, we will cease to be intimidated and overwhelmed by our problems. Praise may not change our circumstances, but it changes us. C. H. Spurgeon, called the prince of preachers, said, "When we bless God for mercies, we prolong them. When we bless Him for miseries, we usually end them."

Now there's a nugget of truth! When we praise God for the blessings in our lives, however great or small, they multiply. And when we give Him thanks and glorify His name in the midst of trying situations, our troubles turn trivial in the light of His ability to work them out for us.

The next time you're under pressure, try thanking and praising God. Not for the trial but for His promises and willingness to deliver you from your difficulty and provide for your need. First Thessalonians 5:18 instructs us this way: **In everything** *give thanks, for this is God's will for you in Christ Jesus.*

Note that it does not tell us **"for everything"** give thanks."

When we're new, immature believers we tend to be self-centered as we wait on the Lord. It's normal to go to God with most of the focus being on ourselves and our needs, because we don't know any better. Most of our waiting time is devoted to talking to Him about our problems and praying for His provision in our lives. After we unload our list of concerns and needs, the Holy Spirit prompts us to begin to praise God and give Him thanks for Who He is, not just for what He does for us.

As we mature in our faith, a welcome and joyful shift takes place in our hearts. Praise begins to overshadow our prayer requests. Praising the Lord becomes a larger part of our waiting experiences. We focus more and more on Him and less and less on ourselves. We still have needs that God is more than ready to meet. But because we have experienced His faithfulness, we begin to focus more on thanking Him instead of just asking Him for things.

Something very powerful happens in our lives when we devote most of our time with the Lord to praising Him and giving Him thanks!

Praising God is a spiritual exercise that doesn't come naturally. In all honesty, left to itself our flesh balks and rebels at glorifying its Creator. We discovered in chapter four that our adversary and spiritual enemy, Satan, does all he possibly can to hinder us from waiting on God. He will always adamantly oppose us when we choose to glorify the One who defeated him! Remember and rejoice that *you are from God little children, and have overcome them; because greater is He who is in you than he (the devil) that is in the world* (1 John 4:4). This scriptural truth is worth praising the Lord for! Stop and praise Him right now for your victory over the evil one through Christ.

Praise is our personal responsibility. Choose to make praise an ever-increasing part of your devotional life.

Praising God has not been easy for me. I've struggled with it. I wasn't raised in a home where we practiced open praise and thanks to the Lord.

Growing up I also hung out with people who weren't interested in the things of God. In the denominational church where I was spiritually mentored, people talked about praise, but didn't express praise openly.

I rejoice that two life-transforming things took place in my life. First, through the toughest time in my life, a period of personal heartbreak and deep disappointment, the Lord taught me how to praise Him. I learned firsthand from the Holy Spirit to openly, freely, and joyfully praise the Lord. A major piece to the puzzle of my personal healing, restoration and renewal can be attributed to being set free to love the Lord with all my being. Second, God brought into my life some joyful Christians and a church fellowship that knows how to glorify God in a balanced, biblical, joyful manner. Worshipping with believers who love to praise the Lord keeps the fire within my spirit burning.

I encourage you to do a personal study of what the Bible says on this subject of praise. Search the scriptures. Dig up everything you can about glorifying God, praising Him, and giving thanks. From Genesis to Revelation, you will find God's people worshipping, adoring, praising, giving thanks and glorifying Him. Practice what you discover. Your waiting times with the Lord will become much sweeter and more powerful when you make it your priority to praise His name!

SIX HOW-TO'S ABOUT PRAISING GOD

1. SPEAK HIS PRAISES

The Bible says to use your mouth and lips to praise God (Psalm 63:5, 145:21). When you get alone and away in your waiting place, open your mouth and speak. Tell Him you love and adore Him. Praise Him for His goodness. Thank Him out loud for all He is doing in your life. Verbally rejoice in all He means to you. Tell Him how you feel about Him.

The Holy Spirit comes upon us with fresh anointing and spiritual power when we praise God with our lips.

2. SHOUT HIS PRAISES

Psalm 132:9 tells us: *May Your priests be clothed with righteousness, and may Your godly people shout for joy!* (HCSB) Psalm 47:1 declares: *O clap your hands all peoples; shout to God with a voice of joy.* Psalm 32:11 exhorts us: *Be glad in the LORD you righteous ones; and shout for joy, you who are upright in heart.*

Did you see the theme of these three verses? It is shouting! We're to shout about our God! Not pout. Not doubt. Shout! If people in the stands at a sporting event can shout praise of their team's performance, certainly God's people can stand up and shout their joy because Jesus has saved them from sin, death and the grave!

If you want to know the deep things of God, learn to shout your praises. That's why I like the private, secluded places. It doesn't matter how much noise I make there. Only the Lord, the devil and I hear it. There's power in feeling free to shout His praises. Sometimes in the woods I find myself shouting at the top of my lungs about God's goodness to me. And you know what? My shouting blesses the Lord, rattles the devil, and it makes me feel good!

3. SING TO THE LORD

We don't have to be professional singers to sing praises to God. We can make a joyful noise to the Lord as well as anyone else. Everybody can sing, especially those who love God. Psalm 147:1 exhorts us: *Praise the LORD! For it is good to sing praises to our God; for it is pleasant and praise is becoming.* It's pleasing to God to hear His children sing His praises. Whether you're on key or not, sing to the Lord.

Memorize Bible verses and passages. Learn praise choruses to sing when I you're in God's presence. When a song comes in your spirit, open your mouth and sing it. Singing good songs, songs of praise, songs that uplift, is good for the soul.

Singing ministers to the Lord and to us. The Holy Spirit has inspired so much excellent worship and praise music. Hosanna, Integrity Music, Shepherd's Fold, Maranatha, and Hillsong have produced outstanding praise choruses that usher you into the presence of the Lord. Those advancing in their faith make singing His praises an important part of their times of waiting upon God.

4. LIFT YOUR HANDS TO THE LORD

You'll find a lot freedom in your walk with the Lord when you get over your timidity and pride and start lifting your hands in praise to God. Whether in private, or in public, you'll discover the liberating power of humbly, yet joyfully standing before God, rejoicing in Him with outstretched arms. The following Scriptures encourage us to lift our hands in prayer and praise.

> Psalm 28:2: *Hear the voice of my supplications when I cry to You for help, when I lift up my hands toward Your holy sanctuary.*
>
> Psalm 63:4: *I will bless You as long as I live; I will lift up my hands in Your name.*
>
> Psalm 88:9: *My eye has wasted away because of affliction; I have called upon You every day, O Lord; I have spread out my hands before You.*
>
> Psalm 119:48: *I will lift up my hands to Your commandments, which I love; and I will meditate on Your statutes.*
>
> Psalm 134:2: *Lift up your hands to the sanctuary and bless the Lord.*

By the example of David, the master of writing and singing praise to God through the psalms (songs), we are encouraged and exhorted to lift our hands to the Lord. When we lift our hands toward heaven, we're acknowledging Jesus' Lordship in our lives. We're also surrendering and submitting ourselves to Him as our Master and King. It's hard to feel nervous or worried when we lift our hands to God.

A tremendous spirit of freedom and joy comes over my spirit when I praise Him with uplifted hands. Try lifting your hands to the Lord. Jesus will be pleased; you'll enjoy it, and your waiting times will step up a notch too!

5. GIVE THANKS

Immature believers give God their troubles, while mature believers give Him thanks. Thanksgiving is a mark of spiritual maturity and Christlikeness. We saw earlier from the Word that we are to continually give thanks to God. When we start thanking God for everything we can think of, burdens lift, troubles flee, inspiration comes, and peace floods our spirit. Giving thanks just makes you feel good. Why? Because it's the right thing to do. Psalm 92:1 declares, *"It is good to give thanks to the Lord, and to sing praises to Your name, O Most High."*

If you've slipped into the habit of being a complainer, griper or whiner, start today to begin giving thanks. Whiners turn into winners when they learn to give thanks!

People who know how to praise the Lord fill much of their waiting time with thanksgiving. It's incredible how fast the time flies when we focus on thanking God for His goodness to us. Be a thanks-giver!

6. WORSHIP WITH A CONGREGATION THAT PRAISES THE LORD

Life is too short and eternity is too long to sit in a spiritually dead sanctuary or auditorium. If the local church you attend is shy about praising God through music and singing, make a change. The Holy Spirit will direct you to a place where you can praise Jesus openly and freely.

If you want to grow and advance in your faith, put into practice the power of praise. *Sing the glory of His name; make His praise glorious.* Psalm 66:2

LISTENING TO THE LORD

Sam Rayburn, for many years the speaker of the U.S. House of Representatives, used to admonish young congressmen, "When you're talking, you ain't learning." That's wise advice for junior congressmen and for young believers. If all we do is talk and not listen, we won't learn. We receive most from the Lord and learn His ways when we listen.

Listening is a spiritual skill. We must become good at it if we want to really grow in our faith walk. When we talk we can only say something we already know or think. But when we listen, we can learn what someone else knows. We need to know what God knows. Our Heavenly Father will give us all the direction we need for our lives if we will just listen to Him. But how rare it is in this day to find a person willing to be quiet enough to hear God speak!

Psalm 62:5 reads: *My soul, wait in silence for God only, for my hope* [expectation] *is from Him.* To listen we have to shift into silent mode — purposefully get still, set aside our own agenda, and listen for the voice of the Lord. Listening requires us to develop a spirit-sensitivity. Your spirit must be sensitive to the Spirit of God. Job's friend exhorted, *"Listen to this O Job, stand and consider the wonders of God"* (Job 37:14). You can consider the things of God best when you listen. Your spirit becomes sensitive to His when you stop talking, quiet down and wait for Him to speak.

Throughout the Bible we're exhorted to hear the Word of the Lord; but we can't hear His Word if we don't listen for it. If we're always talking and never listening, how will we learn anything? It isn't possible. Have you ever heard this old saying: God gave us two ears and one mouth, so we're supposed to listen twice as much as we speak! Advanced believers have learned the priceless value of listening more and talking less before the Lord.

In Isaiah 41:17-20, the prophet wrote about a time when the people of God were in need of refreshment and renewal. Israel was in trouble and God said He would step in Himself to deliver His chosen people from their dilemma by answering them personally and providing for their every need.

> *The afflicted and needy are seeking water, but there is non, and their tongue is parched with thirst; I, the Lord, will answer them Myself, as the God of Israel, I will not forsake them. I will open rivers on the bare heights and springs in the midst of the valleys; I will make the wilderness a pool of water and the dry land fountains of water. I will put the cedar in the wilderness, the acacia, and the myrtle, and the olive tree; I will place the juniper in the desert together with the box tree and the cypress, that they may see and recognize, and consider and gain insight as well, that the hand of the Lord has done this, and the Holy One of Israel has created it.*

When we look to the Lord and listen for His voice, we're seeking His answers to our problems. And that is what we need most…His personal intervention in our lives. Listening opens the doors to divine answers personally designed to meet our particular needs.

I had only been born again in Christ a month when I was invited to attend a Navigator conference in Seattle. New in the faith, I was eager to learn the Word of God from those more seasoned then me. I can't recall the details of the keynote speaker's message that first night at the retreat center at the foot of the Rocky Mountains. But I will always remember the assignment he gave us. It was late in the evening when his message was completed. He told the assembled congregation to disperse, go outside, find a quiet place, get alone, and then ask this question: "Lord, what do you want to say to me tonight?"

I followed his instructions, finding a quiet, isolated place along the road at the edge of the forest. There I knelt down, cleared my mind the best I could and asked the Lord to speak to me. He did. His voice wasn't audible, but I knew I had heard from the Lord. The Spirit of God told me to always trust Him no matter what; that God had a wonderful life planned for me if I would simply trust Him for everything. I left my quiet place fired up that God had actually spoken to me.

That evening revolutionized my Christian life in two ways. First, I learned from the very beginning of my walk with Jesus that trusting Him is the key to success. I strive to trust Him more and more every day because trusting Him really does work! Second, I began the habit of regularly slipping away to be alone with God, getting quiet, and asking that priceless question, "Lord, what do You want to say to me today?" I don't know how many hundreds, more likely thousands of times I have asked that crucial question over the ensuing years. When I ask that question and put my spirit on listening mode, I always hear from Him. Without fail, He answers when I wait and listen for His response.

When we listen for the Lord, we receive the spiritual strength and power we need to go forward by faith. Isaiah 41:1a reads, *"Coastlands, listen to Me in silence, and let the peoples gain new strength."*

How do we listen in silence? Get alone and away. Set aside your agenda. Ask the question, "Lord, what do you want to say to me today?" Stop talking. Listen. Expect to hear from the Lord. Listen, listen, and listen until you hear. Then receive what you have heard. Rejoice and give thanks. Go do what the Lord told you to do!

> *Blessed is the man who listens to me, watching daily at my gates, waiting at my doorposts.*
>
> Proverbs 8:34

Remember, we learn from the Lord when we listen to the Lord.

Fasting

In an age when fast food and feasting appear to be king, for many people fasting has gone the way of the dinosaur. Even in church circles fun, food and fellowship activities draw the largest crowds; fasting is a holy habit that is seldom practiced and rarely looked upon as a key to holy living. But not to those who hunger and thirst after a deep, intimate spiritual relationship with God.

Fasting has its roots in the Bible. Old and New Testament figures fasted regularly in their walks with God. Fasting is a spiritual discipline with self-denial is its core.

Our bodies require and crave nourishment. Fasting involves the voluntary denial of food for a predetermined period of time for the purpose of focusing on spiritual things. There are times when God would have us set aside the physical needs of our flesh in order to direct our attention to our spiritual needs. In the Kingdom of God, relationships and power flow from purity (Matthew 5:8). Therefore, when we fast for a season denying ourselves and cleansing our physical vessels, our bodies— which are the temple of the Holy Spirit (1 Corinthians 6:12-19) — are focused to receive the spiritual food we need to become more like Christ.

Scripturally, fasting occurred on numerous occasions and for a diversity of purposes. In the Old Testament, God's people fasted when they gathered together at the temple (Joel 1:14; 2:15). Jehoshaphat and Judah fasted during a time of national crisis as they looked to the Lord for deliverance from three invading armies (2 Chronicles 20). Ezra proclaimed a fast after the rebuilding of Jerusalem and the reading of the Book of the Law (Ezra 5:8; 8:21). Isaiah laid out in detail the type of fast that is acceptable to God in Isaiah 58:1-10.

In the New Testament, Jesus fasted for 40 days in the wilderness while being tempted by the devil (Matthew 4:1-11). The Pharisees practiced rigid religious fasting according to the strict legalism of the Law (Mark 2:18-19, Luke 18:12). The early church sent its first missionaries, Paul and Barnabas, out into the world after ministering to the Lord through prayer and fasting (Acts 13:1-3). Jesus rebuked the religious hypocrites of the day for abusing the fast and instructed the disciples in proper fasting (Matthew 16-18). In Mark 9:17-29, the demon possessed man being delivered by Jesus provided a platform for the Lord to reprimand the disciples for their lack of spiritual power because they had not fasted and prayed enough. In every one of the above-mentioned instances, you'll find that the results of biblical fasting were closeness to God and spiritual power.

I've found from personal experience that when I fast I'm more spiritually focused and more sensitive to the Holy Spirit. Fasting isn't an end unto itself. Fasting is a means to the spiritual end of drawing closer to Jesus. In Matthew

4 Christ's personal victory over the devil was, without question, due to His steadfast reliance on the Word of God ("It is written"). His fast during the temptation contributed greatly to His ability to remain spiritually sharp.

At times we do lack spiritual power. The whole purpose of these Wait Training chapters is to help us get before the Lord in practical ways so we can be renewed according to His strength. Mark 9:17-19 tells us the disciples were disappointed because they couldn't cast the demons out of the demon possessed man. They should have been able to because Jesus had given them power to cast out devils (Matthew 10:1). But they failed. The Lord stepped in and delivered the young man, setting him free. After the dramatic incident, the disciples asked Jesus why they couldn't do it. He said to them, *"This kind can come out by nothing but prayer and fasting"* (Mark 9:29 HCSB).

The implication is obvious. Christ's followers weren't praying and fasting as they should have been. They lacked power because they neglected these holy habits.

If we're going to be like Jesus, mature in faith, strong in the power of God and triumphant over Satan, then we must add fasting to our regimen of spiritual exercises. And we must fast the way Jesus said to.

> *"Whenever you fast, do not put on a gloomy face as the hypocrites do, for they neglect their appearance so that they will be noticed by men when they are fasting. Truly I say to you, they have their reward in full. But you, when you fast, anoint your head, and wash your face, so that your fasting will not be noticed by men, but by your Father who is in secret; and your Father who sees what is done in secret will reward you."*
> Matthew 6:16-18

Fasting, like prayer, is to be done in secret — privately. We don't fast before men — we don't tell everyone. We fast before the Lord. He is the rewarder of those who deny themselves in order to draw closer to Him. When we fast, nobody should know about it but us and God.

I'm certainly not an expert on the subject of fasting. But I do have some experience I can pass along to you.

- Talk to the Lord about fasting. Hear from Him before you start.
- Study all the biblical references on fasting. Read a good book

about fasting. There are some excellent works available on the subject. Stay away from anything flaky, faddish or foolish!

- Make sure you're in good physical health and have consulted with your doctor if necessary. You need to understand what goes on in your body when you fast for any period of time, whether short or long.

- Resist the temptation to announce your fasts to others. That's a form of spiritual pride the devil can use against you. Follow Matthew 6:16-18. Dress normally. Clean up. Look sharp, like nothing is out of the ordinary. Remember, your fast is between God and you.

- Begin slowly. One meal. Then two. Then move to a day. The general rule for fasting is to start small and expand your fast as the Lord directs.

- There is no formula period of time for fasting. Biblically, people fasted a few meals, for days, weeks, and as long as 40 days. Each period of fasting had a specific purpose and goal. Fast for longer periods of time only as God directs and if you are in good health and know how to properly break your fast and reintroduce food to your body.

- Fast for longer periods of time when you really need to hear from God — when you have to have an answer or a breakthrough. Concentrated focus brings powerful, timely responses from the Lord.

- Remember, fasting is a spiritual tool for bringing us close to the Lord while we wait on Him. Secular people, gurus, "health nuts," cultists, New Ager's, Buddhists, Muslims and others practice fasting too. But Christians fast because Jesus fasted. Our goal is to be like Christ and influence our world for Him in a powerful way!

The next time you prepare to wait on the Lord, consider fasting. God will reward you with rich spiritual treasure as you deny yourself in order to draw near to Him.

WARFARE PRAYING

Scripture tells us that we're engaged in a war — a spiritual war in which heaven and hell are battling for the souls of men. Because *our struggle is not against flesh and blood, but against the rulers, against the powers, against the world forces of this darkness, against the spiritual forces of wickedness in the heavenly places* (Ephesians 6:12), we must *be strong in the Lord and in the strength (power) of His might* [and] *put on the full armor of God, so that* [we] *will be able to stand firm against the schemes of the devil* (Ephesians 6:10-11).

Spiritual warfare is a very real and necessary part of the daily life of the believer in Christ. The Apostle Paul, a mighty spiritual warrior who knew how to fight the good fight, wrote in 2 Corinthians 10:3-4 that *though we walk in the flesh, we do not war according to the flesh, for the weapons of our warfare are not of the flesh, but divinely powerful for the destruction of fortresses*. Being engaged in spiritual warfare requires being equipped with spiritual weaponry. God has provided some very powerful weapons for us to use to bring destruction to Satan and his evil forces. Paul calls them *weapons of righteousness* (2 Corinthians 6:7).

Ephesians 6:10-20 describes in detail the spiritual soldier's armor including the names of each piece of protective equipment (defensive and offensive weapons). We're commanded to *put on* and *take up the whole armor of God* so that *we can resist in the evil day* and *stand firm against the schemes of the devil*. Certain victory comes because we stand firm with all of our spiritual armor in place, fighting the devil in Jesus' victorious name!

In Ephesians 6:18-20 Paul wrote about this powerful piece of spiritual weaponry.

> *With all prayer and petition pray at all times in the Spirit, and with this in view, be on the alert with all perseverance and petition for all the saints, and pray on my behalf, that utterance may be given to me in the opening of my mouth, to make known with boldness the mystery of the gospel, for which I am an ambassador in chains; that in proclaiming it I may speak boldly, as I ought to speak.*

Praying in the Spirit includes praying against Satan, praying for souls (intercession), praying with passion (fire), praying with compassion (tears), and persevering prayer. Those advancing in their faith will find their waiting times being devoted to this type of powerful prayer.

Pray Against Satan

Christ has given believers spiritual authority over the evil one (Matthew 10:1, 8; Luke 10:19; Mark 9:17-29; Acts 16:16-18; James 4:7). In every situation, Christians are spiritually superior to Satan. We always win because of Christ (1 John 4:4). But authority must be exercised to be effective. The secret place of prayer is the front line, the first place for taking charge of the enemy.

Praying against the devil means putting and keeping him in his place, talking back to him, and telling him where he stands. The devil thinks he is somebody he isn't. First Peter 5:8 says to *be of sober spirit, be on the alert* [because] *your adversary, the devil, prowls around like a roaring lion, seeking someone to devour.* Note the devil is *like* a roaring lion, not *a* roaring lion!

When he comes prowling about and growling at you when you're waiting on God, remind him who he is. He's a serpent, not a lion. He crawls on his belly, crushed by the foot of Jesus! He's defeated and headed for hell, a loser who has no authority whatsoever in your life. Remind him and his demons that you're covered by the blood of the Lamb. Resist him in the name of Jesus and he will flee!

Satan's a liar. When he tells you things that aren't true, talk back to him. Set the record straight by quoting God's Word to him. As Jesus did in the wilderness, tell him, "It is written" or "Thus saith the Lord" or "This is what God's Word says." When Satan hears the Word, he's history.

Learn to be very bold and vocal in talking back to the devil. Shout at him if you want, so he knows who's in charge. The devil can't overcome the Word because he was overcome by the Word, who is Christ. Revelation 12:11 declares, *"They overcame him* [Satan] *because of the blood of the Lamb and because of the word of their testimony, and they did not love their life even when faced with death."*

Praying against the devil isn't for amateurs. It's for those who know who they are in Christ and where they stand in Him. Christ-confidence and Holy Spirit courage is necessary to confront Satan. God's people are to push back the gates of hell. Believers are to be aggressive in their fight with the devil. Without hesitation or timidity, tell Satan that you know who he is and what he's up to. Tell him he can't succeed. Bind him and his demonic servants. Set boundaries around them. Tell them to take a hike. Remind the devil of Christ's victory over him. Remind Satan that he's going to spend eternity in hell while you enjoy heaven for all time with Jesus!

Enemies can't be ignored. They must be confronted and defeated. The best way to beat a bully is to stand up to him. In the secret, waiting place of prayer, stay alert, and be bold in praying against the devil and his evil devices. Remember what James said about our victory over Satan:

Submit therefore to God. Resist the devil, and he will flee from you.

James 4:7

Pray for Others

Immature believers spend a lot of time praying for themselves. More mature believers spend a lot of time praying for others. The art of intercession (praying on behalf of another) is a mark of spiritual growth and likeness to Jesus.

In John 17 we saw how Jesus prayed for the disciples and the future church. In James 5:16 and several other references, the Bible tells us to pray for one another (fellow believers). It's a high and holy privilege to lift our brothers and sisters in Christ to the Father through prayer.

Devote a significant part of your prayer time to praying for fellow Christians. Pray regularly for specific individuals and their families and pray for others as the Spirit puts them on your heart. Ask the Lord to watch over them, keep them from the evil one, bless and prosper them, give them wisdom, heal them when ill, guide their steps, inspire their minds, grant them favor with the world and help them resist temptation. Pray they will faithfully use their spiritual gifts and abilities to win the lost to Christ. Sometimes you will know exactly how to pray. At other times, pray in the Spirit and trust Jesus to know how best to intercede for the person's needs (Romans 8:26-27).

Scripture also tells us to pray for those who are spiritually lost. In Romans 10:1, Paul expressed his desire for the Hebrew nation to find Christ as Savior:
Brethren, my heart's desire and my prayer to God for them is their salvation.

God hurts for all people caught up in the consequences of sinful living. He doesn't want anyone who is lost to die and be lost forever. He wants them to turn from their sin and find life in Christ. He does everything He can to show people He loves them. He provides what every person needs to find their way to heaven. When we intercede for the lost, we're standing in the gap for them.

In Ezekiel 18:32, the prophet Ezekiel expressed God's concern for the lost when he exclaimed, *"I have no pleasure in the death of anyone who dies," declares the* LORD GOD. *"Therefore, repent and live."*

In Ezekiel 22, we get a glimpse of our Heavenly Father's heart. Through Ezekiel, God grieved over and bemoaned the nation's morally corrupt conduct. In verses 29-30 the Lord lamented:

> *"The people of the land have practiced oppression and committed robbery, and they have wronged the poor and needy and have oppressed the sojourner without justice. I searched for a man among them who would build up the wall and stand in the gap before Me for the land, so that I would not destroy it; but I found no one."*

God's chosen people were utterly lost. The nation was thoroughly corrupt, headed for judgment. Merciful and gracious, God searched for a man to stand between the people and His righteous indignation and ultimate judgment. He looked for someone to come before Him and plead the people's cause, to pray for mercy, grace, forgiveness and restoration to prevail.

But God couldn't find one solitary person to intercede for Israel. No one in the entire nation to pray for mercy. The result: The Lord poured out His indignation and consumed them with the fire of His wrath (v. 31). Terrible judgment fell because there wasn't anybody to stand in the gap.

Our day isn't much different from Ezekiel's. Sin abounds everywhere you turn. Lost sinners who are wayward and worldly don't pray for themselves. They don't respect God or fear Him. They think they can live without Him. But they don't realize the seriousness of their situation of facing eternity without Jesus Christ.

As Christians it's our responsibility and privilege to pray for people outside of the family of God. We're to present their names before the Lord, pray for the softening of their hearts and for the Holy Spirit to bring them to a point of conviction where they will turn from sin and turn to Him.

Pray regularly for your unsaved neighbors by their names. Rebuke the enemy from their lives, and speak salvation over their families.

As the Holy Spirit brings them to mind, intercede for acquaintances, relatives and friends who need the Lord.

Next to praising the Lord, the highest joy in prayer is to pray for the lost.

When we pray for the lost and stand in the gap for them, we're doing the thing that moves the heart of God more than anything else.

Loving Jesus means loving souls. When we pray for lost people, we pray with the heart of Jesus!

> *Jesus said to him, "Today, salvation has come to this house [Zaacheus'], because he, too, is a son of Abraham. For the Son of Man has come to seek and to save that which was lost."*
>
> Luke 19:9-10

Pray with Passion (Fire)

Joshua 14:6-15 records the story of one of my favorite heroes of the faith. I can't read it and not come away fired up! Eighty-five–year-old Caleb asked Joshua for his inheritance in Canaan. You'd think being a senior citizen, Caleb would want some serene, hassle-free real estate for his retirement, right? Wrong! Caleb pointed his finger to a mountain full of ferocious giant warriors and boldly declared, *"Give me this hill country about which the Lord spoke on that day that Anakim were there, with great fortified cities; perhaps the Lord will be with me, and I shall drive them out as the Lord has spoken"* (v 12).

At an age when we think people his age have nothing left to offer, Caleb was heading up a mountain to drive out some giants who had no business being on God's people's land.

Go Caleb! He was a man of passion and spiritual fire. Note in verse 11 what he said about himself: *"I am still as strong today as I was in the day Moses sent me; [45years earlier at Kadesh-Barnea] as my strength was then, so my strength is now, for war and for going out and coming in."* No rocking chair for Caleb. He was as strong as ever, ready to show them he was the king of the mountain.

Going to war at 85. Why was Caleb so fired up and still able to fight for God? Caleb was of a different spirit than those around him. Caleb followed the Lord His God fully (vv. 7-9, 14). Wholeheartedly. Without reservation or hesitation. Through thick and thin, Caleb was serious about his calling in life. Here was a man of intense spiritual passion. Inside that gray haired man of God burned a heart on fire for the Lord.

We should be as passionate about waiting on the Lord. According to Webster, *passionate* means "easily aroused to anger, capable of, affected by, or expressing intense feeling, enthusiastic, fervor, ardor, zeal, intense emotion compelling action."9

Life in Christ stirs strong feelings that compel Christians to action!

When we go to meet with God, we should charge out with energy and urgency. In our place of prayer, we need to pray like we really mean it — passionately, intensely, energetically, enthusiastically, fervently, zealously, and focused. We should meet with Jesus like we mean it. Fired up, ready to fight for the Kingdom, we should stand up boldly and be counted, not sit and cower.

The secret place of prayer is the place to get excited about your faith. Let your worship, adoration, praise and thanksgiving to the Lord show it. Get mad at the devil and let him have it in the name of Jesus!

Point to the "hill country" where the lost live and say, "Lord, give me those souls. Give me my family, my neighbors, my city, my country, my world for Christ. I'll go and fight Satan in Your Name to set them free. Strengthen me with Your strength and together we will drive the devil out of the hearts of men and women, boys and girls everywhere!"

Get fired up! Passionate! As Christians, we shouldn't want to live any other way.

Passionate people conquer challenges and overcome obstacles. They advance through adversity because their hearts are burning with an all-consuming desire to reach their goal. Passionate people won't be denied, because their cause is worth whatever it takes to fulfill their mission.

Passionate people are powerful people. Jesus was a man of unparalleled passion. His passion took Him to a painful death on a cross. Why? Because He came into this world to save sinners. An empty tomb on a glorious resurrection morning secured salvation for all those who will believe and receive.

> *O DEATH, WHERE IS YOUR VICTORY? O DEATH, WHERE IS YOUR STING?* The sting of death is sin, and the power of sin is the law; but thanks be to God who gives us the victory through our Lord Jesus Christ! Therefore, my beloved brethren, be steadfast, immovable, always abounding in the work of the Lord, knowing that your toil is not in vain in the Lord.
> 1 Corinthians 15:55-58

Are you passionate about your walk with the Lord? Do you get excited thinking about Him and spending time in His presence? Can you barely wait to get away to pray? Do you care about winning the lost? Do you really care that if they aren't won they will go to hell forever? Do you hate the devil with a perfect hatred that only desires his continual defeat? Are you fired-up about your Christian life — full of the zeal of the Lord of hosts? Does the spirit of Caleb burn in your heart?

When we realize what Jesus Christ has done for us, how can we be anything but intensely passionate about our relationship with Him and our calling to help others find Him?

Pray with Compassion (Tears)

If passion puts heat in our praying, then compassion puts heart in it. We need both, heat (fire) and heart (tears) to be effective in prayer. The kind of prayer that moves God, devils and men is prayer that is fired up and bathed in tears.

Jesus is our model of compassion. As the Lord approached Jerusalem…

> *When He approached Jerusalem, He saw the city and wept over it, saying, "If you had known in this day, even you, the things which make for peace! But now they have been hidden from your eyes. For the days shall come upon you when your enemies will throw up a barricade against you, and surround you, and hem you in on every side, and will level you to the ground and your children within you, and they will not leave in you one stone upon another, because you did not recognize the time of your visitation."*
>
> Luke 19:41-44

Note that Jesus saw the city and wept. He shed tears of compassion for those who had failed to understand what God was trying to do in their lives. By rejecting Jesus, the Jewish people missed the moment of the Messiah's visitation. Destruction was coming.

Many people don't realize the Salvation Army began as a church, and is still one today. During one of the Salvation Army's ministerial conventions the pastors were frustrated as to why they weren't winning as many souls as they once had. Founder William Booth was unable to attend the meeting, so they wired him, asking their esteemed leader for his counsel. He sent back a two-word message — Try Tears!

We must weep for the lost if we would win the lost.

Psalm 126:4-6 is a scriptural guarantee that those who weep will reap a bountiful harvest of souls.

> *Restore our captivity, O LORD, as the streams in the South. Those who sow in tears shall reap with joyful shouting, He who goes to and fro weeping, carrying his bag of seed, shall indeed come again with a shout of joy, bringing his sheaves with him.*

Sowing and weeping comes before shouting and reaping.

Jeremiah is known as the weeping prophet. (Read Jeremiah 9:1, 10, 18; 13:17; 14:17; 31:16 and Lamentations 1:2; 2:11, 18.) Feel why he mourned and cried over Judah.

> *"Harvest is past, summer is ended, and we are not saved." For the brokenness of the daughter of my people I am broken; I mourn, dismay has taken hold of me. Is there no balm in Gilead? Is there no physician there? Why then has not the health of the daughter of my people been restored?.... Oh, that my head were waters, and my eyes a fountain of tears, that I might weep day and night for the slain of the daughter of my people!*
>
> Jeremiah 8:20-22; 9:1

Harvest time had come and gone and Judah was still not saved. Jeremiah was heartsick, overcome with grief. He wept because his heart was broken over the sin of the people. They were lost, astray from God, and headed for destruction.

I find it hard to not pray without tears when I look at the spiritual state of our nation. Our country and world is in deep spiritual trouble, headed for eternal destruction unless the people repent and return to the Lord. The Church has the answer (Jesus) and holds the key (the Gospel) to this world's deliverance from sin and salvation.

Why do we seem to be so ineffective in turning our world to Christ?

Could it be that many of our so-called soul-winning ministries are barren and fruitless today because they are tearless? The Bible is unmistakably clear: no tears, no fruit. No compassion, no conversions. Soul-winning soil must be saturated with the soul winners' tears if a harvest is to be reaped.

I have learned some things about tears and weeping for the lost. First, tears flow from broken hearts. Second, tears keep our hearts soft. Satan does all he can to harden our hearts toward the lost. Hard hearts won't win anybody. Hard hearts ruin men. Soft hearts renew men. Third, tears must be spontaneous. We don't just turn them on or work ourselves up into a crying spell. When we're sensitive to the Holy Spirit, He moves on our hearts, stroking the cords of compassion. Genuine, Christ-like care and concern for the lost produces tears that God records and rewards.

Fourth, tears must be genuine and sincere, never for show or effect. Tears aren't something to be conjured up for dramatic impact. Hollywood does that; holy men and women of God don't. Fifth, tears are the Lord's anointing for the man with the broken heart. Tears are the result of feeling the wounds and pain of hurting people. Sixth, tears flow from strength. Weeping is not weakness; strong men cry. We must shed tears for the lost if we want to have the heart of Jesus. Seventh, tears are most effective when shed in private, alone and away with the Lord. Like prayer and fasting, weeping before the Lord is where the reward is. The church needs more weeping and shedding of sincere tears for the lost from our pulpits and in our prayer meetings; but weeping for the lost is sacred when heartfelt tears are gently spilled on the holy ground of the waiting places with the Lord.

Today more than ever we need a mighty outpouring of Christ's compassion on the church. A revival of broken hearts for the heartbroken and lost.

Is there someone on your heart you want to see saved, but nothing seems to be happening? Try weeping for their soul.

Ask the Lord to anoint you with tears and break your heart for lost and hurting people. You'll be amazed at how your witnessing ability and their willingness to listen and receive the Good News will change when you've wept for them before the Lord. Like Jesus who wept over Jerusalem and Jeremiah who wept over Judah, may we be found weeping day and night for the lost!

Pray with Perseverance

Prayer is work. And for prayer to work, we must keep working at it.

Pray at all times, in all places, for all people, and for all things. Remember that in Ephesians 6:18 Paul told us to *pray at all times in the Spirit, and with this in view, be on the alert with all perseverance and petition for all the saints.* The

Part 2: Wait Training

phrase "be on alert with all perseverance" means to be present at your post and remain at your post. Stay wide awake at the place of prayer.

Luke 18:1 tells us Jesus exhorted His followers to pray at all times and not to lose heart (faint KJV; never give up NIV; become discouraged HCSB.). The Master is telling us that prayer is to be our life. We are to endure and overcome everything that tempts us to lose heart, become discouraged, and stop praying.

We conquer by continuing. Jesus said, *"The one who stands firm to the end will be saved"* (Matthew 24:13 NIV). To stand firm means to continue waiting on the Lord whether you feel like it or not, whether it is convenient or not, whether it is popular or not, or whether it's producing visible results or not.

Former heavyweight boxing champion of the world James Corbett was asked what it takes to be a heavyweight champion. He answered, "Fight one more round! When your feet are so tired that you have to shuffle back to the corner of the ring, fight one more round!"

Waiting can be tiring, trying, taxing, and even troublesome at times. The devil "pulls out all the stops"[10] in trying to prevent us from getting away and alone with the Lord. Waiting and praying is to be the Christian's lifestyle, not hobby. We become effective in prayer when we hang in there and pray with all of our might! That's why we need to persevere, especially when the pressure is on. Waiting on the Lord and persevering in prayer every day is fighting one more round in the faith fight!

If you want to be blessed, keep waiting on the Lord. The deep things of God become real to us when we are willing to do whatever it takes to daily meet with Him. Like Isaiah of old, may our spirits within us diligently seek Him.

> *The way of the righteous is smooth; O Upright One, make the path of the righteous level. Indeed, while following the way of Your judgments, O LORD, we have waited for You eagerly; Your name, even Your memory, is the desire of our souls. At night my soul longs for You, indeed, my spirit within me seeks You diligently.*
>
> Isaiah 26: 7-9

A Heads-Up Before We Wrap Up

If you're serious about warfare praying, count on the enemy to counter attack. When you penetrate the devil's domain, he *will* strike back in one way or another. When we spend time pushing back the gates of hell, all hell will break loose. Satan's first line of attack is usually immediately after prayer times. The children might be fighting, you and your spouse might have a stupid spat. The refrigerator expires, the dog has seizures, a toilet won't flush. Are you getting the picture?

The devil can't stand to lose. Learn to expect a reaction from the devil. Realize after a powerful session of waiting on the Lord, that the evil one won't be happy and he will try to do something to disrupt your life and discourage your faith. So stay on spiritual alert, standing strong in the Lord and the power of His might.

Don't worry about the devil. He's already defeated. Just watch for him. Expect him to retaliate. Then simply and firmly rebuke him and go forward by faith!

Fellowship with the Lord

Our primary purpose in waiting on the Lord is to have sweet fellowship and communion with Him. While we're in His holy presence, our Heavenly Father will fine tune us, prune us, and tweak us spiritually! We need all of those things if we're to grow more and more into the likeness of Christ. The Lord will richly reward our devotion and discipline.

No one waits on the Lord in exactly the same way. You should wait on God in the way the Holy Spirit directs you. Keep in mind that even each time will be a little bit different. That's what's exciting about meeting with God — it's always special and tailor made to meet our personal needs.

On the next few pages I'm going to describe in detail a typical hour that I might spend on one of my prayer walks with the Lord. I don't wait on the Lord perfectly, and you don't have to wait on the Lord the way I do. I pray sharing my process and experience will inspire you to establish a regular time to meet with the Lord.

> Leaving the house to enter the nearby greenbelt, I take a deep breath of the fresh air and rejoice that I have the time, health, and opportunity to meet with my Father in Heaven. I express to Him my excitement and expectation of our fellowship today. Watching tree tops sway gently in the wind as squirrels hurry along the branches directly above me, and cardinals calling to each other, I praise the Lord for life and creation.

It's so good to be alive in Christ and to share in the beauty and majesty of the earthly creation and wonderfully unique creatures He made for me to enjoy.

Walking along the path beyond the boundary of our backyard, I stop for a moment, glance back at the house and thank the Lord for my wife, children, pets, home, and everything He has provided for us. I am indeed a very blessed man. My heart is full as I think of and thank God for the people in my life who love me. I pick up my pace and move quickly to cross a ravine that leads me to the open field on the other side of the creek. As I ascend the bank, and start over the rising terrain, I ask, "Lord, what do You want to say to me today?" I'm silent for a few moments, preparing myself to receive whatever God has for me.

Today, I sense first I should take out my Bible and turn to Psalms. I read out loud and sing and shout His praises as I walk along the outer rim of the creek as it winds through my secluded spot. My heart full of joy and rejoicing, I pause for a few moments to lift my hands toward heaven to praise His name. The sunlight is bright and soothingly warm this morning. Skies are blue. A few white clouds dot the horizon. A warm breeze blows gently across my face. A hawk appears out of nowhere and soars effortlessly and majestically on invisible air currents. Oh Lord, life is good! Thank you Jesus for all of the wonderful things You have prepared to bring me pleasure.

I watch the hawk soar higher and higher toward the heavens. Crying out to the Lord, I pray, teach me Heavenly Father how to soar like that on the wings of Your Spirit. I want to spiritually soar through this life. Like the hawk, effortlessly, yet powerfully, above the challenges of everyday living…that's the way I want to live.

The Holy Spirit brings to mind Isaiah 40:31 — *those who wait for the Lord will gain new strength; they will mount up with wings like eagles, they will run and not get tired, they will walk and not become weary.* I quote it and thank the Lord for reminding me where renewal, power, and spiritual strength come from.

Moving on, I walk along the overgrown pathway, pushing aside waist high weeds and tangled grass as I go. The Lord reminds me that He directs my every step and clears the way as I commit myself to follow in His footsteps. I step through an opening in the old, rusty barbed wire fence and make my way to the creek again. Sitting about ten feet above the rushing stream, I get quiet. My soul stills as I take in the sounds of bubbling water, squawking blue jays, and the jackhammer rat-a-tat of a woodpecker looking for insects on a nearby cedar leaning over the creek. It's time to listen.

I sit silently for quite a while, praying in the Spirit, asking the Lord to speak to me. I toss a rock into the creek. In sinks immediately. I throw a piece of bark into the fast moving water; it floats merrily downstream, carried on the current. The Holy Spirit whispers to my spirit, "Steve, be like that bark. Let me carry you through life to all the places I have appointed and prepared for you. If you try to run by yourself and in your own strength and power, you'll sink like that rock. But if you'll trust Me completely, I'll take you where I have planned for you to go. Yoke up with Me. My way is easy and my burden is light."

"Thank you Lord for showing me that I can count on you to carry me successfully through life," I think. I stand and praise Him some more and find myself speaking at the top of my lungs, praising Him, shouting the glories of His name. I want everything within the sound of my voice to hear me bless the Lord. Boundless freedom and joy floods my heart as I make my way back to the path.

Out in the open once again, a spirit of intercession comes over me. I pray by name for those God puts on my heart. I walk and pray, standing in the gap for those who the Holy Spirit has made me aware of who need God's help. I thank the Lord for the miracles He will perform in their lives — thank you Jesus for loving each one of these precious people and for working in their situations.

Coming to a fork in the path, I ask the Lord which way to go today. I feel drawn to the right, to the open space under a highway bridge that spans the creek. It's time to battle the enemy.

Every time I enter this part of my secret place it's time to fight. The Holy Spirit rises in me, and I commence warfare praying. I shout at the devil, taking authority over him and telling him what he cannot do in my life and ministry. It's a powerful time, sensing the spiritual battle going on all around me. I stand boldly on the Word, confessing Scripture after Scripture that declares the devil's defeat! Automobiles pass just overhead as I pray this way for several minutes, but I'm oblivious to surroundings, focused on the forces of evil that seek to disrupt my time with God. I bind Satan and set loose the help of heaven. I rejoice over my enemy, shouting him down, and letting him know I am coming after him in Jesus' name! Glory to God! The battle is the Lord's. The victory is the Lords…and His victory is mine.

My spirit settles down. I retrace my steps listening again for the voice of my Commander-in-Chief. My mood has become meditative and contemplative as I walk and wait for instructions for the next steps in our lives and ministry. I hear His voice, take out my pen and paper and jot down what He has told me. Thank you Jesus for direction. I praise You that the steps of the godly man are ordered by the Lord. I will do what You have said to do.

The wind picks up as I head toward the higher ground of my wooded prayer closet. I ask the Lord to send a rushing, mighty wind of the Holy Spirit over me as he did the disciples (Acts 2). Come sweet Lord Jesus, fill me, energize me, anoint me with fresh oil as you did David (Psalm 92:10). I lift my hands upward and receive fresh power and anointing.

The terrain gets rough now. I have to carefully pick my way through a sprawling, patch of twisted briars that block the path. I move cautiously, pushing aside each thorny tentacle that tries to pierce my skin. I get tangled here and there, but I press on until I clear the obstacle. I feel a sense of "you can't stop me, devil" "as I put my prickly adversary behind me. What an object lesson for me! I learn about pressing on, persevering and ultimately overcoming the obstacles the devil will put in my path as I seek to fulfill God's will for my life. Thank you Lord for encouragement from this object lesson.

Drawn to a small, tree covered vantage point overlooking the expressway, I watch the cars speeding by. A heavy burden for souls comes over me. Where are they all going Lord? How many of these passing by today are on their way to heaven? What about the guy in that Mercedes? The driver of that eighteen-wheeler steaming up the hill? The teenagers in the Camaro? The folks in the beat-up pickup? I weep as I pray for the precious souls passing by on the highway, calling upon the Lord to save them.

Then I pray for revival in America, from White House, to penthouse, to poor house and everything in between. *Oh, Lord, will you not Yourself revive us again that Your people might rejoice in Thee?* Psalm 85:6. I ask the Lord to send a revival of righteousness to our land, cleansing us, purifying us and restoring us to God. So be it Lord. May it sweep over all of us soon. Show me my part in preparing the way for a great spiritual awakening in my beloved United States of America.

The burden for my homeland lifted, I head back toward home, walking swiftly. There's one more place to visit before I leave this holy ground. Over by the pond, there's a place that calls to me every time I come here to wait before the Lord. I call it my surrender spot. Having arrived at the spot where an ant hill used to be, I kneel before the Lord uttering, "Father, not my will, but Your will be done. I submit everything to You again, release it all into Your hands. My life, my family, my ministry, my stuff is Yours. Do with me what You will Lord. I know it will be good, exceeding abundantly above and beyond what I could ask or think. Thank you Jesus that Your plans for Me are far greater than mine."

Rising, I follow the familiar path home. I finish my prayer walk rejoicing in the Lord. Giving thanks for a great time of fellowship with my Father in Heaven, I start thinking about how to apply what I received and brace myself for Satan's retaliation.

Thank you Lord for meeting with me today and renewing my spiritual strength!

Lead me in Your truth and teach me, For You are the God of my salvation. For You I wait all the day long.

Psalm 25:5

Chapter 11
How to Find Peace with God's Pace

Have you ever felt like God was lagging behind a bit in your life? I have.

Most, if not all, of us have tried to hurry the Almighty along at one time or another. We buzz along at breakneck speed, blazing trails for God, ignoring the posted speed limits as we attempt to accomplish something great for the Kingdom. Then, without warning we find ourselves alone on the side of the road, broken down somewhere on the spiritual superhighway, and God seems to be nowhere in sight.

Have you ever found yourself frustrated because the Lord didn't keep pace with you? Dr. Phillips Brooks, one of 19th Century New England's greatest preachers, was known in religious circles as the golden-mouthed orator. He had an impeccable reputation for poise and endless patience in public. But close friends saw another side of Dr. Brooks in private. He often suffered from moments of frustration and irritability. One day a colleague saw him pacing the floor like a caged lion. "What is the trouble, Dr. Brooks?" inquired the friend. Brooks replied, "The trouble is that I'm in a hurry, but God isn't!"

Running the race at God's pace is the key to crossing the finish line victoriously!

This Race Called Life

The writer to the Hebrews tells us in 12:1 to *run with endurance the race that is set before us*. Today people all around us are running the race set before them. But alarming numbers of Christians burn out and drop out of the race. Well-meaning individuals who ran well for a while, find themselves casualties gasping for breath— off the track and out of the race God set before them.

Have you ever wondered why there are so many physically, spiritually and emotionally exhausted Christians in pain, injured, out of gas, no longer able to compete for the prize? It's because we aren't running our race according to God's pace. We attempt instead to keep up with the rat race of life by running the world's way. As a result we lose poise, peace, power and productivity.

Dr. Brooks was right. God is never in a hurry. We might be, but not the

Lord. From beginning to end, God's plan is perfectly timed out and on schedule, whether we believe it or not. No effort on our part can slow the Lord down or speed Him up. Our Creator has programmed His divine pace into His universe.

The plan of salvation is set to God's timetable, not ours. Revelation is made and redemption is completed according to His holy will and perfect timing. Sometimes God acts at what seems to us an accelerated rate, incredibly fast, spinning our head as He carries out His plans. At other times, the Almighty One moves so slowly it seems a turtle could outrun its Maker. Whether swift or slow, both speeds are part of God's pace.

Life moves at varying speeds. At times it zips by so rapidly the days seem to run together. You know those seasons. The pace becomes unbelievably hectic, bordering on frantic as everything seems to happen at once. So much is going on so quickly that about all you can do to keep up is to take a few deep breaths and try to hold on!

Although we might not admit it, most of us like the adrenaline rush that comes from life in the fast lane. We get excited about the emotional high we experience there. We might even find ourselves wishing that life would always stay in hyper drive.

I'm a high-energy person who operates at two speeds…fast and faster! I believe rather than easing into the world, I was launched…with my motor set on speed! Just ask anybody who knows me. I talk fast, eat fast, walk fast, play fast, work fast (and my wife says that I even sleep fast, whatever that means). I have to admit I have even pushed my self-propelled lawnmower around the yard so I could get on to the next project! Pretty ridiculous, I know. But for me, life is to be lived…and the faster the better!

But is faster always better?

Life is a race that is to be run from the starting line (Point A) to the finish line (Point B). We're definitely headed somewhere. (Heaven is God's choice for us.) We're supposed to arrive there in a proper and timely manner (by His grace, Ephesians 2:8-9 and at His pace, Isaiah 40:31). But our race is more than just getting there, more than arriving. Much more.

Our race is about enjoying each step of the journey. Success in life isn't about rushing around, pushing all the right buttons, making all the right connections, and pulling off the right things just so we can say we've arrived.

Lasting, satisfying success is resting in the Lord, running at His pace and enjoying the race as we follow Him.

I have to admit that I've lived most of my life afflicted with destination disease. This dreadful and potentially deadly disease of the spirit and emotions infects us with the deceptive notion that the destination, not the journey, is what really matters. For nearly four decades, the sole, all-consuming focus of my personal, family, and ministry life was arriving. The prizes I ran to win? A holy and disciplined personal life, a happy, prosperous Christian family, and a large, fruitful and influential ministry. Reaching the goal, achieving the desired results, and accomplishing it as quickly as possible was the only game in town as far as I was concerned. Results oriented and destination driven, I pushed myself at a feverish pace to arrive at the destinations I believed God had for me.

I set out with my characteristic fiery enthusiasm, spiritual zeal, and fervent faith to accomplish my goals in as short a span of time as possible. As a believer in Christ and a minister of the Gospel, I tackled my tasks in the name of the Lord. My modus operandi was don't wait, just create and make it happen. I, not God, established an unhealthy pace for myself: Run as fast as you can; never slow down; don't rest. At times the brutal pace was impressive and productive, but it was never peaceful or restful.

I was driven by spiritual passion and an emotional hunger to prove to God that I was worthy of His love, acceptance and approval. Biblically, I had received His love, acceptance and approval in Christ. But because I wasn't into enjoying the journey with my Savior and I didn't slow down often enough or long enough to simply receive, rest in, and rejoice in His unconditional love, I missed out on experiencing first-hand, in my heart, the love God had for me. I was more concerned and consumed with getting to heaven successfully and receiving the promised rewards of a faithful Christian and pastor than I was with getting to know My Heavenly Father. My self-appointed, performance-motivated, race for results robbed me of the wonderfully fulfilling personal relationship God wanted me to have with Him. It's hard to admit, but it's true.

The result of my frantic pace? At age 37, I crashed and burned. A forced resignation from my position as pastor brought me face-to-face with failure, grief, depression, and self-destructive thoughts. Even my depression moved quickly — I rapidly descended into an ever-deepening black hole of despair that nearly took my life. Internal turmoil, torment, confusion, and fear drove peace far from my broken heart and crushed spirit.

I spun dangerously out of control. Trapped in an emotional whirlpool of overwhelming grief and sorrow, I became so lost emotionally and spiritually that, try my hardest, I could not find my way out of depression's icy grip. I admitted myself to a psychiatric hospital for treatment of severe reactive depression.

Though I felt God was a million miles away and not aware of my crisis, the Lord's hand was upon me as I checked in for what would turn into a 30-day stay. I was evaluated by the nursing staff and attending physician. Test results verified I was in serious trouble. Physically, chemically, emotionally, relationally, and spiritually, I was totally depleted. My scores across the board were off the scales in the negative. I was told I was one of the most severely depressed persons they had ever seen.

That day as I sat on a bed in a hospital ward, my life in shambles, submitting myself to God's healing and restoration of my life, a healing process began. It would last nearly three years.

Through a process of grace and mercy, the Lord healed my hurt, rebuilt my heart, renewed my hope, and restored me to Himself, myself, my family, and the ministry.

Steve Roll is a man who has personally experienced the healing, restoring and renewing power of Jesus Christ. He delivered me from the depths of despair and raised me up to new heights of grace and glory! For that I am eternally grateful.

Many factors contributed to my burning out and falling out of the race of life. For our purposes here, I want to look at a key factor that was one of the major players. It's something I've mentioned several times aleady: Pace.

A significant portion of my restoration process occurred at home. The Lord sidelined me from formal, full-time ministry for 27 months. This period was one of the most challenging, but most rewarding times in my life. During this spiritual sabbatical that the Lord appointed, anointed, and used to rebuild my life, I came to know my Heavenly Father in a way I had always longed for but never experienced.

I spent the majority of my time waiting on Him. Hundreds upon hundreds of hours were given to prayer, study of the Word, fasting, meditating, reading, listening for His voice, and seeking His direction. What an incredibly rich time I was privileged to spend with Jesus! God loved this burned out, beaten up, brokenhearted son and servant of His so much that He gave me a gift of two years alone in His presence. My life is forever different because of this special time God set aside for me.

In my healing process some devotional and prayer times before the Lord stand out as watershed moments, major milestones that significantly molded and shaped my recovery. A chilly day in February 1993 became one of those times that transformed my spiritual thinking and changed my future behavior.

As I walked and talked with the Lord, I sensed it was time for Steve to be silent. As I listened for God's voice, I heard the Lord speak to me in my spirit saying, "Steve, be at peace with my pace. I will rebuild your life and restore you to the ministry. You will fulfill the dreams I have put in your heart. But do it My way this time. My yoke is easy and My burden is light. Be at peace with My pace. Learn from Me how to flow in the Holy Spirit. I will teach you to walk and run at My pace."

Revelation of truth is critical to our understanding of how God wants us to live our lives. Kingdom principles and godly wisdom come only from above (James 1:5-8; 3:13-18). We need to know these truths if we are to triumph over the trials of this life. Our Heavenly Father wants His children to know these things. So He waits for us to wait on Him so He can show us the scriptural truths that will transform our lives.

That wintry February day, the Lord met me and revealed to me that success in life and ministry depends on flowing in His Spirit and following the pace He sets for us. Whether quickly or slowly, we are to flow with God as He moves in and through our lives to bless us and others. Whether it is a season for soaring with wings as eagles, or running and not becoming weary, or walking and not fainting (Isaiah 40:31), we need to fully submit to God and commit ourselves to be at peace with His pace.

As the impact and importance of "be at peace with My pace" sank in, a light turned on inside of me. My spiritual eyes opened wide for the first time in a long time. My inner man jumped and shouted, "Wow, so that's how it works! Thank you Jesus for showing me what I needed to see. Before, I was depending on me, not You. Living and ministering in my power, not Yours. Running the race at my pace, not Your pace. I had it all backwards. No wonder I burned out. I will do it Your way this time."

It's wonderful to receive truth. But for truth to be effective in our lives, we have to believe in it enough that we do something about it. Theory is one thing. Taking action is another. The book of James tells us plainly what we are to do with the word of truth.

> *Therefore putting aside all filthiness and all that remains of wickedness, in humility receive the word implanted, which is able to save your souls. But prove yourselves doers of the word and not merely hearers who delude themselves. For if anyone is a hearer of the word and not a doer, he is like a man who looks at his natural face in a mirror; for once he has looked at himself and gone away, he has immediately forgotten what kind of person he was. But one who looks intently at the perfect law, the law of liberty, and abides by it, not having become a forgetful hearer but an effectual doer, this man will be blessed in what he does.*
>
> James 1:21-25

The blessed person, the one who is influential and makes a lasting impact in life, is the one who receives the Word of God with a humble spirit and then goes out and puts it into practice. He not only hears it (revelation), he does it (application).

According to James, God's Word is complete and brings freedom to those who abide by it. The Lord knew exactly what I needed when He told me to be at peace with His pace. He was perfecting me by making me whole and building my character, setting me free from my failure so I could become successful in Him. I now know that success is not only being faithful to fulfill God's call on my life, but also to accomplish it His way, in His time, at His pace, and with His power.

Bouncing back requires doing the new things the Lord reveals to us. You can successfully come back from a serious setback in your life if you will be diligent to obey what God shows you. It isn't always easy. Anything valuable or worthwhile never is. At times you'll have to summon the courage and fortitude to stick with the process. Roller coaster feelings will test your faith and trust

How to Find Peace with God's Pace

that the Lord knows what He's doing. Some healing days will zip along; some will drag; some will seem to just stand still.

I can tell you from experience that your decision to accept His pace and be at peace with it will definitely be tested more than once! Even so, commit yourself to spending the rest of your life implementing this scriptural strategy for success in the daily doing of what the Lord has for you to do.

You might have to learn how to walk spiritually all over again. The first few steps will be pretty tough. Baby steps for sure! But as you plant your feet on the firm foundation of the Word and step out on God's promises, you'll become stronger and stronger. Step by step, do your best with the Holy Spirit's help to rely on Jesus instead of yourself. Choose to accept His pace in the restoration process. You'll want it to hurry up at times when your flesh grows impatient. But as you focus on your spirit and your goal, God's grace will always come through for you. As you submit to God's pace, grace and peace will come into your heart.

John 14:27 tells us Jesus said to the disciples, *"Peace I leave with you; My peace I give to you; not as the world gives, do I give to you. Do not let your heart be troubled, nor let it be fearful."* When Jesus left for heaven, He left behind some very significant things for His followers. Peace was one of them. Note it was His peace that He gave to us. Not the false, shallow peace of this world.

Speaking of Jesus Christ, Paul wrote in Ephesians 2:14, *"He Himself is our peace."* Jesus is our peace; it comes from Him. The only place to find peace is in Christ. The world doesn't know anything about real peace and can't experience it because it doesn't know the God who is our peace (Philippians 4:9). Peace flows from the nature and character of God. It's His gift to us. To receive the gift of God's peace we have to receive His Son Jesus, the Prince of Peace. To know Jesus is to know peace.

I love how He told those He loved that their hearts did not have to be troubled nor fearful because He would fill them with His peace. What a wonderfully refreshing and reassuring word for those who were going to carry on Christ's work in an antagonistic, hostile world!

Peace, internal peace had been a stranger to me for many years. I had memorized John 14:27 and in the heat of the battles I faced, I quoted it often seeking comfort from its soul soothing message. But peace eluded me. The years when I ran my race at my pace trouble, fear, and panic reigned in my heart where peace should have ruled (Colossians 3:15).

But God loves us and has a better way for us. Our Heavenly Father sends His peace to still our troubled hearts and steady our fearful spirits. The peace of God that is above our understanding can flood our spirit, wrapping our hearts in a warm blanket of divine confidence and assurance that everything will be all right.

One thing I learned is that once we fully surrender and stop fighting with the Lord about the speed (pace) of how His will is coming to pass, then the Holy Spirit can flow through us and a fruitful life and ministry is automatic.

The parable of the seed in Mark 4:26-29 illustrates this life-changing lesson:

> *The Kingdom of God is like a man who casts seed upon the soil; and goes to bed at night and gets up by day, and the seed sprouts up and grows — how, he himself does not know. The soil produces crops by itself; first the blade, then the head, then the mature grain in the head. But when the crop permits, he immediately puts in the sickle, because the harvest is come.*

This is a kingdom parable about process. I don't know about you, but I have never been terribly fond of processes. I've usually been too impatient to wait for a process to complete its course. My approach to life left little room for hanging around, exercising patience and allowing things to work they way God ordained them. But life is a process — a whole bunch of processes — that we must come to terms with if we're to be successful and find satisfaction.

In this story, Jesus painted a picture of a farmer farming. He taught that fruitfulness in God's Kingdom is a process that requires a divine/human partnership. Man's part is to sow the seed into the soil. God's part is to grow the seed. The farmer in this story did what a farmer is supposed to do: He put the seed in the ground. Did he stay up all night and worry about whether it would grow? No. On the contrary, he sowed the seed and then went to sleep. When he awoke the next morning, he saw that the seed had sprouted. How it did, he had no idea. All he knew was that he sowed it and God grew it!

Process is all about how. Many times I have asked God how something is going to happen. How can we do this? How will this turn around? How will this need be met? The Lord has always answered my "how" prayers by replying, "The how isn't up to you Steve, it's up to Me. Leave the how to Me. You sow the seed and I will grow the seed."

God has built a process into the very ground He made. Note *the soil produces crops by itself.* It's a miracle of creation the way a small, seemingly lifeless seed can lay in the cold, dark dirt and then spring to life, bursting through the soil, stretching toward the sunlight as it progresses through the blade, head, and mature grain stages on its way to harvest. Our Creator placed the miracle in the seed and the soil.

During the growth process, the seed goes through several stages of varying duration. The first stage is slow. It seems to take forever before the farmer sees that tender, soft green sprout push through the surface of the soil. Though it seems a long time coming, farmers get excited when the sprouts appear. Growth begins in earnest once a sprout frees itself from its soil grave. The second stage moves more quickly. The farmer can see measurable growth almost daily. This stage is fun, watching the stalk stand taller and taller each morning.

The process seems to slow down again as the third stage commences. The head that will hold the grain is nearly invisible for a time. Then at just the right moment, there appears a head that has quietly formed and now quickly fills up with grain. Farmers begin to see the fruit of their labor at this stage. Finally it's time to call in the harvesting crew, cut the grain and get it into the barn. The process that started with some tiny seeds sown into the soil culminates with a bountiful harvest that will provide bread for hungry people.

Did you see the pace in this process? Each stage progressed at different speeds. Harvest was the goal all along, even though the pace of development varied throughout the process.

God's formula for success in both farming and living boils down to man sowing seed and God growing the seed. It's that simple. When followed, this process, the pace of which God has ordered, results in fruitfulness (harvest).

In our passage, the farmer sowed the seed. Having done his part, He trusted God to do His part. The farmer rested peacefully knowing that the process was in place and He could count on God to grow the seed. Each morning, he got up and went to work to care for the grain. He watched it mature, cultivated and cared for it until harvest came. Then he joyfully reaped what he had sown…tons of grain from thousands of tiny little seeds that he was faithful to put into the ground.

After he sowed the seed, the farmer, couldn't speed up or slow down the growth process. By faith, he submitted himself to God's process for crops. The how and when were in God's hands. The farmer accepted the process and worked hard. At the proper time he reaped and enjoyed the reward of God's will for farmers — a bountiful harvest!

Process is no longer my foe. Slowly but surely, I've come to realize God's process works for us, not against us. His pace is something we should respect, not neglect or reject. Running our race at God's pace is good for us because He designed it that way. It's part of His plan for our lives. His pace protects us from burning out and dropping out of the race.

The Bible tells us that God has plans for His people. Jeremiah 29:11 reads, *"I know the plans I have for you," declares the* L<small>ORD</small>*, "plans for welfare and not for calamity to give you a future and a hope."* This verse declares that God's plans are good plans. He has our wellbeing and best interests in mind. Divinely prepared plans are filled with hope and promise a bright and prosperous future. Peace, power, and productivity flow from the life of the person who is at peace with God's pace for their life.

Our adversary the devil has a plan for us, too. It's an evil plan formulated in the pit of hell and founded on fear, calamity, and disaster. There is no hope or future in it. The devil knows he's powerless to overrule or overcome God's plans, so he devises strategies to interfere with and disrupt God's plans by tempting us to take the pace of the game (God's will) out of God's hands and into our own.

The evil one's ultimate goal is to deceive us into believing that running our race at our own pace is better than running it at God's pace. How does he do it? He attacks our peace. He knows if he can get us to become uneasy, anxious, frustrated and upset about the pace of God's work in our lives we will be tempted to abandon the Lord's plan and devise our own. Satan's strategy is very subtle. The father of lies suggests things just aren't moving along fast enough. He casts doubt in our minds that God is doing a very good job caring for us. Then he makes us think that maybe, just maybe we can do things better and finish a little faster our own way. Subtle indeed, and unfortunately, very effective if we don't keep our guard up.

Being the thief that he is, Satan is out to steal our peace. If he can make us become unhappy with what's happening or not happening in our lives, he can rob us of the one thing we need to stay on course — the peace to trust God's plans and pace for our race through life. Being at peace with God's pace boils down to having faith that God knows what He is doing.

We can successfully resist the devil's schemes and strategies by keeping our faith focused on God and trusting His plan. How? Isaiah 26:3 tells us: *You will keep the mind that is dependent on You in perfect peace, for it is trusting in You.* (HCSB)

We're told here that God is the agent of our peace. He, not we, will (not might) keep us in perfect peace. Complete peace belongs to those who trust in the Lord and keep their minds *stayed* KJV (fixed, directed to, riveted, focused) on Him.

Again, we have a divine/human partnership. Our part is to keep looking to Him and trusting in Him. His part is to keep us in a state of complete peace.

A middle-aged couple came to my office for marital counseling after the husband's adulterous affair. The devastated wife was battling bitterness, unsure if she could forgive him…or even wanted to.

The husband was carrying a heavy load of guilt and condemnation for breaking the bond of trust and shattering the covenant that lays at the heart of a holy, healthy, happy marriage. He was struggling with trying to understand how he could have stepped outside of his vows and been unfaithful to his wife of 10 years.

Through their tears and confusion they told me that they were both Christians when they were married. They started out their life together committed to building a Christian marriage and family. They trusted the Lord for the things most couples look to Him for. But God's pace wasn't acceptable to them. As time passed and they didn't see these things come to pass in the way or according to the timetable they had established, they began to take their eyes off Jesus.

Satan took advantage of their disappointment, moved in, and deceived them into thinking that the Christian approach to life doesn't work. Slowly but surely, doubts eroded their faith. Because their minds were no longer directed to God, they compromised convictions and commitments. Their restless hearts sought peace and satisfaction in all the wrong places. They fell away from the Lord and fell into sin.

This troubled couple had bailed out on their faith, believing they could do a better job of running their lives than God could. How did they do? Neither of them had experienced God's peace in their marriage relationship or home life for years.

They reaped what they had sown.

Heartache always visits hearts that turn from God and the people they love. This couple had lost everything sacred, valuable and meaningful. The destroyer came, ripping apart their relationship and all but murdering their hope of a successful, satisfying marriage.

This couple could only find peace and the grace they need to rebuild their lives, reconcile their marriage and restore their family by returning to the One they had turned their backs on. They had to totally recommit themselves to trust God, and determine to keep their minds and hearts on Him. And yes, they had to come to terms with being at peace with God's pace as they worked through the pain of the healing process.

If we're to have perfect peace, we have to choose to keep our minds focused and fixed on God. We must trust in Him and Him alone — not circumstances, not people, not the world, not ourselves. God won't do our part for us, and we can't do His part for Him. We must make the conscious, committed choice to trust Him and look to Him. Then perfect peace will be ours.

Our races are made up of real-life things: dreams, visions, desires, goals, decisions, relationships, health, material needs, finances, marriage and family, careers, ministry, and a whole host of things, large and small. As the Author of life, God knows how to pace our race. If we're going to run in such a way as to win, as the Apostle Paul exhorted us in 1 Corinthians 9:24, then we have to understand how God's pace works and carries us into the winner's circle.

Honoring and glorifying God by finishing the course and winning the race is what Christian living is all about. I've learned a few things about God's pace, mostly through the school of hard knocks. I trust the following insights will help you run your spiritual race successfully.

Pace Is a Part of Life

Whether we like it or not, pacing is woven into every fiber of the fabric of the universe. We can try to deny it, ignore it, neglect it, abuse it, even attempt to manipulate it, modify it, minimize it, disclaim it, or discredit it. But to no avail.

Pace dramatically shapes our race. It can work for or against us, depending on how we look at it. I used to think that the slow times of life in particular were of no redeeming value, so instead of accepting, welcoming, and letting the slower times enrich my race, I tried to eliminate them from my life by refusing to acknowledge that they had any place in my run for glory.

It didn't take long for me to discover I was wrong.

Pace Varies Throughout Life

There is an ebb and flow to life, distinct and differing periods, stages and times when tempo varies. Life speeds up, slows down and sometimes seems to come to a complete stop! Sometimes it even feels like it's going backwards.

But God is always at work. He moves in the fast times and the slow times of our lives. Think about the Lord's pace in His Word.

- God created the earth out of nothing in six short days (Genesis 1); yet human history has spanned six millennia.

- Noah built the ark over a period of 120 years (Genesis 7-8); but the rains that fell to flood and cover the earth only lasted 40 days and nights.

- The children of Israel were slaves in Egypt for over 400 years; then God's mighty hand and His servant Moses delivered God's chosen people almost overnight. The plagues, Passover and Exodus took place in a short span of time.

- Joshua and Israel circled the city of Jericho 13 times in a week's span before the wall came tumbling down (Joshua 6).

- Nehemiah rebuilt the walls of Jerusalem in 52 days, a record setting pace (Nehemiah 1-6). Peter fished all night and caught nothing; but when Jesus told him where to lower his nets, the catch was immediate and broke the nets (John 21:1-11).

- In the New Testament church, thousands were saved in one meeting (Acts 2), a single person in another meeting (Acts 8).

- The Lord Jesus healed everyone who came to Him. Some were healed instantly; others' healing and recovery came through a process over time.

Scripture reveals that God's pace of carrying out His plan varies. We don't get to pick and choose which pace we prefer. In His wisdom, God chooses the timing, pace, and yes, the duration of the variously paced laps of our lives that He knows will contribute most to development of Christ-like character in us. To run victoriously, we have to come to the point where we willingly and joyfully accept the varying paces of life's race.

Pace Proves Our Faith

If everything in our lives happened immediately, then why would we need faith? Why would we need to trust God? Romans 8:24-25 drives home this truth about needing faith when we hope for what we do not see.

> *In hope we have been saved, but hope that is seen is not hope; for who hopes for what he already sees? But if we hope for what we do not see, with perseverance we eagerly wait for it.*

Fast times are the fun times for our faith. But the slow times, the times when moments stand still, test the mettle of our faith.

Abraham is a hero of our faith because *he believed God and it was counted to him as righteousness* (Genesis 15:6). God promised He would bless Abraham, and Abraham would be the father of a great nation, and all the nations of the earth would be blessed through Abraham. He promised Abraham a natural born son. Abraham believed God's word and entered into a covenant with Him (Genesis 15:7-21). Abraham and Sarah waited 25 long years before Isaac, that promised son, was born.

Abraham's faith was proved (established as genuine) not only in the fast moment of the promise and the covenant, but also, and most importantly, in the long, slow season of waiting for the promise to be fulfilled.

Slow times do more for building our faith than fast ones. Anyone can shout "Hallelujah!" when life is happening, the pace is fun and the going is good. But if you really want to become mature, exercise your faith during those slow times. That's where your faith stretches and grows stronger.

We Have to Pace Ourselves to Be Successful

I've never run a marathon. Running 26 miles just isn't appealing to me, but some people love competing in these endurance races. I've talked one of them.

He travels all over the country, running in the big races.

Having won a few races, he knows the thrill of victory. I asked what he believed was the key to crossing the finish line first. Without hesitation he replied, "Pace, Pastor Steve, pace. I pace myself throughout the race. Different stages of the race require a different pace. I work at not running too fast, and not running too slow. Some miles are run in a steady rhythm. Other miles I have to pick up the pace. Marathoners who win understand the importance of pacing themselves throughout the race. The right pace at the right time is critical to winning."

Life is a marathon, an endurance contest. If pacing is necessary for being successful as a physical runner, then for spiritual runners, pacing is certainly vital for victory. God's people must run their races, pacing themselves according to the words found in Isaiah 40:31 which this book is based on.

> *Those who wait for the LORD will gain new strength; they will mount up with wings like eagles, they will run and not get tired, they will walk and not become weary.*

WE MUST AVOID PACING PROBLEMS

Running ahead of God or running behind Him are the two most common problems we have with our pace. Lagging behind is usually the result of laziness or lack of obedience, or both. As undisciplined, disobedient believers, we fall behind the pace God sets for us. It puts us in a catch up mode.

The Lord doesn't bless disobedience. Until we obey, we aren't able to run side by side with Jesus. Study your Bible and you'll see those who disobeyed God didn't prosper, weren't promoted, and didn't win because their disobedience stopped them in their tracks. While they stalled in disobedience, the Lord moved on to run with and bless the obedient.

If you're wondering why some things in your life aren't happening as you think they should, maybe it's because you've been disobedient in some area. Ask the Holy Spirit to search your heart and point out anything that isn't right. (See Psalm 139:23-24.) When God shows you what's wrong, go and make it right. You can catch up with God when you start obeying Him again.

Running ahead of God is usually prompted by impatience. Losing patience with God's pace, we decide to take matters into our hands, believing we can manage our lives better. So we shift into overdrive, put on our blinker, and pass God, travelling down the highway of life in the fast lane, leaving the Lord behind in our dust.

Cruising along at high speed, we soon realize God isn't with us. We can't seem to hear His voice. We don't readily see His provision. Our prayers go unanswered and we have trouble repelling Satan's attacks.

When we move out from under God's protective covering, we get ourselves into serious trouble. Running ahead of Jesus instead of with Him puts us in a place where we become a easy target for Satan.

My greatest blunders, costliest mistakes, and most humiliating experiences have occurred when I became impatient and ran ahead of the Lord. I've learned the hard way that running ahead of God never puts me ahead, and always sets me back.

We win the race by keeping pace with Jesus!

We Sense God's Pace by Being Sensitive to the Holy Spirit

The Christian life is life in the Spirit. The following verses give us a scriptural sampling of the importance of the Holy Spirit in our life.

- *If we live by the Spirit, let us also walk by the Spirit.* Galatians 5:25

- *The Lord is the Spirit, and where the Spirit of the Lord is, there is liberty.* 2 Corinthians 3:17

- *Then he said to me, "This is the word of the Lord to Zerubbabel saying, 'Not by might nor by power, but by My Spirit' says the Lord of hosts."* Zechariah 4:6

- *"You will receive power when the Holy Spirit has come upon you; and you shall be My witnesses both in Jerusalem, and in all Judea and Samaria, and even to the remotest part of the earth."* Acts 1:8

- *When they came up out of the water, the Spirit of the Lord snatched Philip away; and the eunuch no longer saw him, but went on his way rejoicing. But Philip found himself at Azotus, and as he passed through he kept preaching the gospel to all the cities until he came to Caesarea.* Acts 8:39-40

These verses show us that power, pace, and freedom for witnessing for the Kingdom of God come through the person of the Holy Spirit. He sets the witnessing pace for our lives. He shifts the gears from slow to fast, and fast to slow. That's why we must become skilled at waiting on the Lord. While waiting, we become spiritually sensitive and tuned in to the moving of the Spirit of God. We will know how to flow in His power and how to move at the right pace because we spent time in His presence.

You'll become more able and considerably more accurate in discerning the Spirit's movement and pace in your life when you make it a high priority to meet with the Lord regularly to learn from Him how to move in His power and at His pace. Staying sensitive to the moving of the Spirit, and obeying His leading, will keep you running your race at God's pace.

We need to let go and get in God's flow, be moved as He moves. Not ahead, not behind, but right in the middle of God's actions. He is moving all over the world today. He will use those who flow with Him.

CONTENTMENT IS THE KEY FOR BEING AT PEACE WITH GOD'S PACE

Someone once said that every man lives in one of two tents: content or discontent. That's really true, isn't it? Most of us have lived in both tents during our lives. I must say I like accommodations of content best!

The Bible tells us in Proverbs 14:30 that *a tranquil* [peaceful, content] *heart is life to the body.* Paul wrote to Timothy, *"Godliness actually is a means of great gain, when accompanied by contentment"* (1 Timothy 6:6).

Note that life and great gain are the rewards of the contented heart. Godliness is profitable when contentment is its traveling companion. We can be at peace with God's pace when we're content to move at whatever speed He determines is best.

Before we examine how to be content, look at this contentment quiz to see in which of the two tents you reside.

- When life is moving along wonderfully and things are going great, am I dissatisfied and longing for even more?
- When life slows to a snail's pace, do I complain and whine?
- Does frustration or faith dominate my response when God sidelines me from my race for a season?

- Do I boo, or applaud my colleagues when they pass me on the track?
- When nothing seems to be happening and I just spin my wheels in the same spot, do I curse God or bless His name?

Popular author and counselor Gary Smalley made the following observation concerning contentment. It's something worth pondering. It's scriptural too!

Two powerful truths I have learned about contentment. First, if we're not satisfied with what we have today, we'll never be satisfied with what we have tomorrow. Second, contentment is knowing I already have everything I need in Christ.

The Apostle Paul shared his attitude toward contentment:

> *Not that I speak from want, for I have learned to be content in whatever circumstances I am. I know how to get along with humble means, and I also know how to live in prosperity; in any and every circumstance I have learned the secret of being filled and going hungry, both of having abundance and suffering need. I can do all things through Him who strengthens me.*
>
> Philippians 4:11-13

Contentment doesn't come naturally. We must learn to be content. Paul openly admitted he had learned to be content — he had been schooled in the secret of being content no matter what was happening, in every and all circumstances. Paul was satisfied in whatever situation he found himself because he could do all things (handle every contingency and circumstance successfully) through Christ. So can we, because Christ is our sufficiency also.

Contentment springs from experience that knows Jesus and I can handle anything that's happening or not happening in life.

What about you? Are you content with where you are and with what God is doing in you as you run your race? It's a fact: If you're not satisfied with the lap you're currently running, you won't be happy with the next one either.

You need to settle this peace and contentment business once and for all. Choose right now to be at peace and walk in God's wisdom by learning to trust the Lord for your every circumstance. Commit yourself to be content with your current pace so He can trust you with tomorrow's and bless you for your faithfulness.

God's Pace Is Always the Right Pace!

Psalm 37:23 tells us *the steps of a man are established by the* Lord; *and He delights in His way.*

I entered these words into my personal journal as God was teaching me about His pace.

> *Wednesday I spent four hours in prayer. Psalm 37:23 was the focus of my time with God: "The steps of the good man are ordered by the Lord." Steps. God has ordered my every step. Not one giant step. Not leaps. Steps. One step then another, all laid out by Him.*
>
> **Application for me:** *Do the thing at hand. Take the simple step before you, Steve. Let God do the hard thing. He delights, takes pleasure in the way we take, and doesn't require us to do the hard things. He does that. Our part is to do the easy thing before us. Take each step as it is revealed. Obedience to the step directly in front of me is what I am responsible for.*
>
> **Message today from the Holy Spirit.** *Steve, do the simple thing. God will do the hard thing. When you're under pressure while waiting for Me to break through supernaturally, you're tempted to feel that you have to perform. You have to make something happen. You try to force something. Do something. When you're waiting for the big thing, you're tempted to take action when it seems to stall. But you must counter that pressure by taking the simple, single step right in front of you. Whatever it is. Take that step. Then take the next step. Trust me, Your Lord and Savior, for the steps that lead to the fulfillment of My vision and mission for your life.*

Whether the Lord speeds things up (Isaiah 60:22) or slows things down (Habakkuk 2:3), we can be at peace with God's pace because each and every step of our spiritual race is laid out before us. We don't have to panic about which path to take. It's right in front of us. Step by step by step.

God's plan for our lives comes to pass when we step out confidently each day to take the next step of faith on the road to victory.

Trust the Lord with the pace of the your process. Be content. Enjoy your walk with your Heavenly Father. Keep your eyes fixed on the finish line. At the end of the race, when you've taken that final step into glory and see Him face to face, you'll receive the rewards reserved for those who were at peace with God's pace as they faithfully ran their race.

> *I have fought the good fight, I have finished the course, I have kept the faith; in the future there is laid up for me the crown of righteousness, which the Lord, the righteous Judge, will award to me on that day; and not only to me, but also to all who have loved His appearing.*
> 2 Timothy 4:7-8

Chapter 12
Some Things Are Worth the Wait

The very best things in life come to those who wait.

In 1975 a good friend introduced me to the game of racquetball. When I smashed that small ball against the front wall and it bounced back barely missing my partner's head, I was hooked!

Racquetball was invented for high-energy guys like me. I spent my first few years playing hard, but not smart. With characteristic enthusiasm, I charged the front wall, hit shots on the run without being set, dove for the ball, sprawled on the floor, crashed into walls, and found myself out of position more times than not. I tried to look like I knew something about the game, running around in my sweats, perspiring profusely, swinging my racquet wildly, chasing that little ball up and down the court. But my overzealous, under educated style produced few points. And you have to score to win.

Shrewd seasoned players took advantage of my kamikaze approach to the game and skillfully placed shots where I couldn't return them. They scored point after point with ease, while I scratched my head in amazement wondering how they did it.

One day an observant veteran took me aside during a break and said, "Steve, you have the ability to step up to another level of play. But you have to learn to wait for the best moment to take your shot. Don't hurry. Establish your position. Set your feet. Follow through with your wrist. Put the ball into play where you want it to go. Patience pays off when you wait for the ball and then place a shot that's un-returnable. Opportunities to make outstanding shots that your opponent can't reach are worth waiting on. The thrill you get is so !"

Taking his advice to heart, I adjusted my style. Believe me, learning patience wasn't easy. But I really wanted to play better, so I disciplined myself to be patient while waiting for the ball.

The veteran was absolutely right, and patience paid off. Slowly but surely, over the years my game improved dramatically. Of course I didn't win every game. But I won more than before, and I had more fun than ever before!

Eventually, a torn meniscus forced me to quit playing. And that was okay, because I can be successful running my race without racquetball.

Sports, hobbies, and other secular interests come and go. But things worth waiting for, especially things of lasting value — the things of God — require faith, patience, and endurance. The Psalmist wrote to us in Psalm 27:13-14:

> *I would have despaired unless I had believed that I would see the goodness of the Lord in the land of the living. Wait for the Lord; be strong, and let your heart take courage. Yes, wait for the Lord.*

The key to overcoming a spirit of despair and seeing God's goodness is believing that we will! We receive what we believe. The psalmist David believed he would see God's good hand and that everything he was working and waiting for would come to pass…and he enthusiastically and emphatically exhorted us to stand strong and walk courageously while we wait for the Lord.

Jeremiah 31:14 tells us the Lord declared, *"My people will be satisfied with My goodness."* The things in life that God wants each of us to have flow from His goodness. They are worth waiting for because only they can satisfy our needs. So, we should spend our time, pour our energy, and focus our efforts on the things that are really worth waiting for.

Priorities

Priorities are essential to success. People whose priorities are out of order spend major portions of their lives working diligently and waiting patiently for things that in the long run, really aren't worth it. They labor in vain when the Lord is not in the things they think are important. When they finally reap the unfulfilling fruit of their misdirected labor, and wake up to the fact that they've been wasting their lives pursuing the wrong things, despair knocks on the door of their heart.

The purpose of this chapter is to share some things that are definitely worth waiting on the Lord for. But first, think about these five things.

1. **Many people turn and leave the dock just before God's ship comes in.** They give up and quit, compromise, or return to their old ways when what they were waiting for was just around over the horizon. They often miss their breakthrough and God's blessing by just a little bit.

2. **God always has something better for us than what we would pick for ourselves.** His choices are certainly worth waiting for because they are so much better than our own.
3. **We appreciate most what we have to wait for.** Having to wait for something increases its perceived value.
4. **God will keep His Word, but we must be willing to wait.** The Word of God promises wonderful things to those who wait. If we choose not to wait, we shouldn't expect God to perform what He has promised for us.
5. **Waiting on God is a spiritual investment that pays great dividends.** There is no higher rate of return in the universe than our Heavenly Father's!

Let's look at some of the most important things in life worth the wait.

THE RIGHT MATE

Relationships are the most valuable things we can experience. Next to a personal relationship with God through Jesus Christ, the second most important relationship in life is between husband and wife. Who we marry and spend our life with is one of the biggest decisions we ever make.

The Bible tells us *he who finds a wife finds a good thing and he obtains favor from the Lord* (Proverbs 18:22). God's appraisal of marriage is that it is good. It is honorable (Hebrews 13:4). The world belittles marriage while the Lord elevates it to a high, holy and honorable place. A wife is a good thing. A husband is a good thing.

God desires for men to find good wives and women to find good husbands. According to our verse, the married man with a good wife receives favor and blessing from God. This being the case, common sense would dictate that a man who would be wise would want to be very careful in choosing a wife and wait for the right woman.

In 1 Peter 3:7 the apostle wrote:

> *Husbands, live with your wives in an understanding way, as with a weaker vessel, since she is a woman; and grant her honor as a fellow heir of the grace of life, so that your prayers may not be hindered.*
>
> Author's Paraphrase

Husband and wife are fellow heirs in life, joint partners in the journey of faith. They are privileged to experience the grace of God together, as lifetime companions. The Lord said it isn't good for man to be alone, so he made Adam a suitable helper and partner named Eve (Genesis 2:18-25).

Being alone is not God's best plan for anyone. His desire for each of us is to share life with a loving, committed, complementing companion. But some people let their hormones and loneliness override wisdom. Their need to have someone can deceive them into accepting a less than the best choice for a companion. The right someone, not just anyone, makes togetherness work. Because oneness (Genesis 2:23-25) and partnership lie at the heart of holy, healthy, and happy companionship, the right mate is worth the wait.

How important is marriage? It's so vitally important that God presents the husband/wife relationship in Christian marriage as a parallel to, or shadow of, Christ's relationship with His bride the Church (Ephesians 5:22-33). Husband and wife are to conduct themselves in the manner that Jesus and the church relate to one another.

Successfully fulfilling the roles and responsibilities of the marriage relationship as described in Ephesians 5 requires that a man and woman be certain that they are marrying the right person for the right reasons. The standards set by the Lord are demanding enough with the right mate. Trying to make marriage happen God's way with the wrong mate can be disastrous.

In Solomon's search for the meaning to life, he drew some conclusions that could tempt people to become depressed if they didn't keep their perspective positive! He made a long list of things he called vain — things we do that really don't matter in the long run. Through the process of elimination, he sorted through the stuff that is vain, and arrived at an incredibly simple, yet powerfully profound statement about man's reward in life. *"Vanities of vanities! All is vanity"* (Ecclesiastes 1:2).

Solomon proposed that a man's ultimate success, his most satisfying reward is not his work, his hobbies, or anything else. It's finding joy in his mate and their life together.

> *Enjoy life with the woman whom you love all the days of your fleeting life which He has given to you under the sun; for this is your reward in life, and in your toil in which you have labored under the sun.*
>
> Ecclesiastes 9:9

Every man on earth needs to know and embrace the fact that his reward in life is to enjoy life with his wife.

If man's reward in life is enjoying his wife, then men and women who want to experience life's best better give thoughtful, prayerful consideration to who they marry and how they treat them afterward. If we say "I do" when we should have said "I don't," and marry the wrong person, life will not be enjoyable or rewarding.

Solomon had a specific word for wives in Proverbs 31:25-31. The godly, virtuous woman focuses on taking excellent care of her household. Her reward? Her children and husband bless her name. They let others know what a great wife and mother she is.

For varying reasons (communication problems, control issues, emotional immaturity, low self-esteem, obsessive behaviors, adulterous affairs) many marriages are in deep trouble today. Nearly 80 percent of the pastoral counseling I do is with people with marriage problems. It grieves my spirit deeply when I hear the heartbreaking stories of husbands and wives who say they love each other, but they can't live peaceably with one another.

But what troubles me most and causes me to wonder if people even think any more is when, knowing that marriage is supposed to be for keeps and that God has given us specific guidelines in His Word for a successful and satisfying marriage, even professing Christians tell me things like:

- We knew premarital sex was wrong, but we were so in love.
- We didn't wait for sex until we were married. Now it seems like something is missing from our relationship.
- He was so nice and treated me like a lady, his kids took to me, and they all needed me. So we got married.
- It was hard being alone and raising my son as a single parent.
- After dating for three months we decided to get married.
- While dating, we started messing around. She got pregnant so we felt we had to get married. We never really loved each other, but now there's a baby.
- I was tired of being alone. He was handsome.

- Pastor, I didn't have peace. As a matter of fact, on the day of our wedding, I knew in my heart this was wrong and the Lord was telling me no. But I got married anyway.

People can't expect to walk right when they start on the wrong foot! I don't condemn those who have made mistakes. We all fail. Biblical counsel directs us to look to the Lord, learn from our failures, redeem our mistakes, and do better the next time. That's what redemption and restoration are all about. We must do these things if we ever hope to enjoy a mate and receive the rich rewards married life can bring.

I'm convinced God chooses and prepares the right mate for us. If we will diligently and faithfully seek Him concerning a marriage partner and then wait for that person to come into our life when the time is right, then we can choose His choice for us, be at peace, and live happily ever after.

To find the right mate, we have to be the right mate. Here are ten time-tested truths I give as guidelines to people seeking a mate.

1. Pray about a mate. (James 1:5)
2. Keep yourself sexually pure. (1 Thessalonians 4:1-8; 2 Timothy 2:19-22; Hebrews 13:4; 1 Corinthians 6:12-20)
3. Do not compromise God's standards for Christian marriage. (Ephesians 5:22-33)
4. Marry a committed, victorious Christian who's living a Christ-like life successfully. (2 Corinthians 6:14-18)
5. If you've been divorced, be healed from your hurts and learn from your mistakes before considering remarriage. (Jeremiah 30:17; Psalm 139:23-24; Psalm 143:8-10)
6. Receive Christ-centered, Bible-based pre-marital counseling. (Proverbs 11:14)
7. Have the blessing of your parents. (Exodus 20:12)
8. Seek the counsel of at least two trusted, mature believers who know you, love you, and want the best for you. (Matthew 18:19)
9. Wait to be sure. Time is on your side when it is right! (Proverbs 3:5-6)
10. Commit yourself to being the mate your mate can enjoy life with (Ecclesiastes 9:9).

The right mate is worth the wait! I know. I have *an excellent wife* that Proverbs 31 describes. It's nothing short of a miracle that we were married and have stayed happily married for 40 years and counting. I was the product of a broken home, Jo Ann a stable one. My family struggled financially, while Jo Ann's family enjoyed a middle class lifestyle. My wife received Christ as her personal Savior when she was five years old and was a grounded, stable, solid Christian when we met. I was a troubled young man growing up and didn't receive Christ as my Savior until I was 20. I struggled in areas of life that Jo Ann did not.

Our family backgrounds, personalities, religious upbringing, economic expectations and life experiences were so different…and yet God used all of that to make us right for each other.

I enjoy life with my wife! She brings to my life the gifts, graces, godly virtues, and womanly charms that God knew I needed in order to be complete. When I stop to think about all the wonderful things I get to do and experience in this life, there is no question that next to my relationship with the Lord Jesus Christ, my greatest personal joy and rejoicing is found in the wife of my youth.

You'll receive unbelievable blessings and spare yourself a lot of grief if you will trust God and wait for the right mate.

CHILDREN

The Bible is pro-life and pro-children. In a wayward world like ours where many consider children a burden, God declares boldly and unashamedly that children are a blessing!

Look what the Lord has to say in Psalm 127:3-5:

> *Behold, children are a gift of the LORD, the fruit of the womb is a reward. Like arrows in the hand of a warrior, so are the children of one's youth. How blessed is the man whose quiver is full of them; they shall not be ashamed when they speak with their enemies in the gate.*

If you're a parent, have you looked at your children lately and thanked God for giving them to you? God's gifts are always good gifts (Matthew 7:7-11). His gifts are given to enrich our lives, not impoverish them. The man who has many children (full quiver) is considered blessed. His enemies pay him respect and listen to him because of his many arrows (children). Having children (the fruit of the womb) is another one of God's rewards in life.

I'm honored and humbled having my son and daughter in my life. They bless me every day! At every age and stage of development, their uniquely precious personalities have touched Dad's heart like nobody else can. Life would be a lot less rich without them.

Children are a challenge. My arrows, like yours, come wrapped in human flesh that ruffled my fatherly feathers from time to time. The adolescent years were particularly challenging. But from something Dr. James Dobson once explained, I realized that the goal of raising junior and senior high kids through the turbulent teenager waters is for everyone to still be on the raft when adolescence runs its course.[11] I'm happy to say that our family got wet from time to time traveling through life together, but all four of us are present and accounted for. And we love and respect each other too!

Children are a trust as well as a gift. As Christians we are stewards (managers) of all that God has given us. We're required to be found faithful (1 Corinthians 4:2). The Lord gave my wife and me the priceless gifts of a son and a daughter. He entrusted to our care two unique, fearfully and wonderfully made human beings who were created in His image, are precious in His sight, divinely designed for greatness, and destined for eternity. It has been our privilege and responsibility to work with the Lord in the life-long molding and mentoring process that trains and shapes them into Christ-likeness. It is rewarding beyond description to be involved in the making of a man and woman of God.

As with marriage, becoming a parent is an important decision that demands waiting before the Lord for His timing and blessing. God knows when we're ready for the responsibility of parenthood.

My wife and I waited nine years for our son to arrive, then three more for our daughter. I recall with perfect clarity both of their births. Adam was born on a Sunday afternoon in sunny San Diego after 12 hours of intense labor. Stacy was delivered on a cold, snowy Michigan morning after only three hours at the birthing center. Both moments were miraculous!

I will never forget the fragile sound of their first cries, touching their tiny fingers and toes, holding them close to my chest and caressing them, and gently kissing their foreheads. Those two little bundles of love captured my heart in a hurry. They made me a father, and I have enjoyed every minute of it!

Whether you want to have your own biological children, or you want to adopt a deserving child, wait for your children. Trust God for them. Be patient with the process.

While you wait, take your place and stand courageously against a self-centered, immoral, conscienceless society that murders the unborn through abortion, and dehumanizes and de-dignifies children through neglect and abuse.

Returning to a moral position of sanctity of life, respecting the gifts God has given us in our children and resolving to raise them right is the solution needed to stop the abominable slaughter of the innocent unborn, and the hellish indignities and injustices committed against children.

Children are worth waiting for because they are God's gift and they are our future!

Healing

We appreciate health most when we're sick. A period of physical, emotional or spiritual illness has a way of jarring our memory banks and reminding us how important being healthy really is.

Whenever we're afflicted with sickness, it is natural to want to be healed right away. Sickness is part of life, but it isn't God's plan for us. Health, wholeness and well-being are His will for His children. Jesus Christ suffered terribly at the hands of cruel men, receiving a malicious beating that shredded His back and literally left strips of torn flesh and blood (Matthew 27:11-32). The prophet Isaiah foretold this event over 800 years before it actually occurred:

> *He was despised and forsaken of men; a man of sorrows, and acquainted with grief; and like one from whom men hide their face He was despised, and we did not esteem Him. Surely our griefs He Himself bore, and our sorrows He carried; yet we ourselves esteemed Him stricken, smitten of God, and afflicted. But He was pierced through for our transgressions, He was crushed for our iniquities; the chastening for our well-being fell upon Him, and by His scourging [stripes] we are healed. All of us like sheep have gone astray, each of us has turned to his own way, but the Lord has caused the iniquity of us all to fall on Him.*
>
> Isaiah 53:3-6

Jesus was despised, rejected and forsaken. He was beaten and bruised beyond recognition, crushed and humiliated by sinful men.

Even God the Father abandoned His Son during this intense season of inhuman suffering when Jesus became sin for us. (See Matthew 27:46)

Why did Jesus, the Holy One of God, who was innocent and blameless, take such an awful, ungodly beating? The Bible tells us He willingly submitted to it because of His great love for us. He allowed Himself to be nailed to a cross, and have His flesh pierced through with nails and a spear, to save us from our sin. He was scourged so we could be healed from sickness. Peter, an eyewitness of the crucifixion of Christ recorded this in 1 Peter 2:24: *He himself bore our sins in His body on the cross, so that we might die to sin and live to righteousness; for by His wounds you were healed.*

Jesus purchased our salvation and healing at the place called Calvary. Healing is a done deal (*for by His wounds, you were healed*). Healing and health belong to believers through Jesus Christ. We receive the healing that the Lord procured for us by standing in faith, believing that His stripes and blood have made us whole and victorious over sin, sickness, and death.

Jesus rose from the dead in resurrection power! He is alive and is Jehovah Rapha, *the* LORD *who heals you* (Exodus 15:26). David wrote in Psalm 107:20: *He sent His word and healed them, and delivered them from their destructions.* Through Jeremiah, God told the nation of Judah that they would be healed: *"I will restore you to health and I will heal you of your wounds,"* declares the LORD. (Jeremiah 30:17). We all suffer wounds and sickness that we in ourselves can't heal. But the Word of God says Jesus can, and will, when we look to Him with faith and trust Him to heal us and restore us to health.

Sometimes the Lord heals instantaneously. At other times, healing is a process over time. I have seen and experienced both.

How and when the Lord heals is His business. Our part is to believe and receive. Our faith trusts Him for the healing and the process. Symptoms not withstanding, we must stand firm in faith, receiving our healing and recovery because it's ours in Christ.

When I battled depression, the symptoms became so severe that I seriously considered committing suicide. The Lord graciously and miraculously intervened, saving me from self-destruction. The immediate crisis over, I still needed healing and restoration of my spirit and emotions.

The restoration process took nearly three years of standing firm in the faith, working harder than I have ever worked in my life (emotionally and spiritually) and waiting, waiting, waiting. The step-by-step healing process fully and finally resolved some inner emotional conflicts in my heart, bound up my wounds and renewed me spiritually. Was my healing worth the wait? You'd better believe it! I wouldn't trade what the Lord has done in me for anything!

If you or someone you know needs physical, emotional, or spiritual healing, wait for it with faith. Put your trust in Jesus and the recovery process. Hold on to His promises. You are healed in Christ. Lay claim to what is yours. Hang in there. Do whatever you have to do to get better. Wholeness is wonderful! Healing and wellbeing is worth waiting for!

If you're one of those compassionate caregivers who helps everyone else find healing and wholeness, but you need some healing in your own life, it's time for you to take care of yourself.

We can't lead others to healing and wholeness if we aren't whole or healed ourselves, can we? Make a good decision for yourself. Step aside from your ministry for a while so the Lord can minister to you. It's okay. You're worth it. God can take care of people while you take care of yourself. So take some time out for yourself! You and everybody who needs your help in the future will be glad you did.

Biblical Prosperity

When the preacher came to the place in the ceremony where he said, "Will you take this woman for richer or poorer, for better or worse, in sickness and in health?" the groom thought it was multiple choice so he replied, "For richer, better, and healthier!" That guy had prosperity on his mind.

I believe we would choose those things, too, if it were up to us. Why do I think so? One, I know I would and you aren't much different than me. Two, our Heavenly Father built those desires into us. Better, healthier and more prosperous lines up with His will while worse, sick, and poor is definitely not the Lord's will for His children.

Psalm 35:27 tells us: *Let them shout for joy and rejoice, who favor my vindication; and let them say continually, "The* Lord *be magnified, who delights in the prosperity of His servant."*

Proverbs 13:21-22 reads: *Adversity pursues sinners, but the righteous will be rewarded with prosperity. A good man leaves an inheritance to his children's children, and the wealth of the sinner is stored up for the righteous.*

Psalm 37:11 states: *The humble will inherit the land and will delight themselves in abundant prosperity.*

And 2 Corinthians 9:8 says this: *God is able to make all grace abound to you, so that always having all sufficiency in everything, you may have an abundance for every good deed.*

The thrust of this small sample of Scriptures on prosperity is that God is pleased when the righteous prosper. He takes pleasure in blessing the righteous with abundance. And the righteous are pleased that He does!

I was raised in a home that didn't have a lot of money. Our basic needs were met, but abundance and prosperity were foreign language to our family. At an early age, I began thinking and then believing that money and material things were out of reach for guys like me. Only the rich got to enjoy the benefits and privileges of wealth. I had no concept whatsoever that my Maker wanted to bless every area of my life, including the material side.

I grew up hating poverty and envying those who were well to do. I was jealous of those better off than me. I became money motivated. I set my sights on becoming a medical doctor so I could get ahead and live the good life. At that point in my life prosperity meant money and stuff for myself, period. My motives were totally selfish.

Then I became a Christian. When Jesus came into my life, everything changed. Including my ideas about prosperity. A number of years passed before I broke free from my poor man's mentality and began lining up my personal faith with God's Word. I studied the lives of biblical characters to find out how they approached prosperity. The Lord taught me a great biblical principle from faithful Abraham's life. In Genesis 12:1-3, we read of Abram's initial call from Jehovah.

> Now the LORD said to Abram, "Go forth from your country, and from your relatives and from your father's house, to the land which I will show you. And I will make you a great nation, and I will bless you, and make your name great; and so you shall be a blessing; and I will bless those who bless you, and the one who curses you I will curse. And in you all the families of the earth shall be blessed."

God made a covenant with Abraham (see Genesis 15). The Lord's holy agreement with Abraham was based on a promise of faith and blessing. If Abraham would believe God, God would bless Abraham. Note here that the Lord said, *"I will bless you."* Why? *"So you shall be a blessing."* Through Abraham, God's blessing would extend to all the families of the earth.

Blessed to be a blessing. This is biblical prosperity. This prosperity principle revolutionized my motives, thinking and practices concerning money and its purpose. It was a life-changing revelation for me to learn that God blesses His people so they can bless others! Abraham was blessed so he could bless others. Blessed people can bless people. The Lord wants us to prosper (flourish, thrive, succeed) *so we can be a blessing to someone else*.

Biblical prosperity provides the means for God's people to bless others in His name. Material wealth and resources give us the ability to *go into all the world and preach the Gospel to all creation* (Mark 16:15).

Ministry takes money. If I can say it this way, if we don't have the dough, we can't go! But our motives in ministering to others must always remain pure and above reproach. I used to think that prosperity's perks were only for me. Now I know that the Lord prospers me so I can help others prosper (flourish, thrive, succeed) too! I'm not into getting what I can get for myself any more, but getting what I can get so I can give it to others in Jesus' name.

The great Methodist preacher and revivalist John Wesley said, "Get all you can. Save all you can. Give all you can." What an outstanding philosophy of biblical prosperity! Get it so you can give it! Why does the Lord store up the wealth of the wicked for the righteous? So we can use it to win the wicked to Him, that's why!

My attitude adjustment regarding biblical prosperity took a while. But I'm learning more and more each day to walk by faith, believing that it's God's will to prosper me and bless me with material abundance so I can accomplish everything He has called me to do. My family has become faithful tithers (Malachi 3:8-10). We give offerings cheerfully (Luke 6:38; 2 Corinthians 9:6-7) and we get behind worthy Christian causes as the Lord leads us. We never hesitate to give money or materials to people when God says to. We also work hard, spend money wisely, and manage the resources He entrusts to us as faithfully as possible.

Does any of the above pay off? I believe it does in time and eternity. We've been blessed far beyond what I used to ever believe could be possible and it just keeps getting better and better. We have more and are able to help more than ever before.

But do you know what I'm really excited about? It's the treasure we've been storing in heaven (Matthew 6:19-21). What we store in the bank of heaven is secure and available to us in our time of need.

One of my favorite verses is Psalm 37:25. David confessed, *"I have been young and now I am old, yet I have not seen the righteous forsaken, or his descendants begging bread."* David declared that throughout his entire life, from youth to old age, God had always provided for him and his family. The Lord had never failed to prosper David and his tribe with the things they needed to succeed in this life. As I am getting older by the day, I say a hearty "Amen!" to what David said.

Biblical prosperity is far bigger than having personal material wealth. Biblical prosperity means having the resources and ability to accomplish God's will. Biblical prosperity works when we let God go to work to bless us so we can bless others. Prospering and being blessed with abundance in all things so we can be in a position to bless others is something definitely worth working and waiting for.

Fulfilled Dreams

Do you have a burning desire in your heart to accomplish something great for God and His eternal Kingdom? Have you discovered a worthwhile need that is waiting to be filled? Do you have thoughts, ideas and plans for how meeting the need can become reality? Can you see in your spirit with the eye of faith a vision of what the Lord wants to do through you? Does this vision stay continually before you, daily calling to you to do something to fulfill it? Is every extra minute of your spare time consumed with considering how to complete what God has called you to? If you answered yes to these questions, you've hitched yourself to a star and are following a dream!

Dreams get us out of bed every morning, keep us pushing through the day, and tuck us in at night. The Lord has called His people to be visionaries and dreamers who pursue their God-given dreams with the power of the Holy Spirit. Joel 2: 28 tells us: *It will come about after this that I will pour out My Spirit on all mankind; and your sons and daughters will prophesy, your old men will dream dreams, your young men will see visions.* Seeing visions and dreaming dreams of what God wants us to do makes the Christian life dynamic and fulfilling. Divine dreams direct the course of our lives. Everybody needs to dream a dream that can come true with God's help.

Dreams coming true are worth waiting for! We'll spend the next chapter learning how to wait for dreams to come true.

The Harvest

I'm the oldest of six sons. Mom pretty much raised us by herself. As the eldest, I took a lot of responsibility upon myself. One fall, when I was visiting an uncle's house, he took me, and a couple of shovels, to his vegetable garden in the backyard.

He strategically placed his shovel at the base of a plant that had definitely seen better days. Driving the blade deep into the soil, he brought it out and dumped what looked like big dirt clods onto the ground. What I thought were dirt clods were potatoes!

I was eager to help. The more we dug, the more we uncovered. By the end of the afternoon, we had 25 sacks full!

I was so excited about digging up the potato treasure I asked my uncle if he would teach me how to plant and grow my own potatoes. He taught me how to cut out an eye of a potato; how deep to bury it in the dirt; how far apart to space the plants; how much water they would need, and the signs that would signal harvest time had arrived. I hurried home that day, dreaming of the potato patch I was going to plant in our backyard the next spring.

Springtime found me preparing my first potato garden. Visions of bulging sacks packed with big, firm, brown skinned potatoes that would feed our family motivated me to have the best potato patch on our block. I tilled the soil, spaced the plants in perfect rows, and even dressed off my potato farm with a string fence.

I labored faithfully all that summer, watering, weeding, and debugging my first potato farm. While I worked, I dreamed of the monstrous potatoes I was certain were growing beneath my feet!

Just as my uncle had said, when September rolled around, the plants started to die, signaling that it was time to break out the shovel. I'll never forget that first harvest. I had the time of my life!

Plant by plant, I dug for the buried treasure. As I unearthed each mound, I was utterly amazed at the number and size of the potatoes. The more I found, the more I dug. Talk about the joy of discovery! My first attempt at a potato patch produced so much produce my brothers and I spent most of the next day hauling treasure-laden sacks into our basement for storage.

Harvest is worth the wait! How do I know? My family feasted on delicious, home grown potatoes all year long!

In Matthew 9:37-38, Jesus told His disciples, *"The harvest is plentiful, but the workers are few. Therefore beseech the Lord of the harvest to send out workers into His harvest."* The harvest the Lord alluded to wasn't potatoes. The harvest field that is ripe and ready for harvesting is the world of lost souls.

Note that Jesus didn't say to pray for the harvest. He said the harvest is already ripe and plentiful. He told us to pray for laborers. Why? Because it needs to be reaped and *the workers are few*. What an indictment, then, and now!

The only thing that has changed since Jesus uttered these words is the world's population. The harvest is even more plentiful today. There is still a shortage of workers — not nearly enough laborers to bring the lost safely into God's fold. In this 21st Century, the Lord is still looking for soul-winners. We are to pray to Him that more workers will get out into the field.

If you've ever led someone to Christ, you know the harvest is worth the wait. There's no greater joy than the soul-winner's joy! (Luke 15:7). Souls are worth working for. But harvesting is hard work. Just ask anyone who has lived and worked on a farm. Harvest season demands focus, dedication, sacrifice, endurance and a commitment to do whatever it takes to get the crop into the barn.

If that loved one that you have prayed for years becomes born-again into the Kingdom of God, receiving the free gift of eternal life, then the wait will have been worth it, won't it? If that unbelieving neighbor or co-worker you've been witnessing to surrenders to Jesus and is born again, it's worth the wait, isn't it? People coming to Christ are worth waiting for.

I will always remember one young couple in their early 20s. They were living together without being married, doing and dealing drugs, partying night and day, deeply in debt, and not getting along at all. She had become pregnant and given birth to a precious little girl.

This young mother became burdened for her baby and the environment they had brought her into. The responsibility of raising a child began to weigh heavily on her heart. She knew there had to be a better way to live.

Their neighbor was one of our church's faithful soul-winners who visited with those who needed the Lord. God put it on her heart to start praying for this young couple across the street. One afternoon, she took them some homemade cookies and invited them to church.

The young man openly scoffed at her, but the young woman was hungry for the Lord. She attended one of our services while he was away. Tears streamed down her face as she sat in the pew and listened to the Pastor tell of Jesus' love and the power He has to change lives.

When she shared her experience with the young man, he became angry and hostile, forbidding her to have anything to do with "those Jesus freaks."

Their neighbor kept praying and sharing with this young woman whenever she could.

One day after a horrible domestic quarrel, the young woman called my office and asked if a pastor could come visit. She was afraid and needed to talk to someone. When I met their neighbor at the house, the young woman was alone. She poured out her problems, shared her concerns, and then opened her heart to hear about Jesus. That afternoon, she received Christ into her life as her personal Savior and Lord!

She started attending church regularly. He griped and groaned, but he let her go. We kept praying that his heart would soon soften. She asked him if I could come to visit with them. She wanted him to meet me. He said I could come, but he wouldn't be there.

On the appointed night, I took a couple of people with me to their home. He wasn't there. But while we were sharing with her, he showed up. Decked out in leather jacket and boots, a half-smoked cigarette dangling from his lips and beer in hand, Mr. I'm-not-going-to-be-there shoved the front door open, sauntered across the living room, reached out to shake my hand and said, "Evening, preacher. How the 'blank' are you? Would you like a beer?"

First impressions are lasting impressions. I can still see him standing there mocking my presence, trying to intimidate me into a confrontation. Mustering up all the self-control I could, I looked him in the eye, smiled, and replied, "Good evening, sir, my name is Steve. No thank you, I had a Pepsi before I came." My calm response took the wind out of his sail…at least for the moment.

She introduced the others. We chatted for a while. As I turned the conversation to talk about Jesus, the young man pretended not to listen and took verbal shots at me whenever he could. He was antagonistic to the Lord and extremely hostile to preachers and the church. He said the only reason I came was to get their money. He knew that I knew that they didn't have any, so it was just bluff.

I countered his rudeness and spiritual ignorance with compassion and godly wisdom. As the evening wound down, I thanked him for allowing us to visit in his home, invited him to a church service, and told him I would be praying for him. He sat silently in his overstuffed chair, sipping on his beer, sneering at me as she saw us to the door.

Their relationship worsened.

They experienced some really tough times while he tried to fight off the conviction the Holy Spirit was bringing to his heart. One night, he ran into serious trouble. Some of his drug buddies beat him up and stole his drugs and money. He went home and took his frustration and anger out on her. She fled across the street with the baby, seeking safety in her new friend's home.

They separated. Alone, beaten-up, and broke, he had some time to think about how miserable his life really was. The Lord continued to work on his heart. The next weekend he showed up at church. He sat near the back, hoping not to be seen. After service, he quietly slipped out. I called him the next day to see how he was doing, and asked if I could come to see him. He agreed.

I'd been praying for this young man for weeks. The Gospel seed had been sown in the soil of his heart a number of times. He was now in deep personal crisis. As I drove over to his house, I prayed that this might be the hour when he would surrender to Jesus.

A much humbler man met me at the door. He didn't offer me a beer this time, either. Looking like a man who had lost everything, he asked me how he could be saved. I shared the plan of salvation. When I asked him if he wanted to ask Jesus into his heart, he broke down. He wept, and I wept with him. I took his rough, tough-guy hands into mine and led him in the sinner's prayer. He gave his life to Jesus, and Jesus changed his life.

He immediately started coming to church. The young couple made things right and were married in the Lord. They got involved in a small group Bible study. They began witnessing to their old drug buddies and partying friends.

He even set up a meeting in a friend's home, asking the guys to come and hear about Jesus. He invited me and another pastor to come. Thirty-five of his unsaved former buddies showed up and seven of them were saved that night.

One by one, many of this young man's old friends came to Christ!

The harvest is, indeed, worth waiting for. These two precious people were worth the wait. They're going to heaven because laborers prayed, worked, and waited for them to receive Jesus. And because of them, a whole bunch of their friends will spend eternity in heaven too.

When it comes to waiting for the salvation of people you are trying to reach for the Lord, never become weary. Keep praying. Keep witnessing. Keep sharing God's love with them.

The field is ripe. Harvest will come. Souls coming to Christ are worth waiting for.

Christ's Return

Jesus is coming back! How do we know? The Bible tells us so. After His ascension to heaven, a pair of supernatural spokesman told the disciples He would be back.

> *After He had said these things, He was lifted up while they were looking on, and a cloud received Him out of their sight. And as they were gazing intently into the sky while He was going, behold, two men in white clothing stood beside them. They also said, "Men of Galilee, why do you stand looking into the sky? This Jesus, who has been taken up from you into heaven, will come in just the same way as you have watched Him go into heaven."*
>
> Acts 1:9-11

On the night of Christ's betrayal, Caiaphas the High Priest, personally interrogated the Lord. He asked Jesus whether or not He was the Son of God. Matthew 26:63-64 records Jesus' response:

> *Jesus kept silent. And the high priest said to Him, "I adjure You by the living God, that You tell us whether You are the Christ, the Son of God." Jesus said to him, "You have said it yourself, nevertheless I tell*

you, hereafter you will see the Son of Man sitting at the right hand of Power, and coming on the clouds of heaven."

Other scriptural references support His glorious second coming:

I kept looking in the night visions, and behold, with the clouds of heaven One like a Son of Man was coming. And He came up to the Ancient of Days and was presented before Him. And to Him was given dominion, glory and a kingdom, that all the peoples, nations, and men of every language might serve Him. His dominion is an everlasting dominion which will not pass away; and His kingdom is one which will not be destroyed.

Daniel 7:13-14

In those days, after that tribulation, the sun will be darkened and the moon will not give its light, and the stars will be falling from heaven, and the powers that are in the heavens will be shaken. Then they will see the Son of Man coming in the clouds with great power and glory.

Mark 13:24-26

Behold, He is coming with the clouds, and every eye will see Him, even those who pierced Him; and all the tribes of the earth will mourn over Him. So it is to be. Amen.

Revelation 1:7

Reading those verses gets me really excited about Christ's return to earth. I am so ready for His second coming that there are days when I look toward heaven, lift up my hands, and echo John's last words at the end of God's Word in Revelation 22:20. *"Amen. Come Lord Jesus."*

The next great event in redemption's plan is Christ's second coming. When He returns, He will set everybody straight and make everything right. Study the scriptures for yourself and see what they tell us Jesus will do when He comes back for His bride. Then you, too, will find yourself saying, "Lord Jesus, come quickly!"

I can hardly wait to see Jesus. But I will have to wait. So will you. Paul tells us in 1 Thessalonians 1:10 that we are to *wait for His Son from heaven, whom He raised from the dead, that is Jesus, who delivers us from the wrath to come.* His coming is certainly worth waiting for.

We need to wait well while we wait for Jesus to return from heaven. Waiting well means watching, worshipping, working, and witnessing faithfully while we listen for the blast of God's trumpet that will announce His Son's triumphant return.

We wait well by walking by faith. Jesus will be looking for people with faith when He returns. In Luke 18:8 the Lord said, *"When the Son of Man comes, will He find faith on the earth?"* Everything in life worth waiting for, including Christ's return, is to be waited for with faith.

Are you waiting for Jesus to come back? More importantly, are you ready for His return? The only way to be ready is to be certain that you have put your faith in Jesus, personally receiving Him as your Savior and Lord. (See in this order: John 3:3; John 14:6; Romans 3:23, 6:23; Romans 10:9-10; John 1:12; Revelation 3:20; and 1 John 5:11-13.) If you haven't been born again, stop right now, bow your head and pray this simple prayer:

> *Heavenly Father, I realize I need you in my life. I know that You love me. You proved it by sending Your only Son Jesus to live on the earth, die on a cross, and be raised from the grave so I could be saved. Lord Jesus, I believe with all my heart that You are God's Son and that He raised You from the dead. I ask you to forgive my sins, cleanse me from all unrighteousness, and to come into my heart right now as my personal Savior and Lord. From this moment on, I choose to put my faith in You and to obey Your Word. Thank You, Jesus, for loving me and giving me eternal life. Amen*

If you prayed that prayer, Congratulations! You've just been born again. You're a child of the Living God. Welcome to the family! You're now ready for Christ's glorious return. He's coming for you. Follow up your decision by attending a Christ-centered, Bible preaching church, and keeping your eyes on the clouds!

Jesus is coming back soon. His coming is worth watching and waiting for.

Heaven

Jesus is returning to earth to take His children back with Him to heaven. Have you ever thought about what heaven will be like? Here's what some children think:

Heaven is sort of big and they sit around and play harps. I don't know how to play a harp, but I suppose I better start learning that dumb thing pretty soon.

David, age seven

It's like a blue sky with clouds and it's a really fun place because you can play on the clouds. You have to stay away from the edges though, or you will fall off.

Chuck, age eight

I would like to go to heaven someday because I know my brother won't be there!

Tammy, age seven

Heaven's a place where there's money laying around. You can just pick it up and play with it and buy things. I'm gonna buy a basketball and play basketball with my great-great grandmother.

Jason, age six

My personal all-time favorite thought comes from a little girl named Deborah: Heaven should be the happiest part of my dead life.

What will heaven be like? It will be wonderful. I don't know if we'll play on the clouds, but I do know from God's Word that heaven is home for His children.

This earth isn't the believer's permanent dwelling place. Paul wrote in Philippians 3:20, *"Our citizenship is in heaven, from which also we eagerly wait for a Savior, the Lord Jesus Christ."*

Heaven, not earth, is the Christian's homeland. Before the Lord left, He told the disciples He was going away to prepare a place for them. He exhorted them not to worry or be afraid, but to believe and trust in Him. Jesus went ahead to prepare a heavenly home for us (John 14:1-6). The Father's house (in heaven) has many dwelling places under its roof. Its accommodations are out of this world. There is a specially designed place for each one of God's sons and daughters. At this very moment, Jesus is getting the Father's house ready for the arrival of His kids!

Biblically, heaven is a lot of wonderful things. It's a place of worship, praise, and adoration (Revelation 4-5, 15, 19); a place of everlasting life (Revelation 22);

a place of reward (Matthew 25). A place of safety, security, peace and joy where there is no pain, no crying or tears, no death, and no mourning (Revelation 21). The best thing of all about heaven is that we will fellowship with Jesus forever! We will see Him face to face and live in His holy presence for all eternity.

Do you know what else will be wonderful about heaven? No more waiting. That's right. Nothing more to wait for. "Hurry up and wait" will be history. No more waiting around for something to happen. Think about it: no lines in heaven! I once heard someone say they thought that in hell the damned will stand all day every day in long lines, inching their way ever-so-slowly toward the front. As soon as they reach the head of the line, they'll be whisked all the way to the back again. Stand in line, move up, get to the front, boom!, back to the rear….repeated over, and over, and over again for all eternity. Sounds like eternal punishment to me!

There will be no need for waiting in heaven because everything will be complete. We'll have everything we could ever desire because we'll have the Father, the Son, and the Holy Spirit in all their blessed fullness. Won't that be absolutely awesome!

Heaven and Homecoming

Heaven will be homecoming for those who love the Lord.

Evangelist Dave Roever served in the United States Army during the Vietnam War. While patrolling along the banks of an isolated river, his gunboat was came under heavy enemy fire. Outnumbered and outgunned, Dave and his comrades fought furiously for their lives.

In his book *Scarred*, Roever wrote about that fateful day that altered his life forever. A white phosphorous grenade exploded directly in front of him, blowing off one side of his face and parts of his hands, and burning him with second and third degree burns over most of his mangled body. In his book, Roever shares the graphic details of his traumatic injuries, the healing process, and his recovery.

Roever's injuries ignited another war in his life: the fight for faith. Through the agonizing ordeal of pain and disabling disfigurement, Dave Roever put his faith completely and unconditionally in Jesus Christ. Though his body is horribly scarred on the outside, on the inside, his heart is healed and scar free.

He now travels the world as a dynamic proclamation of God's unconditional love, sharing his personal story of victory over adversity through faith in Jesus Christ.

When Dave Roever came to preach and minister at our church, it was my first personal exposure to him. Seeing what had happened to his body, my heart went out to him, knowing how hard it must be to deal with the consequences of his war injuries on a daily basis. But my temptation to feel sorry for him vanished as I watched him minister freely and powerfully out of his former pain. Here was a man of deep love, faith, and gratitude to God for sparing his life so he could witness for Jesus.

Dave Roever did something that day I will never forget. He talked openly to the congregation about the Vietnam War and how, while traveling throughout America, he met thousands of Vietnam veterans every year. He shared how many of them still feel unloved, unappreciated, and unwelcome in America. They fought in a very unpopular conflict. Because the nation was bitterly divided over the war in Southeast Asia, no hero's welcome awaited the men and women who served and sacrificed in Vietnam.

Roever bragged on and expressed his love for the vets. Then he called for all who had served in the Vietnam War to come to the platform. About 20 of us made our way from our seats to the front. Some of us were dressed in suit and tie, others in tee shirts and jeans. Long hair, short hair, professional, non-professional. Three of the men limped to the platform, one using a cane because of his war wounds. One veteran in particular caught my attention as he climbed the steps to the pulpit. He looked so sad, like he didn't have a friend in the world.

Roever personally welcomed each one of us, reaching out with his fingerless and partially thumbed hand to shake our hands. He grabbed each of us in turn and gave us a big bear hug, looking us right in the eye, affirming us, and telling us that he loved us. Then he turned to the congregation of 2,500 people and invited everyone to stand. With tears streaming down his scarred face, he asked them on the count of three to shout, "Welcome Home!"

And they did. The congregation responded with a spontaneous chorus of hearty welcome that nearly swept us off our feet. Again, the crowd shouted an emotion charged, "Welcome Home!" Their standing ovation of acceptance and approval brought down emotional barriers that had been erected over the previous 30 years.

God's healing love and the comforting presence of the Holy Spirit broke out all over the auditorium. What a healing moment — a sacred time of emotional and spiritual release and restoration! It was a holy visitation of God who moved to touch our hearts, heal our hurts, and set our spirits free!

Welcome home! Welcome home! That's what the heavenly host will be shouting when the Lord's soldiers, the victorious veteran's of the good fight of faith, march proudly through the gates of heaven. God's heroes will be home at last.

Going home to heaven is something worth waiting for.

There are so many good things worth waiting for. Will you wait for the good things God has planned for you? Waiting is up to you.

> *As for me, I'm like a green olive tree in the house of God; I trust in the lovingkindness of God forever and ever. I will give You thanks forever, because You have done it, and I will wait on Your name, for it is good, in the presence of Your godly ones.*
>
> Psalm 52:8-9

CHAPTER 13
WAITING FOR YOUR DREAMS TO COME TRUE

You'll never succeed beyond your wildest dreams unless you have some wild dreams. Daring to dream is daring to live. God wants us to dream dreams that will not only influence the here and now, but will be significant enough that the impact of their fulfillment will be felt throughout eternity. Pursuing a God-given dream energizes us and motivates us like nothing else can to accomplish something meaningful in life.

Our Creator is the original dreamer. If you don't think so, just look at creation. This magnificent universe that our Maker created for us to live in is a divine dream turned reality. Almighty God, the dreamer of dreams, is the One who unveils visions and delivers dreams to those who desire to live on the edge of the eternal.

Do you have a dream? If you do, does God to fit in the picture? If we don't possess dreams that are beyond our grasp, then we don't need God. Some people pursue dreams so small that they can be accomplished without divine intervention. A dream that can be achieved without the assistance of the Almighty is more like a human desire than a heavenly dream.

The dreams that matter most, those loft, spirit-stretching dreams that have the potential to change people's lives forever, require the Lord's participation to be successful. Therefore, we need to dream great dreams and attempt something so big, that unless God intervenes, it is bound to fail!

The Bible has several things to say about our dreams and the way we approach their fulfillment.

Proverbs 3:5-6: *Trust in the LORD with all your heart, and lean not on your own understanding; in all your ways acknowledge him, and He shall direct your paths.* NKJV

Jeremiah 29:11: *"I know the plans I have for you," declares the Lord, "plans to prosper you and not to harm you, plans to give you hope and a future."* NIV

Hebrews 11:1: *Faith is the substance of things hoped for, the evidence of things not seen.* KJV

Psalm 37:4: *Delight yourself in the L<small>ORD</small>, and he will give you the desires of your heart.*

Proverbs 29:18: *Where there is no vision [dream, revelation, oracle],*[12] *the people perish.* KJV

WHAT JOSEPH'S STORY TEACHES US ABOUT DREAMS

The Bible is a book about dreams and dreamers. Genesis 37-50 records Joseph's journey toward the fulfillment of his God-given dream. There was no way the dream he dreamed could come to pass without the intervening hand of the Lord. Joseph walked by faith and waited on God for 13 years before his dream was fulfilled.

His personal testimony of trusting in God, no matter what happens, can teach us a thing or two about what to do and what not to do in situations when all we can do is wait. We need to understand five things regarding what happened to Joseph while he waited for his dream to come true.

WE NEED TO BE VERY DISCERNING ABOUT SHARING OUR DREAMS.

Joseph's dream got Him Thrown into a pit! (Genesis 37)

Joseph, Jacob's 11th son, was 17 years old when the Lord gave him a dream. He was the oldest of the two sons of Jacob's favorite wife, Rachel, now dead.

Young and naïve, Joseph shared his God-given vision with his brothers. It got him into some pretty serious trouble. Jacob's family was about as dysfunctional as you can get, and Joseph had already made his brothers angry when he *brought back a bad report* about them to their father.

His brothers knew Joseph was their father's favorite; but when Jacob showed his special love and affection for Joseph by giving him a multi-colored coat — a coat designed not for someone who worked, but for someone who ruled — *they hated him and could not speak to him on friendly terms.*

Then Joseph dreamed, and revealed his dream to his brothers. *They hated him even more* when he told them that he'd dreamed he would rule over them.

Hatred burning in their hearts, Joseph's brothers mocked him (*here comes this dreamer*), and *plotted...to put him to death*. Had not one brother, Reuben, intervened on Joseph's behalf, they would have murdered him.

Heeding Reuben's advice, the brothers took Joseph and threw him into a deep pit…and covered up their vengeful deed by lying to their father.

Jacob mourned and grieved for many days after receiving the bad news about Joseph's death. Even though he had rebuked Joseph for his self-centered, self-promoting dream, the loss of his favorite son broke the elderly patriarch's heart.

Joseph's dream brought out the worst in his family. Envy, jealousy, rebuke, revenge, hatred, plans for murder, lying and deceit rewarded the young dreamer who dared to share his dream. Joseph experienced first-hand from his own household the age-old truth that dreamers will always experience opposition. His brothers did their best to extinguish his dream. Having decided to kill him and deposit his body in the pit, they said, *"Then let us see what will become of his dreams!"* Their strategy: Kill the dreamer, kill the dream.

Visionless people seek to extinguish the fire of those who do dream. They're found everywhere, lurking in the spiritual shadows, waiting for the next opportunity to oppose those who dare to dream. The devil and his demons, jealous relatives, envious friends, and critical-spirited colleagues will attack the dreamer with their negativity. Like wet blankets, they smother and snuff out the flames of the divine desire that burns in the visionary's heart.

We must be careful about how and to whom we reveal our dreams. Because they can be misunderstood, misjudged, mismanaged, and misused, not everyone can be trusted with our dreams. Opposition will raise its ugly head. It comes with the territory when you step out from the visionless crowd to pursue a great dream for God. If you're going to follow a vision, expect someone or something to try and discourage you. You can count on it. But God's dreams don't die.

The Lord knew exactly what He was doing with Joseph. He used Reuben to prevent Joseph's death. Then, at exactly the right time, a caravan of Ishmaelite traders on their way to Egypt passed by the pit. Joseph's brothers, greedy as well as jealous, sold him into slavery. Divine detours are part of dreams coming true. Maybe an all expenses paid trip to Egypt wasn't that bad for Joseph after all!

Our dreams can take us to some interesting places.

Joseph's dream took him to Potiphar's house. (Genesis 39:1-18).

Joseph, an Israelite, was now traveling with a band of Ishmaelites. Abandoned by his brothers, and thought dead by his father, Joseph ended up in Egypt. Potiphar, an Egyptian officer directly under Pharaoh, purchased Joseph from the Ishmaelites at a slave auction. He took Joseph home and put him to work managing the affairs of his household. In a matter days, Joseph the dreamer, went from favorite son of Jacob in Israel to foreign slave of Potiphar in Egypt!

Joseph's dream was beginning to look like a nightmare. How could a slave in Egypt become a ruler in Israel?

I don't know about you, but I don't get excited about highway detours. When I'm heading toward my destination and a detour sign points me in another direction, I start asking some questions: Where does this road go? How far out of the way will it take me? How much time will I lose going this way? How long will it be before it links back up with the main road?

None of us like detours. But they usually serve a purpose. Detours direct us away from construction zones that can delay us, take us out of the path of dangerous accidents and hazardous road conditions that could harm us.

Detours may take us out of our way for a while, but they always lead us back to the main road. Along the way detours provide new scenery for us to enjoy!

Joseph didn't travel to Egypt alone. God went with His dreamer. Even Potiphar recognized that *the Lord was with him and how the Lord caused all that he did to prosper in his hand.* Though Joseph's dream appeared to be derailed, the Lord travelled with Joseph to Egypt and Potiphar's house. Note in verses 3-6 that the Lord's presence made Joseph prosper in his work. Joseph was so blessed by God that he became a successful slave. Potiphar's house also prospered. Joseph's master rewarded him by making him the manager of his business.

People might desert us, but God never does. When dreamers dream, non-dreamers drop out along the way and leave us all alone. Just when Joseph had every reason to have a pity-party in Potiphar's house, the Lord showed up to bless, prosper, and make him a success. God never abandons his dreamers. (See Hebrews 13:5.) From start to finish, He walks with his dreamers until the dream is fulfilled. Other people who are part of the process — whether we know it or not — will recognize God's presence with the dreamer. God blesses his dreamers so those around them can assist them along the road to achieving their dream.

Dreams can be delayed, detoured, and derailed. The discipline of delay builds our character. Patience with the process, waiting for God's timing, is a mark of spiritual maturity. Detours teach us to trust God with the bends in the road and the side roads we don't understand. And don't forget, detours will take us back to the main road where we can get back on track pursuing our dream. A bend in the road is not the end of the road. But we have to be on guard against derailing our dream. Serious consequences can occur when our dream jumps the track.

Joseph's commitment to his dream was severely tested in Potiphar's house. Mrs. Potiphar had a problem. It's called lust. While Joseph faithfully carried out his responsibilities and behaved himself around the house, Potiphar's wife conducted herself in a shameful manner by tempting handsome young Joseph.

Joseph refused her invitations to, *"Lie with me."* Still, she approached him every day. Under constant pressure from her persistent attempts to seduce him, God's dreamer never compromised his conviction. Not once! He resisted her seductive advances for all the right reasons. Genesis 39:8-9 tell us:

> *He refused and said to his master's wife, "Behold, with me here, my master does not concern himself with anything in the house, and he has put all that he owns in my charge. There is no one greater in this house than I, and he has withheld nothing from me except you, because you are his wife. How then could I do this great evil and sin against God?"*

Joseph did what was right. God's dreamers don't sin against God by doing things that break God's moral law. Joseph respected Potiphar. But more importantly, he reverenced (feared) the Lord.

Spurned by Joseph's stand for righteousness and his rejection of her advances, Mrs. Potiphar falsely accused him of sexual misconduct. Joseph went to jail. But the Lord worked through all of this to position him so he would be in the place where he could be promoted so his dream could be fulfilled.

Joseph waited on the Lord, knowing his integrity and uprightness would preserve him.

His position at Potiphar's house had been a test to see if he would stay on track. To rule rightly, a man has to be righteous and moral. The devil knows that sin derails and destroys dreams. Dreamers have to be on guard against compromising their beliefs and giving in to the temptations around them. They have to keep themselves detached from other people's nightmares.

The surest way to derail your dream, and maybe even destroy it, is to sin. When David committed adultery with Bathsheba and had her husband murdered to cover his sin (2 Samuel 11-12), horrible consequences followed. King David, Bathsheba, their families, the nation of Israel, and God's great name suffered tremendously because of his sin. It was a long, painful road to restoration before David got back on track and started dreaming again (Psalm 51).

Joseph didn't let Mrs. Potiphar's problem become his problem. Joseph walked with God, worked for God, was blessed and prospered by God, stood strong for God, and waited on God again as life in Egypt sent him on another detour that appeared to drive the dream even further from fruition.

When a dream comes to a standstill, keep serving the Lord.

Joseph's dream landed him in prison. (Genesis 39:19-41:13)

Falsely accused, unfairly judged, and unmercifully thrown into jail, Joseph sat behind locked bars as a man without a family, country, career, resources, or a foreseeable future. His trust in the Lord was about the only thing he had left.

His faith was all he needed!

Dreamers have to keep believing if their dreams are to come true. Joseph not only believed, he also behaved like a man of faith while imprisoned.

While Joseph was in jail, the Lord was with him, extended kindness to him, and gave him favor with the chief jailer: Scripture tells us when the head jailer made Joseph a supervisor in charge of the other prisoners *the Lord was with him; and whatever he did, the Lord made to prosper.* At the lowest time of Joseph's life, the Lord was right there taking good care of His dreamer. God was positioning Joseph for the promotion that comes to those who remain faithful to the dream.

What did Joseph do while he waited behind bars? He ministered to others when he could have used some ministry himself. Instead of sitting around his cell complaining about all the bad things that had happened to him, he chose to take his eyes off himself, keep them on the Lord and serve those around him.

He was concerned enough about the baker and cupbearer who were in prison for disappointing Pharaoh to ask them, *"Why are your faces so sad today?"*

He explained the meanings of their dreams. And he asked the cupbearer, who would be restored to his position of service at Pharaoh's side, to remember him, put in a good word for him, and try to get him out of jail.

> *Only keep me in mind when it goes well with you, and please do me a kindness by mentioning me to Pharaoh, and get me out of this house. For I was in fact kidnapped from the land of the Hebrews, and even here I have done nothing that they should have put me into the dungeon.*
>
> Genesis 40:14-15

The scenarios played out exactly as he said they would. But Joseph had to wait in jail two more years before the cupbearer remembered the dreamer who correctly interpreted his dream.

An absent-minded man may have forgotten about Joseph, but God didn't forget. He remembered his faithful servant. Isaiah 44:21 states: *"Remember these things, O Jacob, and Israel, for you are My servant; I have formed you, you are My servant, O Israel, you will not be forgotten by Me."* Isn't it reassuring to know that the Lord always knows where His servants/dreamers are? God also knows what needs to happen to get them to the place where they need to be.

THE LORD USES OUR SPIRITUAL GIFTS AND NATURAL TALENTS TO MEET NEEDS.

Joseph's detour took him to the palace (Genesis 41:14)

While Joseph was still incarcerated, Pharaoh had a dream that deeply troubled him. Actually it was one dream with two parts. He summoned the magicians and wise men of Egypt. None of them could tell Pharaoh what the dream meant. This reminded the Pharaoh's cupbearer of Joseph. He told Pharaoh about the young Hebrew named Joseph who had correctly interpreted his dream and that of the baker!

> *Then Pharaoh sent and called for Joseph, and they hurriedly brought him out of the dungeon; and when he had shaved himself and changed his clothes, he came to Pharaoh. Pharaoh said to Joseph, "I have had a dream, but no one can interpret it; and I have heard it said about you, that when you hear a dream you can interpret it." Joseph then answered Pharaoh, saying, "It is not in me; God will give Pharaoh a favorable answer."*
>
> Genesis 41:14-16

Reading the rest of the story in chapter 41 reveals that Joseph did indeed interpret the dream. His godly wisdom was recognized, and resulted in Joseph being promoted to second in command over all Egypt. He would oversee the collection and distribution of food during the bountiful, and famine years.

From prisoner to prime minister in one afternoon — that's moving up the career ladder in a hurry! From the pit, to Potiphar's house, to prison, to Pharaoh's palace. Strategic positioning by God brought Joseph to the fruition of his long, frustrating wait.

Joseph's dream was coming true. Egypt needed Joseph for what God had prepared him to do. At 30 years of age, he was now a ruler. Men bowed before him.

The Bible tells us in Proverbs 18:16 that *a man's gift makes room for him and brings him before great men.* And in Proverbs 22:29 we find these words: *Do you see a man skilled in his work? He will stand before kings; he will not stand before obscure men.*

Working diligently and using his gifts as the Lord directed, Joseph waited faithfully for 13 years before his dream came true. Then, at the right time, his God-given gift brought Joseph into the presence of the one person on earth who could put him in the place where he could fulfill his dream.

Pharaoh needed a dream interpreted. Joseph's gift was interpreting dreams. Pharaoh's need combined with Joseph's gift equals ministry.

God is the giver of gifts. Our gifts make room for us. That's why it is so vital to keep using our gifts while we wait for doors of opportunity to open.

Note that Joseph gave the Lord the credit for all that happened through him. *"Do not interpretations belong to God...."*; *"It is not in me, God will give Pharaoh a favorable answer...."*; *"God has told Pharaoh what He is about to do...."*; *"The matter is determined by God, and God will quickly bring it to pass."*

Before the famine came, Joseph married and had two sons. He named them Manasseh (making to forget) and Ephraim (fruitfulness) because, he said, *"God has made me forget all my trouble and all my father's household"* and *"God has made me fruitful in the land of my affliction."*

When Joseph's brothers eventually came to Egypt in search of food, they found forgiveness from a compassionate brother who said to them, *"Do not be afraid, for am I in God's place? As for you, you meant evil against me, but God meant it for good in order to bring about this present result, to preserve many people alive."* In every instance where God worked on his behalf, Joseph gave God the glory!

God never wastes His gifts. Often, when our dreams are delayed and we seem to be sitting on the shelf, out of service, watching everybody else do their thing for the Lord, we're tempted to think that our gifts don't matter and will never be used again. That's just not true. At exactly the right moment, God promoted Joseph to a position of service where his gifts could be used in ways he would never have imagined were possible.

Do you desire to be promoted in God's work? Pray about it. Wait for His leading. Then seek people and organizations that need your gifts. Promotion in the Kingdom of God is founded on who you know (the Lord) and what you do (your gifts). Don't become discouraged with the process of lining up needs with gifts. The Lord knows how to put needs and gifts together.

I like to refer to Joseph's meteoric rise to rulership as a "slingshot" promotion.

My great-grandfather had a woodworking shop attached to his garage. He presented me with a handmade slingshot on one of my birthdays. He had engraved my initials on the smooth, varnished handle. But for me, what really made my slingshot slick was the big, elastic rubber band attached to the handle. Load a stone, marble or whatever into the sling, pull it back, and fire away! It was fun knocking pop cans off the fence!

What I enjoyed most was standing in the middle of Clark Park near my home and pulling the sling back with all my strength. I would stretch the rubber band as far as my little arms could and give that rock wings as I let go. It thrilled me to see how high and far into space my trusty slingshot could hurl that stone.

I discovered the secret of rubber bands because of that slingshot: Rubber bands are of little value until they're stretched. The farther back I pulled the sling, the farther forward the rock flew. The more you stretch a rubber band, the tighter it gets, the more energy it releases.

Joseph's sling was pulled backed at the pit, stretched further back at Potiphar's house, and stretched to the limit when he was imprisoned. When the Lord released it, Pharaoh sent for Joseph and, just like that, a nobody became a somebody everybody knew about!

Joseph's ride to the top fulfilled a dream that met a number of needs. Joseph saved Egypt and the world from starvation; he saved his family; he was fully restored to his relatives (recorded in Genesis 42-50); and his wise leadership provided for the continuation of God's covenant with Israel.

What became of the dreamer who was forsaken by his family, sold into slavery, mistreated by the world, and seemingly forgotten by God? His dream came true! And, Joseph's dream took him to the Promised Land. (Genesis 50:22-26 and Exodus 13:19)

G OD ALWAYS FINISHES WHAT H E STARTS.

Scripture supports this statement:

Isaiah 46:11	*Truly I have spoken; truly I will bring it to pass. I have planned it, surely I will do it.*
Psalm 138:8	*The LORD will accomplish what concerns me.*
Isaiah 25:1	*O Lord, You are my God; I will exalt You, I will give thanks to Your name: for You have worked wonders, plans formed long ago, with perfect faithfulness.*
1 Thessalonians 5:24	*Faithful is He who calls you, and He will bring it to pass.*
Philippians 1:6	*I am confident of this very thing, that He who began a good work in you will perfect it until the day of Christ Jesus.*

Divine dreams progress through a three-step process. First, the dream is born. Next the dream appears to die. Finally the dream is resurrected! We've seen how Joseph passed through these steps pursuing his God-given dream. The dream was born in his heart at home. It appeared to die in the pit, Potiphar's house, and prison. Then the dream came to life at Pharaoh's palace. Birth, death, resurrection…

Those who see their dreams come true come to terms with the process. They willingly submit themselves to it, totally depending on the goodness and grace of God to successfully see them through.

If you're currently dreaming a God-given dream, whatever stage you find yourself in, the Lord is with you, and He will bring your dream to fulfillment!

Let's summarize Joseph's success.

- The Lord gave Joseph a dream.
- God was with Joseph every step of the way. He prepared each step Joseph would take. He strategically positioned Joseph in the right places with the right people at just the right time.
- Joseph always did what was right no matter what price he had to pay.

- Joseph had a heart for people and ministered to their needs with his gifts.
- Joseph accepted Pharaoh's promotion and used his position to glorify God and be a blessing to men.
- Joseph possessed a teachable spirit, learning valuable lessons from his ordeal that made him a wise leader and righteous ruler.
- Joseph did what was right and forgave his brothers for their sin against him.
- Joseph never gave up on his dream. He kept his faith in the Faithful One who finishes what He starts.

Often a winner is a dreamer who never gave up.

Americans will most likely remember the 1996 Summer Olympic games held in Atlanta, Georgia two diverse events: the deadly bombing that shook crowded Olympic Park, and the courageous performance of a petite, but powerful young gymnast named Kerri Strug, who catapulted the American women's gymnastic team to their first ever team gold medal.

The competition for the team gold was tight. Entering the final day of the event, the vault, the United States was in second place but in position to win if one of the team's two super stars, Shannon Miller and Dominique Dawes performed well. Neither did. Strug, who had stood in the shadows of Miller and Dawes for years, suddenly found herself in the Olympic spotlight, her team's last hope for the first place medal.

Two vaults stood between her and every Olympic athlete's dream, the gold medal. On the first vault Kerri injured her left ankle. As her score flashed up, her coaches couldn't figure fast enough if it was enough to win the gold. So, ankle swelling rapidly, Kerri Strug made her way to the end of the runway, for a second and final vault. It needed to be almost flawless.

She ran full-speed toward the vaulting box, grimacing with pain as she took each step. Hitting the springboard, she pushed herself off the vault, propelling her body skyward, twisting. The crowd went wild as she stuck the landing perfectly. She'd done it!

But unknown to the crowd, Kerri had suffered a third degree lateral sprain and tendon damage in the first landing. Before her score flashed on the scoreboard, she lifted her injured foot off the mat, saluted the judges, lowered herself to mat, and started crawling toward the sidelines.

Kerri Strug had made that second vault, knowing full well that she had seriously injured her ankle and would have to land on it again with her full weight. But an opportunity of a lifetime was before her. Even though it meant risking further personal injury, Kerri, having stared destiny in the face, gave it her all, and the gold medal was placed around her neck.

Kerri's injuries forced her to withdraw from the rest of the competition. During an interview the next day, she said she'd been waiting in the wings for years for her dream to come true. Despite having had four different coaches, inconsistent training in various gyms, a serious injury in an Arizona pre-Olympic trial that nearly crippled her for life, and standing in the shadows of Miller and Dawes, she had kept dreaming and working. She went on to say that this was not the way had she thought it would happen, but her dream had come true.

The day came for Kerri Strug when preparation and perseverance met opportunity. Courage and a strong will to win carried a dedicated, determined dreamer to the gold medal ceremony.

Dreams frequently don't come to pass the way we think they will. Maybe you can identify with Kerri Strug's story. You've been waiting in the wings for a long time, standing in the shadows of others, working your hardest to be the best you can be at what God has called you to do. Obstacles seem to pop up everywhere, tempting you to become weary of the process and stop dreaming! But the desire to go for the gold God has for you keeps burning in your heart. So when will your dream come true?

The Lord excels in making things turn out in wonderful ways that exceed our wildest imagination! Paul wrote in Ephesians 3:20-21:

> *Now to Him who is able to do far abundantly beyond all that we ask or think, according to the power that works within us, to Him be the glory in the church and in Christ Jesus to all generations forever and ever. Amen.*

God has something for you to do that nobody else can do. A dream, tailored specifically for you, waits to be fulfilled. He is more than able to make it come true. All He needs is you…a determined dreamer who will trust Him to do what He says He is going to do.

Fellow believer, faithfully wait on the Lord. Courageously follow Him wherever He leads you. Your day of unbelievable opportunity will come when all the preparation and perseverance pays off. You will be recognized and promoted to the place of service where you can spend the rest of your life doing what you do best for the glory of God.

The fulfillment of your dream is worth waiting for. Wait for your dream to come true.

> *The vision is yet for the appointed time; it hastens toward the goal, and it will not fail. Though it tarries, wait for it; for it will certainly come, it will not delay.*
>
> Habakkuk 2:3

Conclusion
It's Never Too Late to Learn How to Wait!

Whatever was written in earlier times was written for our instruction, so that through perseverance and encouragement of the Scriptures we might have hope.

Romans 15:4

You can go anywhere from where you are. You really can become the person you want to be!

I may have written a book on waiting on the Lord, but I'm an author, not the ultimate authority on waiting on God. I admit I am continually learning how to wait on Him.

I'm still learning that if it's going to be, it's up to God and me. Nobody else, not even God, will do for me what only I can do for myself.

Proverbs 13:4 tells us *the soul of the sluggard craves and gets nothing, but the soul of the diligent is made fat.* In Solomon's day, fat meant success and prosperity. If you want to be fat in the biblical sense, you can be. If you really want to be successful at something and are willing to pay the price to achieve it, it can be yours.

It's true that success can be elusive, but even if you've pursued success in the past and fallen short, you can start over again. Henry Ford said, "Failure is the opportunity to begin again, more intelligently."

The God of the Bible is the God of second chances, new beginnings, and fresh starts. Isaiah 43:18-19 declares: *Do not call to mind the former things, or ponder* [dwell on] *things of the past. Behold, I will do something new!*

And Paul wrote in Philippians 3:13-14:

> *Brethren, I do not regard myself as having laid hold of it yet; but one thing I do, forgetting what lies behind and reaching forward to what lies ahead, I press on toward the goal for the prize of the upward call of God in Christ Jesus*

God is in the business of doing something new. But doing something new is also up to me and you. Our future is forward. That's why Paul reached forward

Conclusion

— toward the future — not back into the past. Paul knew God doesn't want us to brood over past failure. He desires for us to achieve success by trusting Him to do something new in our lives.

So if we haven't waited very well up to this point, there's good news! It's never too late to learn how to wait.

Waiting before the Lord must become a habitual lifestyle that grows and expands with life. As long as we remain humble, teachable and moldable, there is no limit to what we can learn from waiting on Jesus — and life never fails to provide us opportunities (over and over and over again) to learn.

I will always remember when watching Home and Garden Television motivated us to have some remodeling done in our home. Of course we'd heard a few homeowners' horror stories about makeover disasters, but we really wanted to make our home's space more multi-functional and add to its value.

Our plans called for building a study, expanding the laundry room, replacing the carpeted areas on the lower level with hardwood floors, fresh paint, mini-blinds, and new furniture for the study and refurbished living areas. Also included in the project were adding some sidewalks and new flowerbeds, and re-sodding part of the yard.

We contacted a contractor, discussed our desires, designed a workable plan together, and agreed on a price and a timetable for completion. We were assured everything would be finished in three to four weeks — just in time for the Thanksgiving holiday.

I knew when we began that our lives would be disrupted while the project progressed. I reminded myself that I would have to be patient.

What an understatement! When framers, electricians, plumbers, painters, floor layers, finish carpenters, and insulation installers invade your space, order flies out the window. So does privacy and your things staying neat and clean!

I thought we were pretty well prepared. But it wasn't too long before we were buried up to our eyeballs in surprises that would stress everyone and stretch our patience levels to the max.

The first few days went great. The smell of freshly cut lumber, piles of sawdust on the garage floor, and delivery of construction materials created an atmosphere of expectation that the project was going to work fine. Day and night, subcontractors came and went, putting their piece of the remodeling puzzle in place.

With wallboard hung, plumbing plumbed, heating and air ducts installed and electrical boxes wired, it was time for the hardwood floors. The process — installation, sanding, staining, and finishing — would require us to be out of the house four or five days. The dust created by the sanders, and the chemicals from the stains and polyurethane finish would make the air unbreathable. In addition, because we wouldn't be able to walk on the floors, we wouldn't have access to the majority of the house.

Our neighbors suggested we stay at their house for the week. Because they would be gone house hunting in Chicago, they welcomed the idea of having us house sit in their absence.

Staying there was a blessing. We could be right next door in a cozy, fully furnished home. We would be able to take our two dogs out without hassle and keep an eye on the progress at home at the same time. It was convenient and an answer to prayer.

Having packed up our suitcases with what four people need for five days, we moved out and the floor guys moved in.

Things went downhill from there.

The first crew wasn't very motivated, was slow and didn't care about how they treated our home. The sub flooring they put down wasn't level. They installed cracked and broken pieces of oak slats, and applied the stain unevenly — some places were thick and dark, others thin and light because of the uneven subflooring.

Outside, one of the workers spilled the stain on the front porch, leaving a huge dark spot in the center of the entryway. Then he left his used staining rags on the side of the house. It rained. The rain-soaked rags leaked stain all over the newly poured concrete, but the workers didn't think anything about it.

The fourth day, the floor was covered with three coats of a dull, streaked, and milky satin finish when I had explicitly told them I wanted gloss finish (because I'm a shine freak). To make the milky-way look even worse, they hadn't allowed enough time for it to dry between coats, so in some places, the finish was already peeling off in chunks.

I couldn't believe my eyes! My impatience level began rising.

Contrary to their promise, they hadn't covered and draped the house and its furnishings, and the entire upper and lower levels of the house were buried

Conclusion

in powdery white wood dust. The entire house looked like it was covered in a light snowfall. The walls were blemished with black marks from their boots, the white baseboard was spotted with brown stain, and the carpets bordering the hardwood floor were badly stained.

After five days out of the house, I called the company's owners over. They assigned another crew to come and re-do the floors. By then our neighbors had returned so we moved out of their house and into to a nearby hotel.

Hotels are nice for visits; living out of a suitcase isn't as romantic as it is cracked up to be, though. Our then elementary age children were hyperactive the first two days. It was an exciting adventure for them. They loved the pool and candy machines. But when our stay stretched into nine days, all of us began getting pretty testy. Living that long away from home, but not being on vacation, the walls of the cramped room began to close in on us.

Jo Ann and I went to work, the kids attended school, and we carried on with our normally hectic family life and ministry schedule; but not being at home in our regular routine raised the stress levels considerably.

I was allergic to something they were cleaning the room with, so I sneezed, wheezed, sniffled, coughed and couldn't sleep well. Having to go out to eat every meal, drive ten minutes each way three times a day to let the dogs out, and not having access to a washer and dryer got old fast. What we missed most was not being able to kick back and relax in the familiar and comfortable surroundings of our own home.

It took three attempts for the company to get the floors finished to both our satisfaction. The owner took full responsibility for the fiasco, reduced our bill substantially, paid for half of the painting that had to be re-done, and picked up the tab for the hotel and restaurant bills.

We moved back into the house and were welcomed to the dust bowl! It took us weeks of cleaning and re-cleaning to remove the last traces of super fine dust. Everything after the floors was behind schedule. We waited and waited some more for the sub contractors to fit our revised schedule into their construction calendars.

I was working 12-hour days at the ministry, the cost of our remodeling project kept escalating, and in the middle of it all, stressed to the limits and so tired I couldn't think straight, I did something I'd never come close to doing.

Early one morning I pulled my car up to our local convenience store gasoline pumps and filled the tank. I went in, purchased a chocolate donut and diet Pepsi, and left. Fifteen minutes down the highway it hit me — I'd forgotten to pay for my fuel! I returned, apologized, paid my bill, and muttered something about being a little fatigued!

In addition to our life being out of sync, Jo Ann became ill; I injured my arm so I couldn't lift the heavy furniture that had to be moved; our refrigerator died; and on election day, my brand new car sank in a parking lot at the polling place. All four wheels stuck in a foot of Oklahoma muck!

As if all the above wasn't enough, I was working on this book when the remodeling process hit the skids. The thoughts were flowing when the floor work stopped me. I really struggled with not being able to write. I couldn't get to my computer. I was distracted by the house project. I found myself becoming very impatient, extremely frustrated, and even resentful that the floor guys were keeping me from writing my book.

One evening when my frustration level had peaked, Jo Ann turned to me and asked with an impish smile, "What's the subject of that book you're working on?"

Her well-chosen words hit me right between the eyes. I was frustrated because the situation was totally out of my control and all I could do was wait. I finally let go of writing the book, released it to the Lord, and kept telling myself it was okay! It's a good thing I did; I would be interrupted for almost nine weeks before I could start writing again!

Mercifully, when Thanksgiving arrived we had put our home back together, and we feasted with friends on turkey and football. As a fitting end to our waiting process, Jo Ann and I both contracted a severe case of intestinal flu the next day! At least we were home!

I learned something from our remodeling experience. I learned that I still have some things to learn about waiting!

It's worth repeating: It's never too late to learn how to wait.

In the Kingdom of God, those who wait are those who win! When life seems out of control and there is nothing you can do but wait, go ahead and wait on the Lord. Wait on Him and He will renew your strength. Then you'll mount up with wings as eagles, soaring high above your problems; you'll run the race set before you and not become weary, and you'll walk hand in hand

Conclusion

with the Lord and not faint.

As Robert Schuller said, "You'll never win if you never begin."

So get started. Begin to win. You can triumph over the trying times when all you can do is wait!

> *Wait for the* Lord; *be strong and let your heart take courage; yes, wait for the* Lord.
>
> Psalm 27:14

Endnotes

[1] William Barclay, *The Gospel of Matthew*, Vol. 2, *The Daily Bible Study Series*, Revised Ed. (Westminster John Knox Press 1975), 233-234

[2] *The New Testament From Twenty-Six Translations*, (Zondervan Publishing House 1967), 668

[3] Thomas Toke Lynch, *The Rivulet: a Contribution to Sacred Song*, 1855

[4] *Webster's, New Collegiate Dictionary*, (G. & C. Merriam Company1975), 1322

[5] *Webster's*, 402

[6] W. E. Vine, *An Expository Dictionary of New Testament Words*, (Fleming H. Revell Company1966), 193

[7] Many have asked me how I happened to write this poem. I tell them I only held the pen. The Father put the words there. My second son, Chris took the poem to school for a poetry class. I did not even know he had taken the poem from the house. He came charging in the door one day exclaiming how well sister liked the poem, *The Difference* and knew where it could be published. I declined as I was a little shy about my writings being seen by others. I guess God had his own plan for it wasn't long and it began to appear in published papers. So the poem became public domain and has no copyright. I have always felt much gratification knowing how much happiness and comfort the poem has brought to others. My husband passed away…at the age of 56 of cancer. One of his last wishes was for me to try to get my name on the poem as the author. I would be very pleased if anyone who sees the poem could help me with his wish by passing on this writing. I happily give permission for the poem to be published and enjoyed but please place my name as the author. Thank You, In Gods Love, Grace L. Naessens

[8] *Webster's*, 605

[9] *Webster's*, 838

[10] Stops are the knobs on an organ that control the airflow through the pipes. Pulling them out increases the volume.

[11] *Dr. Dobson Answers Your Questions* syndicated column, 2004

[12] *NAS Exhaustive Concordance of the Bible with Hebrew-Aramaic and Greek Dictionaries*, (The Lockman Foundation 1981, 1998)

www.ingramcontent.com/pod-product-compliance
Lightning Source LLC
Chambersburg PA
CBHW060504090426
42735CB00011B/2104